BANDSTAND
The Untold Story

by

Stanley J. Blitz

as told to

John Pritchard

BANDSTAND
The Untold Story

by
Stanley J. Blitz
as told to
John Pritchard

Cover design by: Mark Woodruff
Cover photo courtesy of the Ann & Robert Horn Estate

Library of Congress Catalog Number: 97-65075
ISBN No. 0-914207-14-8

CORNUCOPIA PUBLICATIONS
4234 West Hearn Road
Phoenix, Arizona 85023-5333
(602) 938-9112

Manufactured in the United States of America

DEDICATION

This work is dedicated to my hero,
my recently deceased brother, Richard W. "Dick" Blitz.
In my years of research and gleaned information processing
my brother was my biggest fan in every way.
After his death I decided that now is the time to have this
work published as a book that should have some effect
upon everyone who lived through the "Bandstand" era.
Richard's memory will always be with me and it is in his memory
that I can say, I hope each and every person who
reads this book will enjoy the assemblage of historical facts,
published accounts, memories recalled, and 'reasonable' hearsay
that would never have reached the light of day were
it not for my brother having encouraged me onward through
the fourteen years needed to gather and compile
the historical information you hold in your hands today.

S.J.B.
1997

ACKNOWLEDGMENTS

Ann Horn
Helen Bianchi
Barbara Horn
Marianne Kinsey
Christine Sanders
Peter Horn

Jack Steck
Agnes Mamarella
George Koehler
Dick Clark
Bill Weaver
Pam Mammarella

Ed Hurst
Joe Grady
Cheryl D. Johnson
Kathleen "Bunny" Gibson
Brenda Wright
John Cooney

Mike and Mickey, early publishers of "BEHIND THE SCENES"
A Radio and Recording Industries NEWSLETTER

Temple University, Urban Archives, Samuel Paley Library

Jerry Blavat
Harvey Sheldon
Dolores Steigrod
Tommy DeNoble

*Frank Spagnuola
Fran Saddic
Bobbie Young

Ron Joseph
Justine Carrelli
Ralph Gary Brauner
Barbara M. Wilston

The City of Philadelphia, Office of the Mayor

Mark C. Kissling, V.P., A. C, Kissling Co.

The Public Relations People at Tasty Baking Company, Bakers of TASTYKAKE

Bob Horn's Grandchildren:

Chuck Sturgis
Grant Gay

Alexa Kinsey
Brooke Stugis
John Sanders

Robert Graham
Greg Gay

* Frank Spagnuola is the male dancer on the cover of the 1997 book, *Dick Clark's American Bandstand*

PREFACE

Certain powerful Americans of the 20th century have reached some of their goals by immoral, devious, illegal and criminal ways — and they have gotten away with it. Some such "in power" figures have even been able to obliterate their paths used for getting what they wanted from the annals of contemporary American history. The have done it in ways so devious and skillful that the great American public has quickly lost any and all awareness that anything criminal or grossly immoral even took place.

It is true, as P. T. Barnum discovered, that Americans are and will remain a nation of gullible people. But then, when all things are considered our very gullibility might be one of our nation's great assets, a major strength. We're not fearful of trying things. We get things done. We make mistakes and we remedy our mistakes. We forget or we forgive and we move on — and, yes, we even tend to swallow well conceived, well timed and tactfully placed propaganda. We of the general population have been led on occasions to believe that victims are the guilty ones, and the culprit or culprits only did what was necessary at a given time. We have bought that sort of garbage in the past — and we still tend to do it once in a while in this supposedly more sophisticated era.

Consider How Some Employees Are Terminated In The America....

A frequent example of good deeds and bad deeds by people in power in the United States, as well as elsewhere in the world, is the manner in which loyal employees are fired by owners and bosses. Of course, in the span of a century with its tides, ebbs and flows, the general patterns for the way personnel terminations occur tend to vary in a cyclic way. We go through periods of "Get the dead wood out of here," to other times of "Let's be kind to a departing employee. We can afford it and, besides, our stock holders, our customers and our public are watching how we treat our employees."

Forty to fifty years ago, in the 1940s, '50s, (and even today) it was and is commonplace to terminate a company underling — perhaps even a highly productive individual who falls out of favor with management. Board of Directors members or upset stockholders might even bring about the firing of a corporate president or CEO. Terminating an employee is not at all unusual. It is the "how a firing is planned and carried out," the exact how-it-happens, that differs from decade to decade.

In the 1940s and 1950s, that were economically good times in America with plenty of jobs for those who wanted to work, it remained frequent that a termination would be almost as simple and as quick as a superior saying to the target employee, *"Here's your hat. Here's your final paycheck. There's the door."* with little or sometimes no advance notice. Many such firings were also with no termination pay beyond already earned wages (and possibly earned vacation time paid for, too). And some of us may recall that such firings could and often did literally ruin a terminated individual's career and his or her lifestyle. Some deposings tended, too, to negatively impact the former employee's spouse, his or her children, and even the grandchildren. That kind of firing, friend reader, describes a termination situation that is now — thank goodness — pretty much **a former years termination story.**

Regardless of whether it was labor unions, new labor laws, some of the saddest cases made public, employers putting higher value on good employees, a continuing upswing economy, a disgruntled public, or just kinder and gentler bosses taking command — most firings today aren't handled like they were as recently as 40 years ago or before then. Terminations of the 1980s and '90s are handled differently — and in many situations today, that would have earlier on been reasons for immediate firing, bosses tend to look the other way if the offender is a key, contributing employee and such bosses merely penalize or punish the offender in some way while keeping him or her on the job. It is surely different today than it was back a quarter-century or before then

Reasons for terminations today may well be the same as in years before but the manner in which today's firings are handled and paid for varies significantly. To wit:

Almost all of the adult American public of the 1990s have been made aware of the millions of dollars paid to Ross Perot when the Board of Directors at General Motors wanted him to leave his administrative position with that firm.

The public is aware, too, of the vast sum paid to Connie Chung when she was fired from a major television network as an important and popular news reporter and interviewer after she "strayed" away from the network's interviewing philosophies and policies.

And how about recent firings of NFL and NBA coaches and players before their contracts are ended? Most of them have been paid huge sums of money to walk away and to become replaced by someone thought to be better for a particular team. In most instances their contracts have been bought up when pushing them out, to open doors for other personnel who may (or may not) prove to be better in the fired individual's former position.

We see often today, too, businesses, organizations and teams tolerating a key employee or employees doing wild, stupid and sometimes hazardous things that would surely justify termination, but then letting them off the hook with only a minor penalty. If such an employee were not a major link in their employer's business chain, would they be let off so lightly? We think not.

Today's employers tend, too, to provide remedial treatment or care for employees (particularly for employees whose contributions to the business are substantial) who get into or border upon alcoholism or drug addiction. Psychiatric counseling or medical treatment is also made available to employees in need of such assistance — instead of rushing into termination.

Then there was the matter of the Walt Disney Company's former president, Michael Ovitz, being awarded cash and stock options valued at a combined $128 million when he was forced out of the company in December of 1996 after a little more than a year on the job.

Even more recently, as reported in newspapers on May 12, 1997, when a business news article headline read, **"$11 million check for ex-Dial exec."** Last summer (1996) John Teets, former president and CEO if the Dial Corporation (formerly the Greyhound Corporation) was wanted out by the Dial Board of Directors and many of the corpopration's stockholders. Reportedly the company had to make the $11 million payout because it terminated Teets' employment agreement "without cause" in December of 1996. What really happened was simply this: His bosses wanted to replace him with another CEO before his contract would end in 1998 so, rather than just fire him (and call it that) he became unemployed (except as a consultant to the corporation) "without cause" and has been allowed to say he resigned. The Board members got what they wanted, and John Teets retains his dignity by "resignation" and he's getting a bunch of dollars, and other benefits included in his "termination package," such as company paid medical care for himself and his wife, consulting pay for two years, and an office for five years. On the other side of this coin, John Teets earned his money during the years he was top gun at Greyhound and then at Dial when the corporation name was changed. **This revelation is important to this book's historical mystery because:** While John Teets has been fired — he has been given full credit for the good things he did for the corporation — his dignity and reputation is fully retained and intact — and he is being well rewarded for his past services (for which he was also pad quite well during his top office tenure with Greyhound and Dial.)   What a tremendous contrast from this book's story.

*With this preface in mind as you peruse the pages of this book
the author hopes you will come to agree that:
Bob Horn, undisputed creator of "Bandstand," and one of
the true fathers of Rock 'n' Roll should be named into
the "Rock And Roll Hall Of Fame," in Cleveland, Ohio.*

And that the "Rock And Roll Hall Of Fame" should be in Philadelphia....

So the world may know, this book's author will do everything he possibly can to generate support for Bob Horn's posthumous nomination and selection into the *Rock And Roll Hall Of Fame,* in Cleveland, Ohio. This, even while I believe this hall of fame should be in Philadelphia, the true 'melding place' of rhythm and blues music into rock and roll. Philadelphia, not Cleveland, can be remembered as 'home performing territory' to so many of America's early rock 'n' roll artists and to so many of the small recording companies that produced and struggled to market rhythm & blues and early rock 'n' roll recordings that were the early-on turn offs to the major recording companies.

*This work is an effort to "bring back a segment of mid-century history" that was hidden away for the past 40 years and to restore, posthumously, full remembrance and recognition of the creativity and the 'earned the hard way' true professionalism of Bob Horn. He was the sole creator of Bandstand and a father of rock 'n' roll in America. This story, an American historical mystery, is built upon certain lost and **forgotten truths** now recovered and substantiated, upon elements of **author conjecture** arrived at from information gained from reliable source memories of people who were there 40 to 50 years ago, and clues which came from "**same subject, same responses**" stories repeated time and time again by different source people during 14 years of questioning and formal interviews. As represented, this story is a mystery with most of the players deceased but with left-behind evidence and clues to make this author and readers of the book knowledgeable jury members — each of us to arrive at our own determinations of guilt, innocence, misdemeanor or felony. I wish each reader of this work, "Happy Sleuthing."*

Stanley J. Blitz   1997

CONTENT

x

Notice: All efforts have been made to trace the sources of illustrations and photos.
Any omissions will be rectified in later printings, upon notification.

FOREWORD

Culminating 14 years of research and digging, the stowed away tablets have been found and are recovered; enough of them at least to give back to North America and to the world 7 long years, (mid-1949 to mid-1956) of a culturally important segment of American history. A segment of contempory history that one, two or a handful of powerful men erased with well calculated, well timed and perfectly placed propaganda.

This book speaks not only to 7 years of common people's "Americana history" lost and now recovered — but also to how the erasing of that period literally destroyed the man targeted. He, the man chosen by the same owner-management 'powers.' to create, to format, to develop, to conduct, to embellish and to perfect one of the best – 45 years running (with no significant format changes in all those years) television shows of the 20th century.

And, after the target was destroyed, he was never even given "**created by**" credits on subsequent presentations of the show (as is Merv Griffin for *Jeopardy* and *Wheel of Fortune).* No, another man who took over the hosting of the show has allowed, even subtly encouraged citizens of the U.S. and the rest of the world to believe that he was the man who created the magical show, *Bandstand.* Why, even O. J. Simpson, accused and acquitted of horrendous crimes has retained his rightful place in the Football Hall of Fame. But not so for Bob Horn, the acknowledged creator and original host of *Bandstand.* Did Walter H. Annenberg, his big, big boss rise to his support? No. Did Roger Clipp, his second down the chain of command, lift a finger to help him? No. Did George Koehler, his third down the line boss, and most closely involve with him, come to his support? No. And those who did support him, like Anthony "Tony" Mammarella, *Bandstand's,* first producer, and Jack Steck, program director, and others who worked with him and favored his support – were not in positions to do a damned thing about it except make efforts to console the target, his wife, and his family. For his supporters to have done more, at the time, would have jeopardized their own livelihoods, and their own families.

Negatively impacted, too, have been the innovative *Bandstand* creator's wife, who passed away on February 1, 1997, his son, Peter, daughters, Marianne, Christine and Barbara, and now seven grandchildren. These are grandchildren whose peers scoffingly say to them, "Your granddaddy didn't begin that TV show, BANDSTAND, Dick Clark did."

Now, and until the truth of this book becomes circulated, **92 % of Americans** asked, "Who created the TV show, Bandstand?" will respond, "That's easy, Dick Clark did."

-   -   -   -   -

In the late 1990's, not significantly unlike in years before, few Americans question the tremendous power of the media, and the power of those individuals and families who own and control segments of what we commonly call, "*The Press.*"

The self-created or family acquired *sovereign-like power of media magnates,* and their 'in-favor' underlings, has diminished to some degree in recent years with, today, more public and government watchdogs keeping tabs — but *media moguls'* capacities to make or to ruin individuals or their projects — and to literally shape history — remains intact with only more subtleties and better camouflage. For proof of the ongoing power, one only needs to look back to the most recent major election. Or look to what can happen regarding publicized controversies involving well known figures — when a media mogul's voiced opinion, the nod of the head, or wave of a hand can, and frequently does, mean such things as: "Build it up!," "Cool it.," "Thumbs up.," or "Thumbs down!"

Whether accomplished by lengthy conspiracies at a staff meetings, by rendezvous, or by the giving of secret orders via intercom, telephone, messenger, FAX, epistle, cable, wire, or e-mail — *media owners' power,* this very day, over international affairs , politics, crime, our economy, entertainment, the judiciary, sports, our laws, race relations, *and, yes, even individuals* cannot, and should never be, underestimated.

"BANDSTAND, The Untold Story," expresses this book author's long standing and ongoing concern pertaining to but one classic example of positively and negatively employing three facets of **media-mogul power,** as applied in Philadelphia, Pennsylvania, just 10½ years after the end of World War II:

First came a positive and constructive step, using same ownership, multi-media facilities in a major market area to support the creation and perfecting of a long-living segment of television entertainment that became a segment of American music, dance and youth-inspiring history.

Second, the records are indicating, was the dastardly, contrived, and media induced (and protected) act of destroying the **BANDSTAND** creator's life and career, as well as causing undue and severe suffering within that man's family going into three and soon four generations.

Third was the inexcusable (convenient at minimal cost) obliteration – as far as the general public would be concerned – of the records of creativity, development, and the who, the why, and the how of 4½ history-making years utilized to commence, develop and perfect **Bob Horn's BANDSTAND**, the smooth running, perfect hit television show – that with only partial name changes, and with zero format or procedural changes of any significance whatsoever, beyond going nationwide and relocating point of origin, would entertain millions of people around the world , and particularly in the USA and Canada , for more than forty years.

- - - - -

The, announced sudden suspension from hosting the show, *Bandstand,* and the two months later (apparently happy) acceptance of the resignation of Bob Horn from employment at WFIL-TV (Philadelphia), in 1956, by general manager, Roger Clipp, was (reportedly) for violations of the morals clause in Mr. Horn's contract. Granted, Bob Horn was arrested twice and possibly three times for purported driving while intoxicated (DWI). That's an easy thing to set up with a cooperative policeman and pertaining to a target whose very work takes him to dancing and entertainment places several nights of each week – and who isn't a tea-totaler.

With regard to one of those arrests, by way of example, there was an accident when on a foggy night Bob turned the wrong way into an unfamiliar one-way street and ran an auto in which there were two young girl passengers. One girl was apparently hurt quite seriously, and a law suit ensued, from which Bob's insurance company paid the injured girls family $100,000.

This author learned, too, that Bob served several months in jail in connection with one of the DWI arrests. That time in jail, however, was long after Bob had resigned from WFIL-TV and when the Horns were living in Texas. But that arrest, one of the two or possibly three such arrests mentioned, above, may have also been a fixed or set-up arrest. Indications of that possibility are supported (reflected) in this information given the author by Mrs. Ann Horn during a recorded interview several years before she passed away. What she tells, incidentally, was supported by Mr. Jack Steck, who was Program Director at WFIL during the period this book covers. This is Ann's statement regarding a Bob Horn DWI arrest:

"With regard to one of Bob's summons' for DUI or DWI, (the one for which he would return to Philadelphia from Texas to serve 90-days incarcerated) it actually <u>had the date on the officer's summons changed twice by the police or by the court,</u> I'm not sure which, before Bob's court appearance. That was because on the first two dates police selected to put on the summons – a date on which it was supposedly issued – it became established that Bob was not at the place where his arrest was documented to have occurred on the dates chosen to be on the summons. After changing the summon's date twice, however, they picked a third date when Bob couldn't prove he was elsewhere and he was found guilty."

Then there was the huge publicity charge with headlines and news leaders that ran for weeks on end through three trials, the charge of Bob's statutory rape of a (then) 13 year old girl whose name (perhaps different in 1997) was - - - . But, ahhh, that's for on into the story.

Scottsdale, Arizona, June, 1997
S.J.B.

PART ONE

THE WELL AIMED
RISING STAR

CHAPTER ONE

PREPARING FOR GREATNESS

Given the name Donald Loyd Horn at birth by his father and mother, Loyd and Anna Badman Horn, the man most mentioned in this book was born in Pine Grove, Pennsylvania, near the intersections of Highways 78 and 81, on February 20, 1916. Donald Loyd Horn would change his name twice before his untimely death at age 50, in Houston, Texas on July 31, 1966. Numerous media reports and several books about his era have given his birthplace as Cherry Run, West Virginia but his birth certificate, shown on the following page, reflects his true place, date and time of birth. We can learn from Bob's (Donald's) birth certificate that he was the second child of his parents but we do not know if his elder sibling is (or was) a boy or a girl. Nor do we know, either, if any other siblings came along after Bob, or where one or more of them might possibly be today. For purposes of this story, however, all occurring when Bob was an adult, the whereabouts of his birth family members is of no known significance to this work.

Information about Bob Horn's youth is sketchy at best other than viable hearsay that most of his growing up years were in and near Reading, Pennsylvania. We have reports of his having attended the University of Michigan but upon inquiry, that university has no record of either a Donald Loyd Horn or a Robert or Bob Horn ever having been a student at U of M for either undergraduate or graduate studies. Too, as recently as April of 1997 this author heard by telephone from Bob Horn's son, Peter, that his father never finished high school.

As for a first time name change, Donald Loyd Horn to Bob Horn, that probably occurred when he was a teenager and getting an early opportunity to be a radio announcer at a small, low wattage, local area station and where the name, "Bob Horn" was thought of as being a better radio announcer name than "Donald Loyd Horn." Without delving deeply into Bob's early life events and activities it has been learned that he became a busy announcer at a very early age – as when still a teenager. He probably worked for next to nothing, was a willing worker and for those two reasons was no doubt kept quite busy. And that seems to be *where the best announcers and disc jockeys came from* – from among the radio guys and girls who learned the hard way; being on-the-air lots and lots of hours and being taught by old timers

Form HVS-34—150M—12-41
(Fee for this Certificate, $1.00)

N° 12188

This is to Certify, That the following is a true and correct copy of a certificate of birth filed in the Bureau of Vital Statistics, Pennsylvania Department of Health, as directed by Act 402 of the General Assembly, 1915, P. L. 900.

MAY 24 1943
Date

(Director, Bureau of Vital Statistics)

800

HVS-11   Primary *1443*
                Dist. No.

COMMONWEALTH OF PENNSYLVANIA
DEPARTMENT OF HEALTH
BUREAU OF VITAL STATISTICS

CERTIFICATE OF BIRTH

File No. *25461*
Registered No. *21*

1. PLACE OF BIRTH
County *Schuylkill*
Township
Borough *Pine Grove*
City

No. _____ St., _____ Ward
(If birth occurred in a HOSPITAL or INSTITUTION, give its NAME instead of street and number)

2. Full name of child *Donald Loyd Horn*

3. Sex *Male*	If plural births	4. Twin, triplet, or other	6. Premature	7. Legitimate? *Yes*	8. Date of birth *Feb. 20*, 19*16* (Month, day, year)	
		5. Number in order of birth	Full term			

FATHER

9. Full name *Loyd Horn*

10. Residence (usual place of abode) (If nonresident, give place, county and State) *Pine Grove*   P. O. Address

11. Color or race *W*   12. Age at last birthday *24* (years)

13. Birthplace (city or place) (State or Country) *Pa*

OCCUPATION
14. Trade, profession, or particular kind of work done, as spinner, sawyer, bookkeeper, etc. *Agent*
15. Industry or business in which work was done, as silk mill, sawmill, bank, etc.
16. Date (month and year) last engaged in this work _____ 19 ____
17. Total time (years) spent in this work

MOTHER

18. Full maiden name *Anna Badman*

19. Residence (usual place of abode) (If nonresident, give place, county and State) *Pine Grove*   P. O. Address

20. Color or race *W*   21. Age at last birthday *22* (years)

22. Birthplace (city or place) (State or Country) *Pa*

OCCUPATION
23. Trade, profession, or particular kind of work done, as housekeeper, typist, nurse, clerk, etc. *Housework*
24. Industry or business in which work was done, as own home, lawyer's office, silk mill, etc.
25. Date (month and year) last engaged in this work _____ 19 ____
26. Total time (years) spent in this work

27. Number of children of this mother (At time of this birth and including this child) *2*   (a) Born alive and now living *2*   (b) Born alive but now dead _____   (c) Stillborn _____

28. If stillborn, period of gestation _____ months or weeks
29. Cause of stillbirth _____
Before labor _____
During labor _____

CERTIFICATE OF ATTENDING PHYSICIAN OR MIDWIFE

I hereby certify that I attended the birth of this child who was *Born Alive* at *9 0* m. on the date above stated.
(Born alive or stillborn)

When there was no attending physician or midwife, then the parents, householder, etc., should make this return.

Given name added from a supplemental report _____
(Date of)

(Signed) *W. C. Huss*   M. D. D. O.
or _____ Midwife
Address *Pine Grove*
Filed *Mar 1*, 19*16*   *Harry W. Bolig*   Registrar

_____ Registrar

THIS CERTIFICATE MUST BE FILED WITH THE LOCAL REGISTRAR WITHIN TEN (10) DAYS AFTER BIRTH acceptable word usage, how to get to the meat of a story and how to fill in with anecdotes and patter when story copy is too short for the time to be filled on air. The actual doing of broadcasting or telecasting and working alongside 'real professionals' was and remains the best of all means for learning the business. A broadcast candidate learns to be better and best by making mistakes and discovering remedies, and discovering, too, how to say over and over, better each time, things like "*rubber baby buggy bumpers*," "*Peter Piper picked a peck of pickled peppers*," or the lesser known, "*I slit a sheet, a sheet I slit, and on the slitted sheet I sit*." In other words, few people ever learned to be a top notch radio or TV announcer, weather person, disc jockey or broadcast show host in a classroom. The learning place is on the air doing it repeatedly and getting better and better with every hour worked.

Young Man Of The Nights At An Early Age....

Bob Horn, growing up, was also very much a young man of the nights because of his oddball work hours on radio during late nights when the senior announcers elected to be off work and home in bed. Many a 9:00 p.m. to midnight work shift would find young Bob Horn at the microphone with recordings to play and lots and lots of commercials to read. With Bob would be only an engineer and perhaps a janitor still at the station working with everyone else gone home. When the shift ended the engineer, usually an older married man, would go home and, Bob, still full of energy and oats would seek out something to do, someplace to go. Some nights he would sit for hours in an all night cafe eating, drinking coffee and talking with policemen, railroad people, newspaper pressmen and bundlers, ambulance crews, health care people just off work, ladies of the night or strangers in town. Lots of times conversations would be with an announcer from another station who just off work as he was.

When he had a few spare dollars, Bob went to late night and after hours clubs, and late night entertainment places. He frequented these places often enough so that the owners, bartenders, waitresses, musicians and entertainers all knew young Bob Horn. He talked with all of them, but more, he listened to them. He learned from their conversations, from their professional patter and from their music – music still unheard in the more conventional and so called 'proper nightclubs,' concert halls and dress dance places that he couldn't even afford to visit. No school has ever taught the lessons young Horn gleaned from all of these hundreds of people of the nights. Then, too, he was learning from broadcast professionals, at varying levels in their careers, in stations where Bob Horn was also employed.

About the music young Mr. Horn was listening to in late night spots he frequented, a lot of it was written and performed by African American artists. Theirs were great rhythm and blues songs with solid beats, one might say soul music in a way, that came from the heart with origins going back like forever. In this music, not then found in radio stations' music libraries because, if recorded a all it was done at some tiny recording studio, with record pressing at some out of the way facility with little to near zero distribution capabilities. A lot of these recordings when done, were sold by the recording artists themselves as best they could be, and through back alley and brave record stores willing to take on non-ASCAP composed and performed records and being asked for by mostly African Americans and "digging the music" Caucasians, the likes of young Bob Horn or an Alan Freed.

Working With On-Stage Performers Was An Asset....

Because people in the food, beverage and entertainment business knew and liked Bob– and discovered for themselves that, while young, he was still a darned fine announcer – it followed that from time to time he was paid a pittance to be the MC for some of their programs or to step in as MC when someone scheduled to appear couldn't make a performance . We have learned that Bob wasn't then (or ever became) a particularly funny man on stage or on a nightclub floor – but he was a great Master of Ceremonies because he knew how to present performers so that an audience would be eager to see and hear what was coming up. Too, he always had in mental store enough true stories about musicians and entertainers so he could hold an audience' attention when an act was slow about coming on to perform or if there were some other "time to fill in" on a program for which Bob Horn was the MC.

These were times in his young life when he was learning about life and about people of every race, color and creed. He talked, but he was a better listener. People like a good listener. People liked Bob and they spilled their guts out to him. He learned something from every single one of them. He heard and he learned some of the filthiest language known to man. Parallelling that, however, he was also learning radio airways language usage adn adult conversation use of the proper English language that went well beyond the English being taught in schools to young men his age.

Bob Horn, as has been verified repeatedly by people who knew him well, didn't have a bigoted bone in his body. He didn't care if someone he met was black, brown, yellow, red, green or white, if they were Jew or Gentile, Buddhist, Muslim, Atheist or Agnostic. In Those regards people were all the same to him. What counted with Bob was what each individual person he met, associated with or worked with was like as an individual. His "university of the streets and entertainment business" education proved, over the years, to be superior to the teachings of most higher learning institutions. And his learning that continued until the day he died – was liberal but discerning. As a result, and for most of his life, Bob had lots of good to strong acquaintances and a few damned good friends, as this book bears out.

People who know, told me Bob was radio announcing and emceeing events in and around Reading, PA. when he was seventeen. As years moved by he kept working at his chosen profession in smaller cities throughout Pennsylvania and New Jersey until at age 21 or 22 he found radio announcing employment in the big city of Philadelphia. And in Philadelphia, too, he was soon moonlighting from his radio job to MC entertainment at dances, picnics, parties and wherever his services could earn for him a few dollars while giving him still more exposure and experience working with different audiences. By age 24 Bob Horn was a proven fine voiced, well speaking radio announcer, product spokesperson, and sought out MC in a multi-million population, major metropolitan area. By that age of 24 Bob Horn was already a true and seasoned professional with a career well under way. Like with some other local on-the-air professionals of that era still in broadcasting there today, he could have probably stayed right there in Philly and continued to grow and to earn increasing dollars. That sort of patience, however, would not be one of Bob's main virtues.

About his personal life in those early years this author knows little more than what has been stated, above. Somewhere along the way during those years and a few beyond Bob Horn was married and became the father of a boy, named Peter, (now residing in the Portland, Oregon area) and of a daughter whose name I do not know and who now, according to Peter Horn, lives in or near Reading, PA. As to the whereabouts of Bob's first wife, that presently remains unknown and should be of no consequence to this book's historical mystery message.

Somewhere around the time of the Japanese attacking Pearl Harbor on Dsecember 7, 1941, Bob received an offer to come to work for a radio station way our west in Hollywood. The money sounded good adn opportunity for advancement sounded good, so Bob accepted the offer and moved west. It was while he was in California that he met and married, in Mexico, a beautiful blonde lady, the former Ann Davidow, whose stage name as a nightclub entertainer and USO performer in the South Pacific and Orient during World War II, was Linda Stevens. Ann (as Linda), while performing with a USO show troupe, was the first Caucasian woman to arrive on the island of Iwo Jima aftr the Allied Forces (mostly our own United States Marines) forced the surrender of that island by the Japanese. [A small photo of Ann, singing and playing maracas with a "GI Band" appears in this book's picture pages.] Bob and Ann's wedding photo, by Bruno of Hollywood, is on the page facing this one. Ann and her sister, Helen Davidow Bianchi, who has been helpful in the preparation of this book, were both born and raised in Massachusetts.

A few years after their marriage, when the glamour of Hollywood was worn off, Bob and Ann decided to return east, where Bob would no difficulty getting a radio job offer as soon as radio people there, the ones who knew his talents, would hear he was availble. Bob, who had done it all – pitch man, weather man, announcer, newscasting and being a cracker-jack DJ and program emcee would be returning to Philadelphia as a seasoned professional and a contender for the title (if there were such a title) of "best radio announcer in Philly."

All the while on the West Coast, Bob had kept up with the gradual increasing popularity

and listener interest in rhythm and blues music — by then incorporating into it, in addition to its principal African American artist's creativity and performance skills, touches of county, cowboy, hillbilly, jazz, gospel and other elements of American folk music. While Bob remained attracted to this music in Hollywood and was ready to bring his liking of it back east — in Cleveland, Ohio, another man, Alan Freed, a popular disc jockey there, was playing more and more of that '*music on the way in*' for his fast growing audiences. Audiences who were, then, mostly teenagers and young adults tired of the pre-war and WWII ballads, love songs, big bands and novelty recordings being produced and sold by record companies and artists, most of who believed that *freaky rhythm and blues music* will never catch on with most Americans. That's the way it was during the 1940s while Lawrence Tibbett was singing on "Your Hit Parade, *"Don't Fence Me In."*

By the time Bob and Ann Horn arrived back in Philadelphia in 1945, just after the end of World War II, Bob would be able to walk into almost any broadcast announcing audition at most any station and be able, too, to walk out with the job. And in Philly, where he was known by reputation, he wouldn't even need to go through an audition — if the job was open, he was available, and chose to accept it. Bob Horn, in 1945, was that good, and he was back in Philly where thousands of people still remembered he belonged. Welcome home, Bob Horn.

Additionally, Bob was involved as an impresario periodically with his friend, Nat Segall. Together, they bought to Philly traveling jazz concert groups from time to time or actually assembled performers to stage concerts. They were active in presenting African American artists and their music to audiences becoming more and more attracted to the new brand of music for listening and dancing. The following article appeared in the *Philadelphia Bulletin* on **December 15, 1945**:

JAZZ CONCERT AT ACADEMY
Musical Notables Heard in All-Star Performance

An All-Star Jazz Concert in a series presented by Nat Segall and Bob Horn made the Academy of Music a gathering place for devotees of the "hot" and the "sweet" last night.

Among some 30 performers were several notables in the realm of jazz music. "Georgie" Auld displayed his solo stuff on the tenor "sax" and led his own aggregation. Oscar Petiford, string bass "virtuoso," took a prominent part in the performance and guest stars were Rex Stewart, trumpeter from "Duke" Ellington's band, and J. C. Heard, drummer with Cab Calloway's outfit. "Buddy" Powell handled the piano business adroitly, and throaty-voiced Lynne Stevens did some songs with the Auld ensemble. Another feature was "Jimmy" Golden's Quintet. Bob Horn was master of ceremonies.

For radio, Bob Horn had something special going for him at that time. something that was lacking among most of his competitors in the disc jockey field – he possessed a real liking and feeling for rhythm and blues music. It was that sense of "beat" and "musical expression" new to the era that Bob had known and appreciated for years. It was partly because Bob knew and liked lots of the people who were the makers of that brand of music new to Caucasians. As mentioned earlier, Alan Freed in Cleveland, and a few other DJs around the nation recognized the rhythm and blues music, mostly from African Americans, to be the music wave of youth for the future. These forward seeing DJs – willing to risk possible loss of listeners (and air time ratings) to play those rhythm and blues recordings that older Americans, including the era's recognized orchestra leaders, vocalists and instrumentalists, scoffed at as being unfit and unprofessional – were courageous enough to spin those records anyway. They played those new-to-the-public recordings that young people liked and would soon adopt as their own. These forward-acting DJs, who were contemporary music gurus, were America's fathers of rock and roll. In fact, it was Bob Horn's peer, Alan Freed, who coined the name for the music they were playing. Freed called it "Rock and Roll."

Once back in Philadelphia, Bob Horn first went to work for the Metromedia radio station, WIP, where he worked as an announcer with Jim McKay and Jack Whitaker. While there he was also accepting live show emcee gigs whenever he could in the greater Philadelphia area.

Next, in 1948 or early 1949 Bob was hired by Jack Steck, Program Manager for WFIL-Radio stations (AM and FM), to be a daytime announcer and late night DJ at Walter Annenberg's, Triangle Publications' WFIL-AM radio station. It was at a time when Mr. Annenberg was just getting really started into television with his new WFIL-TV. His TV station, the 13th licensed station in the United States, as Channel 6 in Philadelphia, was at the time Walter Annenberg's pride and joy. Annenberg's Triangle Publications also owned and operated the *Philadelphia Inquirer* newspaper, the *Daily Racing Form* and other radio stations and periodical publications across the nation. Bob had joined a big operation and it was his hope that one day he might break into television on WFIL-TV. Lord knows he had the experience to handle on-the-air television chores. Time would tell.

On radio WFIL-AM Bob was given the task of starting and hosting an afternoons, dance to recordings DJ show for teenagers. It became a combination of Martin Block's long running show, *Make Believe Ballroom*, except that Block's program was for adults and Bob's was for teenagers, after school hours. The new radio show was called Bob Horn's Bandstand and it became popular with teenagers in a hurry. On his show, in addition to spinning standards-of-the-day ballads, big band recordings and dreamy love songs by all of the popular vocalists with sometimes novelty tunes thrown in as well, Bob also played a goodly share of upbeat rhythm and blues songs. These were recordings he obtained from sources he knew best and seldom to be found (yet) in the WFIL-Radio music library. They were also recordings that his youthful

19

audience quickly learned to love as both danceable and "alive" music. His radio dance show, keyed to teenagers (but also appealing to lots of mothers, fathers and older siblings) rapidly became "the" music and dance show to tune to in the 8-million people Delaware Valley. Teenagers, especially like Bob Horn's tastes in music because he played "lots of their music" rather than just the *standards* and their 'parent's music' of the WWII and pre-war years. Along with a mix of what the kids called "slow" and "romance" tunes to listen to and slow dance to, Bob played the jive and jitterbug music — and the rhythm and blues music they could only hear, otherwise, on the few African American radio stations of the 1940s and on into the 1950s.

Bob Horn's Bandstand of 1949, 1950, 1951 and the first nine months of 1952, from WFIL-AM radio, Philadelphia, was a young people's version of Martin Block's *Make Believe Ballroom*, as that adults' dance show emanated from New York on network stations. Horn incorporated into his radio show, also, elements from Joe Grady and Ed Hurst's long-running "records, local news, and local commentaries program," *The 950 Club,"* aired on Philadelphia AM station, WPEN, 950 on the radio dial. All through Bob Horn's broadcast years in Philly, Joe Grady and Ed Hurst would remain friendly competitors. In fact, Ann Horn told me before she passed away, how much respect Bob had for his talented competitors, Grady and Hurst Today, 40-plus years later, Grady and Hurst still have a weekly radio show from New Jersey that can be heard in Philadelphia on weekends. That was then, now is almost to the end of the 20th Century mystery lives on.

The Introducing Of Rock 'N' Roll
To The U.S.A. By Disc Jockey
Pioneers Like Alan Freed & Bob Horn

While there were other disk jockeys around the nation who would occasionally play rhythm and blues recordings for their listeners in the years during and immediately following the end of World War II, there were two memorable DJs who learned well before 1950 that America's teenagers liked and wanted to hear and dance to what was fast becoming a post-war music phenomenon, the rhythm and blues records, the upbeat versions of gospel music, country music, and what some people termed hillbilly music. These recordings, at the time, were predominantly performed by African American artists and were produced by small and often little known record manufacturers with limited distribution capabilities and no huge promotional budgets.

Teenagers and college kids of that era, while tolerating, for slow dancing and listening, the ballads and love songs of the war years, 1940 to 1945, wanted upbeat and lively

20

danceable music they could claim as their own — instead of just hearing and being able to buy the tunes and songs of their parent's generation.

Alan Freed, broadcasting first and well into the 1940s. from Cleveland, Ohio and then, making his move to New York City where he could reach a larger audiences, was the #1 DJ to feature more and more of "kids wanted" rhythm and blues recordings on his broadcasts. As mentioned earlier, it was Alan Freed who coined a name for the r&b records increasing popularity. He called the wide scope of r&b records from their varied sources, "rock and roll." Then at one point during the 1950s Mr. Freed attempted to register his name of "rock and roll," as a trade mark. His application was refused, however, because by the time he got around to filing his application so many DJs around the nation were already describing the r&b records they were playing as "rock and roll," Wherever the Alan Freed named term would appear in print, however, to avoid using his exact expression it would appear as "Rock 'N' Roll." And that's how we usually see and hear the expression today, "rock 'n' roll." Unquestionably, Alan Freed earned his title, "A father of rock and roll.'

But just a few hundred miles distance from Cleveland, from where Alan Freed was introducing one new r&b recording after another to post WWII young people eager to hear and dance to this new music with the great beats, was another man, another DJ and another "early-on" father of rock 'n' roll. In Philadelphia, PA, disc jockey, Bob Horn, the man who created Bob Horn's Bandstand on WFIL-AM radio, – was also spinning these 'catching on' " r&b" recordings for young people of his huge market area.

Freed and Horn both recognized that teenagers of the late 1940s and into the 1950s wanted music of their own to identify with – these, the first ones of the 'baby boomers.' These DJs, ahead of most others, caught early the feeling of their teenage audiences wanting "*music for their own generation*" even though it didn't yet have a name for its style. These two men, and the few more like them around the country, watched and listened carefully to their young audiences wanted. Then, acting upon their audiences wants, these DJs were literally introducing rock 'n' roll to America. Freed and Horn also developed and honed that unique top DJ's knack, a fifth sense or whatever one might choose to call it, for being able to hear a new recording once — sometimes only the first 16 or 32 bars of a record — and knowing almost immediately whether or not what they heard (or were hearing) would be a "hit recording" with their audiences of American youth.

The move toward acceptance of rock 'n' roll in the U.S. was moving right along, Bob Horn knew that, Ann Horn knew it and some hands full of Americans across the country knew it, but the majority of the nation's adults didn't recognize early that a new kind of music (that had truthfully been around for years but was always well hidden away) was moving to the forefront and their children were "gonna be a rockin' soon."

-   -   -

CHAPTER TWO

HIRED INTO A MEDIA EMPIRE

When **Jack Steck**, Program Director at radio stations WFIL-AM and WFIL-FM, in 1949, hired **Robert Horn** to be a daytime announcer and evening and night hours "DJ" for the AM station, Bob Horn became an employee in a single company or facet of Triangle Publications. Other Triangle Publications firms in the Philadelphia area at the time included the *"Philadelphia Inquirer"* newspaper, WFIL-TV, the thirteenth licensed television station in the U.S., and *The Daily Racing Form* and another racing periodical, *The Morning Telegraph*. Other media-entertainment businesses to become a part of the empire, while Bob Horn would grow in stature with increasing audience appeal and in on-and-off-the-air responsibilities at WFIL-Radio and TV, would be the publications, **"TV-Guide"** and **"Seventeen Magazine."** Triangle Publications belonged to the Annenberg family and was headed by **Walter Annenberg**, an amazing publishing and entertainment businesses "expander" of the era, and one of the world's most powerful media moguls of the 1940s, '50s, '60s and on into the 70s.

To Solve The Mysteries of This Book You Need To Meet The Players...

As this story is brought back anew out of mid-20th century historical archives and in words from memories and scrap books of some "old timers" who were there when it all took place — we have opportunity to meet and to form our own personal opinions about a small but intriguing cast of players who performed roles in this unraveling tale. We have here, as it becomes written out, what can best be described today as an **"end of a millennium historical mystery**." This Original Bandstand story is easy to follow because left-behind tracks of incidents throughout a hidden-away to be forgotten seven year period in history (and now forty plus years beyond) afford us the clues to be members of a jury and to individually decide whether a contemporary age musical guru and entertainment creative genius was heinously shot down in mid-flight — or self destructed. This book's author, based upon the materials and evidence here passed on to you, drew positive conclusions concerning whether

23

or not crimes were committed by corporate heads in their dealings with and treatment of Robert "Bob" Horn or whether what happened to him was brought on by his own actions and attitudes. There is much to be considered on both sides of the discussed 1950s series of circumstances, of accusations, of criminal charges (trumped up or real), and of results devastating to a handful of people, like the repair of an aching tooth to others, a must stay and watch it happen by a few others, and to yet another individual, a relative non-participant in the events, being handed a winning bonanza to last a lifetime.

This work, gentle readers, relates solely to a mostly cruel results piece of American history that was buried away between July of 1956 and mid-August of 1966 with the hope, since the end of that period by most of the story's perpetrators that it would never again be brought out into the light. As these words are written only two of the original cast members remain alive and they are elderly — but there are young people, the offspring of two generations (with more to be born) who still must bear the brunt of being called prevaricators or worse when saying to peers or others, "My father, my grandfather, or my great grandfather was the creator and original host of one of the most popular and longest running TV shows of all time — and he was one of the father's, too, of a popular trend in music that caught on and has effected America and the rest of the world since World War II heros put away their arms, their medals and their uniforms.

Now Meet The Cast, Not In Order Of Appearance...

Robert "Bob" Horn

You have already met **Bob Horn** in previous pages of this work and we must be aware that he was, indeed, an experienced and well qualified radio announcer, newscaster, weather man and disc jockey ("DJ") before he came to work for Triangle Publication's radio stations WFIL-AM and WFIL-FM as a new member of the Walter Annenberg multi-media and entertainment interests empire in the organization's headquarter and flagship city, Philadelphia, Pennsylvania, U.S.A. About the, then, 31 years old Bob Horn, much more will be revealed as the story becomes laid out in these pages so that each reader may solve, to his or her personal satisfaction, the too long hidden mysterious details of **"what really happened to Mr. Horn between mid-1949 and July of 1956?"** — the details that meant so much to so many people throughout the U.S. and throughout much of the rest of the world as well.

Walter Hubert Annenberg
(with words, too, about his father, Moses Annenberg)

Mr. Walter Annenberg, lived much of his adult life on a mission, a mission to repair his family's name, its reputation and its fiscal assets following the imprisonment and heavy fines levied upon his father, Moses "Moe" Annenberg , for racketeering and tax evasion. Moses had amassed the family's multi-millions fortune and its successful entry into the publishing business with the launching of his first major publishing ventures in producing and distributing *The Daily Racing Form* and a racing newspaper, *The Morning Telegraph.* Prior to the time of Moses' conviction and incarceration, following lengthy and mass publicized trials, he had also acquired ownership of the *Philadelphia Inquirer*, a solid and influential daily paper with wide circulation (that he increased substantially) and that he used for both financial gain and to convey his opinions in national and international affairs to a vast audience. Prior to his incarceration Moses Annenberg had built his publishing enterprise into a lucrative, multi-million dollars venture in years before World War II, when a million dollars was still a tremendous amount of money.

Politically, Moe Annenberg stood supportivly strong on the Republican side of the fence and when Franklin Delano Roosevelt sought Moe's help to gain the U.S. presidency he found no help from the senior Mr. Annenberg. Upon becoming the president, one of the people FDR definitely didn't like was Moses Annenberg. It was shortly after FDR was in office that the U.S. Justice Department (very possibly upon FDR's suggestion) came down, loaded for bear, on every possible criminal charge of which Moe might have been guilty during his long climb to success. The government did turn up some conviction winners during a lengthy and costly series of spectacular and scandalous hearings and trials of the senior Annenberg, among them, tax evasion. Moses Annenberg was heavily fined and, in disgrace, was sent away to prison for a lengthy stay. His father's sentencing left Walter Hubert Annenberg to carry on the family publishing enterprises and to, as best he could, gradually clear the slate of family shame.

At the time of Moe Annenberg's sentencing and incarceration thousands of people shared Walter Annenberg's opinion that his father had been unjustly and unfairly treated by the American Government in charges, in manner and conduct of trials and in final adjudications. At that time in his life (not that he didn't lean in the direction before) Walter Annenberg became a strict, self-proclaimed "moralist." Walter, to this day, has remained a strong moralist while he has gained the personal friendship of U.S. presidents (mostly Republicans) and government heads from around the world, while he increased the family publishing interests and recovered and increased family wealth, while he was the U.S. Ambassador to the United Kingdom, while he repaired his family's discredited reputation, and on into his retirement.

Yes, Walter Annenberg has been a moralist during his adult life except for one thing – Walter inherited a temper that would occasionally flare up in spite of his usual capacity for keeping it under control. His temper may have been a factor to this historical mystery, just as the occurring story (while it was happening) did cause him to set aside his proclaimed morality while the events ran their course. Walter was in a position to call the shots. There is a strong possibility that he did. With certainty, it was Walter Annenberg who, in a suggestion to his radio and TV stations manager, Roger Clipp, started the wheels turning to cause this story to commence — and simultaneously motivated creation of the longest running, major daytime television show of all time.

Roger W. Clipp

Roger W. Clipp, who had been hired by radio station WFIL as its business manager in 1935, and he remained with the station when it was purchased by Walter Annenberg's Triangle Publications in 1946 from Lit Brothers department store. Clipp would remain with the station, and under Mr. Annenberg was named general manager of WFIL radio and television operations. In 1955, an important year to the story told in these pages, Mr. Clipp was moved up by Mr. Annenberg to be general manager of the radio and television division of Triangle Publications. In that elevated position Roger Clipp, who would maintain that title until his retirement in 1968, was in charge of not only the WFIL properties but also of the corporation's five other television stations and four other AM and FM radio stations throughout the U.S. Roger Clipp was, additionally, made responsible for the organization of *TV Guide* magazine for the company, as first published as a Triangle Publication's periodical on April 3, 1953 with early distribution to 10 cities. Other employees of WFIL-TV who were interviewed by this book's author said of Roger Clipp, he was a sour individual who seldom smiled and who tended to try to run everything at the station personally. "Why," one former employee said, "we couldn't even buy so much as a paper clip without Mr. Clipp's permission." Another former employee said, about Clipp, to an author writing a book about the Annenbergs, "Clipp was one of those men that people are afraid of. He intimidated everybody (at WFIL and) even people outside the organization.

As far as Walter Annenberg's attitude toward Roger Clipp, it was unfriendly but highly practical: As written in a biographical book about the Annenbergs, "Annenberg didn't like Clipp or his methods, but he put up with him because he was hard working and his operations always showed a healthy profit."

Roger Clipp, who had been in the broadcast business since joining NBC in 1929 knew many of the key people in broadcast facilities around the nation and knew, too, the business side of radio and television. We seem safe in saying that he had many acquaintances in the broadcast business but very few friends. According to Dick Clark's autobiography, "Rock, Roll and Remember," (1976) his father was apparently an acquaintance or friend of Roger Clipp and he called Mr. Clipp to help arrange an audition for Dick at WFIL when Dick was seeking a major market announcing job. Dick said in his book, also, that he and Mr. Clipp got along very well right from the first time they met. This may also have some bearing on events of this book.

At WFIL employees jumped to do Roger Clipp's bidding when asked to do something— anything. By that same token, though, it was Roger Clipp who would jump to his master's voice whenever Walter Annenberg so much as suggested something be done. While Mr. Clipp was a major factor, as participant, as a major influence, or both pertaining to the events of this story, after the episodes of this story were over and hidden away (in hopes of never being seen or heard of again by a majority of individuals involved), he would go on to become a major influence in the U.S. broadcasting industry right up to the time of his retirement in 1968. For reasons known only to him, just as he seemed to like Dick Clark from the day the two first met, he tended to dislike Bob Horn. One viable reason for differences in posture may have been that Clark was an entry level employee to be molded as Clipp would see fit, while Horn came to WFIL as already a proven broadcast professional able to take on and handle any announcing, news reporting, emcee, weather man or "DJ" assignment at the stations without Clipp holding his hand. About the broadcast end of the business, excluding the fiscal and management areas involved, Horn was probably more knowledgeable and far more experienced than Roger Clipp. Mr. Clipp maintained a semi active status in the radio and television industry right up until the time of his death in May of 1979. One of Mr. Clipp's early claims to fame was his arranging for and supervising the first televised conventions of both the Democrat's and the Republican's Conventions from Philadelphia in 1948. While Clipp must have done so, no former WFIL employee spoken to by this author could remember ever seeing him smile.

George A. Koehler

It was in November of 1945 when **George A. Koehler** became a new employee at the WFIL radio and television stations in a position we would today call "executive trainee." At first he was a 'special events reporter' and then he worked, over several years, in the management of essentially every department in the WFIL radio and television stations. When, in 1949, Bob Horn came to work for WFIL-Radio, Mr. Koehler was manager of WFIL-TV and an understudy of Roger Clipp to eventually move up to manage WFIL-AM, WFIL-FM radio stations and WFIL-TV. In his biodata from WFIL-TV, we learn these things about George Koehler: He was a graduate of the University of Pennsylvania and was active in alumni fund-raising organizations. He was a member of the Union League and a director of the Navy League of Philadelphia. During WW II, Koehler was a captain in the Army Air Corp and pilot of a B-17. At home, in the days of this story, he was a member of the official board and a trustee of the First Methodist Church of Westmont, New Jersey, where he resided with his wife and two sons. Koehler was a young executive highly respected in Philadelphia, a joiner and an active member of influential local organizations. Although a man who took part in management decisions at WAIL, he knew where he wanted to go within Triangle Publication's radio and TV divisions and he knew he needed Roger Clipp's blessings to attain his goals. Thus, when Mr. Clipp said, "Jump." George Koehler would (during the 1950s) respond, "How high?" That, in time would change so that both Clipp and Koehler would be on top rungs of the Walter Annenberg organizational ladder and on a near equal footing exclusive of seniority held by Roger Clipp. Typically, during years of this story, Clipp would call the shots and Koehler would carry them out — not as a 'gopher' but rather as an obedient junior manager or junior officer. In the goings on of this historical mystery the author was not able to learn anything about Mr. Koehler's personal feelings or concerns (if any) during the course of the events between 1949 and 1956 and somewhat into subsequent years on up to 1966. On an occasion when this book's author met with Mr. Koehler for an interview several years back he either most forgetful of the historical events written about in these pages – or he chose not to be reminded of them. The interview resulted in being a conversation about our luncheon food, the weather and things past but totally unrelated to the subject matter sought. He is a nice, elderly gentleman who simply chose not to talk about the mysterious WFIL goings on of some forty years back.

Jack Steck

Jack Steck, Republic Wire Services said of him when he passed away in June of 1994, "... had been a producer, programmer and talent scout for WFIL radio stations and WFIL-TV, in Philadelphia, that would some years later became WPVI, an ABC affiliate. .....Mr. Steck worked as a dancer and singer in variety shows before starting in radio in 1925." At the time Bob Horn was invited to come join WFIL radio, it was Jack Steck who hired him in 1949, with no audition necessary. Jack new Horn's professionalism well and was happy to bring Bob to WFIL stations in 1949.

Later, in 1951, Roger Clipp asked Jack to audition Dick Clark - which, coming from Clipp, pretty much meant hire the kid if he's any good at all. Jack brought Dick in for the audition and he was good for a young announcer. Jack hired him for WFIL radio. Before Jack Steck passed away in 1994 this book's author had the pleasure – no, it was the honor – of interviewing him to gain his personal opinions about the goings on that were the basis for this story's remaining a mystery until now. As the interview with Mr. Koehler produced nothing – the interview with Jack Steck was most enlightening, as will be brought into these pages in appropriate sequence. Ed McMahon is another performer who must certainly remember how Jack Steck helped his career along.

Anthony "Tony" Mammarella

Tony Mammarella was a skilled, respected and well-liked producer for live shows presented from WFIL-TV, Channel 6, Philadelphia, PA. during the years of this story's taking place . When necessary, Tony Mammarella was capable, too, of filling in for on-the-air people working the shows he produced. Concerning the hit show, BANDSTAND, he was producer of the TV version of the show from 1952, when the Bob Horn created radio show, **"Bob Horn's Bandstand,"** was brought to WFIL-TV from WFIL radio on October 12, 1952. The TV version of BANDSTAND was first co-hosted by Bob Horn and Lee Stewart with Tony Mammarella, producer. Then, later, when it was decided by management to drop Lee Stewart from BANDSTAND in 1954, it continued to be hosted by Bob Horn with Tony staying on as producer, and Tony filling in as host when Bob needed a day off or went on short vacations. Then, in June of 1956, when Bob Horn was placed on suspension from the show, it was Tony Mammarella who hosted BANDSTAND until July of that year, in which month Bob Horn resigned from WFIL-TV and young Dick Clark was designated by management to be the new host of BANDSTAND. Tony Mammarella would remain with the show as producer for three more years, until repercussions from the "Payola Congressional Hearings" caused Tony to resign from WFIL-TV in 1959. At the time of Bob Horn's untimely death in Houston, Texas, in 1966, and before his own demise, Tony Mammarella, who had produced BANDSTAND with Bob Horn as host, followed by being the producer for the show after Dick Clark became the host as well – had wonderful things to say about Bob in an open letter to the broadcast industry and to Bob's widow, Ann Horn. His letter, published in the August

29

10, 1966 edition of **"BEHIND the SCENES"** "A Radio and Recording Industry NEWSLETTER" still published and mailed monthly, from Buffalo, NY, to people in the radio, TV, and recording industry throughout North America. With permission from today's publishers of "BEHIND the SCENES," the letter from Tony Mammarella is reprinted on a page in this book. The reason? Tony's letter expresses his feelings about the goings on of this book better than any author could say it following an interview. During an interview with Tony's widow, Agnes Mammarella, during which access was given to some of Tony's memoirs he was writing, before he passed away, to be parts of a book describing his years in television and telling about some of the events and people he knew in the industry, it was learned that his widow very much shared Tony's feelings about the events and results of the incidents which brought about this historical mystery.

Dick Clark

This cast member differs from the others in that he has said publicly and in writing on several occasions that he knew nothing about any conspiracy among management people at WFIL to fire Bob Horn as host of BANDSTAND. Nor did he know of any plot to force unpleasant things upon him and to anger him enough to cause him to resign. Similarly, Clark has said in his books and in public that he knew absolutely nothing about himself being a contender to replace Bob Horn as host of BANDSTAND until he was called into Mr. Clipp's office by Mr. Koehler and, there, told by Mr. Clipp that he (Dick Clark) was selected to take over as the WFIL-TV host of BANDSTAND.

Frankly, after 14 years of researching the almost day-by-day history of BANDSTAND and the people who made it work, I doubt the truth or at least the full truth of such statements made by Dick Clark or made for him by others. .

On the other hand, I have found no evidence whatsoever that Dick Clark had anything to do with any conspiracy to "dump Bob Horn," so I accept his "lack of prior knowledge" at face value. Too, I admire Dick Clark for saying, in each of his now three books about himself and BANDSTAND, "That if it hadn't been for Bob Horn's creation of BANDSTAND, first on radio and then on TV, he (Dick) doesn't know where he might be today."

While Bob Horn's heirs are not happy about a few of the things Dick Clark had to say about their husband, father or grandfather – depending upon from which generation of Horn heirs one might be speaking with – but they each must admit that at least Mr. Clark has acknowledged Bob Horn's creation of BANDSTAND (even though that truism isn't flashed on screen or stated at the end of each BANDSTAND showing, like the name, **Merv Griffin**, comes across as "Created by" at the end of each showing of "**Jeopardy**" and "**Wheel Of Fortune**." Yes, Mr. Clark has given credit to Mr. Horn for his creativity, while all others connected with the historical mystery, including the "big boss" and his lesser "underling bosses" seem to have done the scores of things within their power to obliterate the history of a king and help the public forget that their king ever existed.

And though, as far as this author is aware, Mr. Clark hasn't yet done anything constructively or in support of it, there are many reasons to cause one to think that Dick Clark must believe (as many readers of this book will come to believe), that *Bob Horn's name should be in the **Rock** and **Roll Hall of Fame***, right there beside the name of Alan Freed, as another man who definitely helped to bring *rock 'n roll* to the United States and to the world ahead of most others — and as Dick Clark, himself, would do during the late 1950s and beyond.

Ann Horn

Ann Horn, the second wife, then the widow of Bob Horn and the mother of their three daughters, Marianne, Christine "Pinky," and Barbara, passed away as this book was being written, in Jacksonville, Florida, on February 1, 1997. Ann, whose name in some accounts was spelled Anne, an whose stage name was Linda Steven, was a celebrity in her own right as a dancer and entertainer in night clubs and with USO shows-for-the-troops during WWII. While Ann was prejudiced, as she should have been, when speaking about her husband, his accomplishments, his goals and his burdens to bear after 1955 — this books author found her to be 100% truthful during the interviews and conversations with her going back, now, 14 years and with a latest conversation with her just days before she succumbed to cancer in 1997.

One lengthy interview with Mrs. Horn, some years back, was tape recorded and in years since that recorded interview — many other people interviewed and others who have simply volunteered additional information have substantiated the truth of everything said by Ann Horn. There were occurrences during the course of the story events of which she had little or no knowledge but even these things, when matched with what she did reveal, further established the honesty and rationale of information given to us for this work by Mrs. Ann Horn. One of Ann's heartfelt wishes for all of her widow years was that one day soon her deceased husband's name, Bob Horn, will be included in the Rock and Roll Hall of Fame.

And There Were Other Bit Players, Too...
(Whose contributions to this work, while small, were meaningful)

<u>Dick Clark's father</u> who, through his acquaintance with Roger Clipp, was able to arrange an audition for his son with Jack Steck at WFIL radio in Philadelphia.

<u>Mrs. Lee Annenberg</u>, who may have put a 'buzz' into her husband's ear about getting a younger host onto his publishing/broadcast empire's WFIL-TV afternoon music and dance show for teenagers.

<u>Mrs. Agnes Mammarella</u>, who's husband was producer for two different hosts on the top popularity WFIL-TV program, BANDSTAND.

<u>Messrs. Joe Grady and Ed Hurst</u>, co-hosts of the afternoon radio show *"The 950 Club,"* heard over WPEN-AM radio, Philadelphia, at 950 on the radio dial. These gentlemen were friendly competitors to announcers and disc jockeys on WFIL-AM afternoon programs.

The All-Important Teenage Dancers....

<u>And many of the (1952 through mid-1956) "Young Dancers"</u> on BANDSTAND, including but certinly not limited to such show dancers as: **David Feldbaum, Pete Capobianco, Rita Capobianco, Dolores DeFelice, Robert Ailes, Joan Arnaud, Jerry Blavat, Marie De Lullo, Elaine Biselli, Pete Stevens, Adeline Catucci, Marie Allman, Jerry Bradley, Barbara Marcen, Ed Curry, Tom De Noble, Jr., Bobbie Miluzzo, Adam Valleriani, Jo Mazzu, Jackie Chirico, Harvey Sheldon, Ron Joseph, Justine Carrelli, Bobbie Young, Ralph Gary Brauner, Dolores Steigrod, Frank Spagnuola, Fran Saddic, Barbara Marsten Wilston, Jim Hudson, Ed Tobin, JoAnne DeMayo, Peggy Scarlota, Lane Avenall, Bill Vogel, Carol McDonald, Tom Gilen, Judy Mezey, Betty Mezey, Jack Ferrell, Herb Vernick** — and the hundreds of other teenage dancers who appeared on TV's BANDSTAND when it was hosted by the show's creator, Bob Horn, four years before Dick Clark had anything to do with the regionally popular show. Some of those same youngsters did continue appearing on BANDSTAND after Clark became host and only they can render honest and personalized, young dancers' opinions about the two men's hosting of the exact same formatted show.

Since the word got out that this book's author was writing about the original version of BANDSTAND, and that he is doing all he can to get Bob Horn enrolled into the Rock and Roll Hall of Fame, letters from more dancers who were on the early BANDSTAND keep arriving in the mail. *The kids all loved Bob Horn* in a way similar to how the players who were coached by him at Notre Dame loved Knute Rockne. Some of the dancing teenager's letters (now in their 50s and 60s) appear in this book. More will be included in the next edition.

TV Shows Don't Last Long Without Sponsors....

Some of "Bob Horn's Bandstand" Sponsors are parts of the historical mystery picture, too: Written on March 22, 1956, just weeks before Bob Horn went on a vacation from which he would never return to "his show," he received a letter from **Thomas Edward "Ed" Hicks**, Vice President, *Pepsodent* Division, Lever Brothers Company, which said:

> *"Dear Bob: Congratulations again! During January and February, competitive activity was the greatest in the history of the toothpaste business and yet Pepsodent held its own with the consumers. In certain markets we made substantial gains.*
> *"Undoubtedly, your handling of Suzie Q and Billy Brown and "your public" are the major factors in this success story." Sincerely, /Ed Hicks/*

Another sponsor, who appreciated and benefitted from sponsorship of Bob Horn's Bandstand was **TASTYKAKE**, **Bakery Fresh** products, of Philadelphia, a firm grown to distribute its products, today, nationwide.

Yet another Philadelphia sponsor of Bob's afternoon TV show was **Kissling's Saurkraut**. In a recent telephone conversation with the senior **Mr. Kissling**, now several years retired, he remembered Bob Horn and his advertising on Bob's show with favorable and fond recollections. He liked Bob and remarked that advertising on his show was good for his saurkraut business..

The attitude of former sponsors toward Bob Horn's Bandstand and its host, Bob Horn, is of significance because it has been implied that Horn didn't get along well with his show's sponsors. In actuality sponsors liked Bob personally, and his show very much.

Fellow Employees Were Heard From, Too....

Lesser Known WFIL-TV employees sensed something amiss, too. Dick Clark, who didn't honestly know Bob Horn well at all, has said in two of his books, **Rock, Roll and Remember**, his 1976 autobiography, and in his book written in 1985 with Michael Shore, **The History of American Bandstand**, that Bob Horn did not get along well with the other employees of WFIL-TV. That is not a true statement according to the scores of people this author has interviewed concerning the Bob Horn era. The only people, it turns out, that Horn disliked at WFIL-TV and who were not fond of him either were his two immediate bosses, Roger Clipp and George Koehler. Clipp tolerate Horn because Horn was a thorough broadcast professional and an all-around announcer, disc jockey and on-the-air communicator. Clipp also appreciated as fact that his station had Bob Horn as their employee, because at the time he was probably the best announcer/"DJ" in the greater Philadelphia area and was in that regard a feather in Roger Clipp's leadership cap. George Koehler disliked Bob Horn because Horn, not nearly as well educated as he, and not having management responsibilities as he, was earning more money than Koehler was. It's true, as I learned from many sources, that Bob enjoyed flaunting his fiscal success. He drove a nice Cadillac automobile, wore fine wardrobe, and relaxed on his cabin cruiser that people tended to refer to as being a yacht. Envy, of course, is not justification for dislike. But then Bob had a way, too, of not jumping to accomplish every little task or whim proposed by Koehler or Clipp unless they firmly ordered something to be done — or when what they said made a hell of a lot of good sense. Horn did his job well, he did it creatively, and he had the respect and friendship of everyone who worked on or appeared on his shows. His listeners and viewers — except those who couldn't stand his playing lots of what was to become rock 'n' roll music — loved Bob, too.

As for Walter Annenberg, the big, big boss, liking or disliking Bob Horn, all was well as long as Horn was bringing high ratings to the station, was liked by his public, was maintaining the station's good reputation, and was earning money for Triangle Publications. Failure by any WFIL on-the-air employee in any one of those areas could spell trouble from Mr. Annenberg.

Local Organizations and Foundations Knew Kindnesses....

Local Organizations benefitted by Horn's support. Bob Horn, who hadn't had an easy or well funded time when growing up himself — or help from family in going about earning his career and professionalism in broadcasting — was always an easy touch for helping an organization to benefit others, or to help out an individual boy or girl who couldn't afford a suit or dress for a special telecast. *In the pictorial section of this book are a few letters and photographs telling or showing appreciation for their benefits from Bob Horn's personal concern and generosity.* Whenever he could earn it and had it, he was willing to share.

There Were Still More Bit Players Who Counted....

While there were still others playing minor rolls, the foregoing named or mentioned people comprise the bulk of the cast of players who participated in the events of **seven years of a disappeared, regional segment of American music and dance history**. Upon having a feel for who the participants were (and including, too, the few who remain alive today) we can step back into 1949 through 1956 to recall the true (or most logical circumstantial truths) of events contibuting to the historical mystery of **Bandstand, The Untold Story**.

- Was it <u>an individual mogul's moment of anger</u> that brought about destruction of a career?

- Was it <u>a conspiracy by two bosses</u> calculatingly plotted and carried out to satisfy their business desire?

- Was it the tale of <u>an individual who came too far, too fast only to self-destruct</u>?

- Was it the result of <u>a suggestion by an active-in-social-circles wife</u> of an empire owner, seeking to make a popular happening more esthetically acceptable among her peers?

- Was it a matter of the '<u>ways of the era' and a chain of coincidental events</u> that lead to the devastating downfall of a king followed by the crowning of a new king, upon purloining the jewel of the kingdom?
- Was it <u>the number one, top boss, getting really mad at an employee and firing that individual immediately</u> — with no caring what would happen to the poor devil?

You Are The Judge.... You Are The Jury....

The evidence, tangible, circumstantial and oft repeated hearsay from trusted people has been painstakingly recovered, piece by piece, tidbit by tidbit, over a long period of time for inclusion in this work. Recently, with the help of scores of people, all of the pertinent information has been assembled into the pages of this book. As a result, the author has reached definite conclusions as to what happened that caused, or permitted the early years history of BANDSTAND to have become, literally, erased from history as far as the general public might be concerned. Up in the Boardroom, in the era during which this crime was quite surely committed, the skullduggery carried out could only have been judged as 'masterful' for all except the victim who was to die — while the perpetrators moved onward and upward to prosper and to then to, in time, retire or ultimately die as stalwart, and purportedly outstanding and respected citizens. These individual executioners who moved right on after their crime to bigger and better lifestyles and to earn obituaries or résumé kudos to make of them model American citizens - not the criminals that they were,

Each reader of this book can determine for himself or herself what truthfully happened in the sudden departure of the creator-host, Bob Horn, from Bandstand, that would become the longest running daytime television show of all time.

- - - - -

CHAPTER THREE

THE BIG BOSS STARTED THE BALL ROLLING

In 1952 WFIL-TV, Channel 6, in Philadelphia was still an infant in the field of telecasting. The station, the 13th licensed station in the nation was a pet business venture of Walter Hubert Annenberg, President and CEO of Triangle Publications who was proud of the fact that he had obtained the license for the station for the cost of a 13¢ postage stamp. He was pleased, too, that he'd had the courage and foresight to go ahead and get that license in spite of the fact that his management employees, at a staff meeting, had advised him against the venture as "television being too new and also being a risky, and high cost proposition."

Walter went ahead anyway and entered the infant field of television in 1950. At the time he already owned WFIL-AM and WFIL-FM radio stations (Philadelphia), that he had purchased from a local department store, and he had acquired Roger Clipp along with his radio stations purchase to manage them. Next, Roger Clipp was named, also, manager of the new Triangle Publications (Walter Annenberg's media corporation) TV station. In 1952 and for some years to follow, WFIL-TV was a pet operation of Mr, Annenberg, who's Triangle Publications properties owned operations included as well, The *Philadelphia Inquirer, The Daily Racing Form* and several other lucrative publications and radio stations across the nation. Early in 1952, Philadelphia, the early home of American television insofar as television manufacturing was concerned, could also boast having two other new TV stations besides Walter Annenberg's station..

WFIL-TV was beginning to do fairly well financially, but of the three Philadelphia TV stations, WFIL-TV's afternoon audience counts were the lowest. Viewers had tired quickly of old movie reruns being shown by Walter's station to fill the afternoon hours. Concerned about low afternoon ratings of his pet venture, Mr. Annenberg, who paid other people to figure out what shows to run or cancel, put on his own thinking cap as to what might be done to capture more viewers in the afternoon — and to also justify increasing afternoon advertising rates to enhance profit potentials. Roger Clipp, who was by then Triangle Publications' overall radio-TV stations manager, and George Koehler, Mr. Clipp's WFIL-TV station manager, weren't coming up with afternoon audience-builder program ideas fast enough to suit the big boss. That's when, according to one of Walter Annenberg's autobiographies, Walter said to Roger Clipp, in mid-summer of 1952, "Try a dance program aimed at teen-agers." He couldn't have known it at the time, but Walter Annenberg, the publisher who some years hence would be named U.S. Ambassador to Great Britain by President Nixon, had just suggested the premise for an afternoon TV program that would soon become an all time winner in U.S. afternoon television.

We have observed earlier that when Walter Annenberg spoke to Roger Clipp — Clipp jumped into action immediately. Shortly after hearing Mr. Annenberg's "suggestion," Roger Clipp contacted the co-hosts of Philadelphia's popular afternoon, teenager's radio program, *The 950 Club*, conducted by the Messrs. Joe Grady and Ed Hurst. He asked them if they would be interested in producing and hosting a program like their popular afternoon radio show at 'his' station, WFIL-TV? He spoke with them about great growth opportunity in television and about the good money they would earn.

For whatever reasons Mr. Grady and Mr. Hurst chose to turn down Mr. Clipp's offer. One reason cited for their turndown, I was told, was that to accept Clipp's proposal would be in conflict with or would violate their long standing contract with WPEN-AM radio. Another reason they turned him down (but didn't say so) might well have been 'not enough money' being the real reason for rejecting Clipp's invitation. This is said because Roger Clipp was known, even to his boss, Mr. Annenberg, to be a tight fisted money manager that was, for security, an asset. For growth and expansion, however, Clipp's not wanting to invest money was, by Mr. Annenberg's modus operandi a real negative. Regardless of the reason or reasons Joe Grady and Ed Hurst thanked Mr. Clipp for his prpoposal and told him the were not interested in bringing their teenager's music and dance program or a program like it to WFIL-TV. According to Ann Horn, incidentally, her husband, Bob, was never made aware of Clipp's offer to Messrs. Grady and Hurst until a long whil later when it was Joe Gady (she thought) who told Bob about Mr. Clipp's offer made to him and his show partner.

The turndown by Grady and Hurst left Roger Clipp and George Koehler scurrying around, with a limited budget, to obtain and get soon on their station a afternoons, teenager dance show — like their big boss had suggested.

In days, it seemed, the teenager's summer vacation was ending. The the kids would be returning to their schools and the program the boss suggested isn't ready for airing. In fact there is no program even on a story board or outlined yet. Clipp and Koehler are desperate. It had to have hurt both of them to consider Bob Horn to do an afternoon dance show but that's exactly what they did. They talked it over and it would be George Koehler to convey their want to Horn — their employee who they both knew to be the best announcer and DJ in Philly but who was also a man neither of them particularly cared for personally. And that rhythm, blues and jitterbug music he kept playing, neither Clipp nor Koehler could force themselves to like that either. They had to admit, though, Bob Horn's audiences and ratings kept climbing up and up as did the revenues being earned from Horn's air hours. And there's the other side, these two bosses aren't Horn's kind of people either.

Regardless of personalities and music choices, Bob Horn was the most qualified person of WFIL radio or TV employees to pull off what had to be accomplished. Horn was an established broadcast personality in Philadelphia — in fact all up and down the Delaware Valley. If he could come up with a good show, he would be an easy personality to promote because so many Philadelphians already know Bob Horn. Clipp and Koehler had to decide before hand what they wanted Horn to do, then it would be up to Koehler, Horn's immediate boss, to convince him to do what they decide. Like him or no, Robert Horn is a thorough professional in the broadcast business, they agreed. Give him some good parameters and a loose rein and he will come up with a good afternoon show. Of course we have to insist upon making the new show more like the Grady and Hurst *950 Club* than like Horn's radio show, **Bob Horn's Bandstand,** on which he plays all the rhythm and blues and African American music all the time. He's got his big following at night but we sure can't have that garbage music over WFIL-TV in the afternoons when thousand of mothers will be viewing it along with their kids. No-sir-eee, that wouldn't do at all.

Some Rational Conjecture

Here we arrive at an author conjectured conversation between Roger Clipp and his TV station manager, George Koehler, concerning how BANDSTAND on television came into existence. The words may not be accurate but the events before and after Bob Horn and Lee Stewart would first carry **Bob Horn's Bandstand** from radio onto WFIL-TV fit perfectly the the events known to have occurred just before and soon after BANDSTAND came to television:

"We have the answer, George," Clipp spoke first, "Have him (Bob Horn) use those "Snader Musical Films" and our films from the "Official Films Library" that we bought early this year, the ones we've paid for and haven't yet used."

"Those damned things. Roger, they're terrible."

"I know, but Horn will put them to good use. They'll slow down all his jitterbug music, and at the same time we'll be getting some use out of our investment."

"Well, maybe? I guess it's worth a try."

"Yeah, George, let's do it. Get him into your office in the morning and let's have him give those films his best shot. If anyone can pull it off, Bob Horn can. And, George, one more thing. We're talking about a two hour show, right after school lets out five afternoons a week. That's more than one man can handle day after day. We have to use co-hosts like Grady and Hurst been doing it so well on WPEN-Radio. Who do we put in there with Horn?"

After a pause, Koehler responds, "Lee Stewart, our *Mad Man Muntz pitchman.* He's been asking me about something I can put him into in daytime television. Lee's kind of funny sometimes. He could be the comic relief and Horn his straight man. They can share the hosting chores. Why, with a little humor every day, the Snaders and Officials for the music part of the show, and Horn continuing to bring in musical artists for interviews every few days — or interviewing them by phone when they can't come in . Roger, we've got a show!"

"It should work, George. Now it's up to you to sell Horn on the project in the morning. We should be able to bring **Bob Horn's Bandstand** to afternoon TV within 5 days. Be sure to sell Horn on the concept first — then invite Lee Stewart into the picture. By golly, I like your idea of using funny looking Lee Stewart, I like the idea of that healthy *Muntz TV ad account money* coming in right away to help cover costs of the show from its day." Yes. That's how we cn do it. Good luck, and let me know how it goes after your meetings with Horn and Stewart tomorrow."

"Yes, it can work. I'm not too much for those doggoned Snaders and Officials but — why not give it a good try. We know the old movies we've been running aren't taking us anywhere."

"Right. You can make it work, George. Let's talk about this tomorrow afternoon, after you have Horn and Stewart primed to start within a week."

Bob Horn's Bandstand Goes Onto Television At WFIL-TV, Channel 6...

Their plan must have hurt Clipp, a man already known and respected in radio and television management circles nationwide and an officer in the Philadelphia Chamber of Commerce, and Koehler, recently out of the Navy, head man of Philadelphia's Navy League, an Elder in his church, and active in several city service organization — and both graduates of the University of Pennsylvania — to even consider an afternoon TV show for youngsters hosted by Bob Horn and Lee Steward.

The next day George Koehler called into his office the one announcer-"DJ" at WFIL-AM who neither he nor Clipp liked very well, and who was on his radio "DJ" show, **Bob Horn's Bandstand**, playing a lot of [too many as far as these Clipp and Koehler were concerned] those rhythm and blues recordings, with even hillbilly and country music tossed in. Music, that for some dumb reason teenagers seemed to like, music like was also being played on Philadelphia's popular African American radio station, WDAS.

Clipp, Koehler and their ilk didn't care for this sort of music at all but their job was to broadcast and telecast programs that would capture and hold the greatest possible number of Philadelphia and Delaware Valley listeners and viewers. On that September date in 1952 and before teenagers of Philly and teenagers all up and down the Delaware Valley were tuning in to **Bob Horn's Bandstand** on radio. Listener charts telling broadcast managers in the area that more and more listeners were tuning to WFIL-AM and Bob Horn's kind of music every month. Horn show advertisers, his show sponsors, were happy with the results of his show — and those advertisers were paying shares to keep WFIL-AM radio profitable.

On another occasion Mr. Clipp had said to Mr. Koehler, "Horn, is playing the same kind of recordings made by those African American and country and western artists in back alley record pressing plants, that *Billboard* magazine tells us that guy, Alan Freed, is playing on his *Moon Dog Show* up in Cleveland." Now, whether Clipp said such words to Koehler, or Koehler said them to Clipp, we'll never know for sure (even though George Koehler is still alive and in economically comfortable retirement as these words are written) — but we can be certain that such a conversation took place between these two managers. The words convey the attitudes and postures of the two rather stuffy gentlemen. And they might well have added, in such a conversation, "But we have to admit that Alan Freed, while being criticized by almost every contemporary pre-WWII era musician and first post war years musicians, too, Freed is bringing the station he works for top popularity ratings and some healthy advertising dollars. In research I heard from one person after another that where music was concerned both Clipp and Koehler, both UP grads pillars of the community were total squares. But, then, so were most other adults of the era.

An example of what the 'staid' and 'proper' musicians were saying of the recordings that would lead to rock 'n' roll, the following is a quote from band leader & composer, **Meredith Wilson**:

> *"Rock & roll is the music of idiots, rock & roll is dull, ugly, amateurish, immature, trite, banal, and stale.*
> *It glorifies the mediocre, the nasty, the bawdy, the cheap, the tasteless."*
> *Then he went on, laughingly to add, "**Mitch Miller** was responsible for rock & roll. "The beard did it.""*

Meanwhile, Back At Stations WFIL-AM Radio And WFIL-TV...

Nearly a whole summer had passed since Walter Annenberg suggested a kid's dance show for the afternoons on his TV station. By the time Clipp and Koehler admitted defeat in finding a show from 'outside' and felt backed into a corner far enough to search inside their own organization for help to bring an audience-builder, afternoon show to KFIL-TV it had to be accomplished in a hurry. Certainly not these not these managers' first choice, but a process of eliminating other stations personnel for the new project, one at a time, brought them to Bob Horn. Maybe Bob Horn could be experienced one who could dream up a successful young people's music and dance show like the big boss had suggested.

Bob Horn had been with them for three years as a proven audience-builder announcer and "DJ." He had served his time at WFIL-AM doing daytime and nighttime announcing chores, and by the day George Koehler would came to Bob Horn for a solution to a WFIL-TV daytime programming problem, Bob had for over a year hosted his successful "DJ" program, **Bob Horn's Bandstand,** on radio.

Further, Bob Horn wouldn't be entirely new to television. A year before, according to Roger Clipp in a news release he ad sent to local newspapers for release on August 19, 1951, he said, after telling about WFIL-TV educational programs, "Other local programs (include) Bob Horn and Jeff Scott serving as musical film jockeys; (he probably had those dumb Snaders in mind) .... also will figure importantly in the Channel 6 picture." This lets us know that Bob Horn was making some appearances on WFIL-TV before the end of 1951, a year before the September, 1952 urgent meeting would be called.

Thus, a morning meeting was convened in Koehler's office with George Koehler, Bob Horn and possibly Jack Steck in attendance. The day was a week before the Fall school year would commence in Philadelphia public and parochial high schools. At the meeting Horn was asked (more realistically he was told, according to how Dick Clark described this meeting in his 1976 autobiography) to move his **Bob Horn's Bandstand** radio program onto television ASAP.

According to Jack Steck, when this author interviewed him 13 years ago, before he passed away, Bob could probably have said "No" to Koehler's proposition, but why would he when he was longing to get onto television anyway. This offer was his first real opportunity. He'd take it. But there would be some strings attached, some restrictive conditions. Told briefly about these conditions, Bob was not pleased by what was demanded but decided to go along with the opportunity anyway in order to be regularly on TV — on WFIL-TV — five afternoons a week — two hours an afternoon — with his own show. Well, almost all his show.

One condition was that Bob Horn would have a partner, a co-host on the show. That partner would be **Lee Stewart**, a hard working radio (and already with a little TV time, too) sales pitch person who would bring to the new, afternoon **Bob Horn's Bandstand,** a first sponsor that Lee Stewart had "locked up." Lee Stewart sold the TV sets of *Mad Man Muntz TV* for a little down and a little a month. The price per set was around $300 and Lee is reported to have sold thousands of them for Mr. Muntz..

Koehler explained to Bob that management wants this new show to be a lot like the Grady and Horst *950 Club* program on radio. The reason, according to Koehler, was that he and Mr. Clipp believed a two hour TV show would go best with two hosts instead of leaving it all to one. Their idea, Koehler explained, was that Lee would provide comedy, as the new show's comic, and Bob would be the straight man, the host working with guest celebrities, and the music 'spinner." Then came the bombshell, the other condition. There wouldn't be many recordings to spin. Bob would instead be the playing "Snaders," and "Officials" the 1950s versions of today's popular MTV music videos.

The difference between then and now, however, was substantial. Snaders were unimaginably and inexpensively produced, 4 to 6 minute film strips using performers like Doris Day, strolling through a garden while singing a song — or perhaps Bing Crosby walking beside an artificially moonlit ocean while he crooned *"Lovely you and blue Hawaii."* The "Officials" were similar artists performing on film strips but of even lesser quality than the Snaders. A few weeks with those three to six minute films and Bob Horn wouldn't have any fans left but WFIL-TV management bought the batches of Snaders and Officials many months before and had never yet found a way to use them. The managers felt, at last, maybe we've found a way to justify our purchase of those horrible films, the films that caused people who knew how bad they were to give them another name. The name was "FIL's folly."

Why would Bob Horn consent to air those films to afternoon audiences? There are two apparent reasons. First, he wanted onto television badly enough that he would be willing to face any audience criticism that might come his way when he must present those almost amateurish music films. Secondly, knowing the films were that bad, and that there were only some set number of them — once played through, that would be the last of them because they surely didn't warrant any replays to a same audience — with perhaps a handful of exceptions.

As for doing the show with Lee Stewart, who Bob only knew through seeing him around the studios once in a while, why not give it a try? If Lee is capable, maybe they can make a good show together. If not, a way will come up to bring the show back to being his alone.

The last week of September and the first week of October was a trial run for **Bob Horn's Bandstand** on WFIL-TV in the afternoons, 2:30 to 4:30. Featured were Bob Horn, Lee Stewart, the boring Snaders and the more boring, still, Officials and a couple of local entertainment celebrity guests Bob had come in to be interviewed. He wasn't rushing to invite in the major celeb's he knew before he ha a feel for how the show was going to work out. It bombed immediately. Those boring films were enough to make any viewer turn away and they were burning up some 75 minutes of the 120 minutes show. To make it worse, Lee Stewart's comedy wasn't at all funny — and Bob Horn was no straight man, at least not with Lee.. Within the first week Bob and Lee, who might have liked each other under other circumstances, were onto each other's cases, each putting blame on the other for a show losing viewers faster than Triangle Publication's media outlets could attract new viewers to watch Channel 6 in the afternoon. The two week test results were from hunger. Bob wanted Lee off the show. Lee didn't know what he wanted and didn't know he wasn't funny (and that even wearing crazy costumes couldn't help much). But both co-hosts knew, after about their third

43

day of telecasting, those damned Snaders and Officials have to go — and they'd have to let Bob get back to spinning his records that the kids liked.

Koehler agreed that the music film strips had to go. He talked to Clipp about it, who agreed the Snaders and Officials should be declared dead. But then what? What are Lee, Bob and the cameramen to do while Bob's recordings play? They could learn to juggle, do acrobatics, twirl ropes like Will Rogers used to do, show the scenery of Yellowstone National Park or headlines of the day's *Philadelphia Inquirer*. But those things, too, after a couple of days programming make for more bored viewers.

Then came "steal and idea" and we don't know who to credit with coming up with the "idea to swipe an idea" — whether it was Bob Horn, George Koehler, Lee Stewart, Anthony "Tony" Mammarella, who had been named producer of the TV **Bob Horn's Bandstand**, or Roger Clipp. This is one idea we probably need to credit to Clipp because he was the one who wanted the team of Grady and Hurst in the WFIL-TV time slot earlier. The idea to steal was part of the latest Grady and Hurst formatting when they were inviting high school kids into their studio while they were on the air. Their show was still only radio but they found time some days to interview the kids somewhat, as to their names, their schools, their hobbies, what teams they were on and stuff like that — and they let the kids dance in their studio when they played records. Why not do that on television? The kids being there and interviewed would eliminate the need for juggling and sword swallowing by the hosts — and, who knows, there might be a good camera shot once in a while panning to the kids dancing. Sure will be better than the Snaders and Officials.

Invite the kids in. We'll switch to the big studio out by the parking lot, get a set built over a weekend and promote the hell out of the new, TV, **Bob Horn's Bandstand.** We can advertise the new program on TV, on radio, and in the *Inquirer* starting Monday. We've got four high schools within easy walking distance of our new studios, two public high schools and a girl's Catholic high school and a boy's Catholic high school. With gymnasium type roll-away bleachers along one side of that studio we can seat about 160 to 200 kids in there with enough room, still, so that 30 or 40 kids can dance while records play. It's better than now with nobody watching the Snaders. With 200 kids in the studio we're bound to have a bunch of mothers, sisters, brothers, grandparents, aunts and uncles at home watching the show to see their kin. Let's do it!

At that moment Bob Horn knew something the others hadn't even thought about. With his choices of "music for post-war youth" and kids being able to see other kids dancing. Wow! This can become not only a popular show but a great show. To himself he must have said, "Just watch guys. You'll see." And Lee, if he'll stay out of the way we'll do just fine.

- - - - -

CHAPTER FOUR

TURNING THE "DJ" INTO A "MAESTRO"

When Messrs. Clipp and Koehler decided to move **BOB HORN'S BANDSTAND** onto afternoon television for high school age youngsters, it was a bold step into unexplored territory. They would exploiting the talents of two men stepping pretty much cold into television from radio.

For Bob Horn, whose career we've been following as this story unfolds, a true broadcast professional who we know came up the slow, hard way on radio by performing in every known and imaginable phase of on-the-air radio assignments, was then a youthful 36 years old. He was married and the father of a son, Peter, by a previous marriage, who was away serving in the air force during Korean conflict days. In this anticipated new assignment Bob Horn would be doing work quite similar to the DJ sort of job he'd been doing for years already but now in front of cameras.

Contrary to the way Dick Clark has described Bob Horn, as *"a man in his late thirties, heavyset with a double chin, long, narrow nose and greased-back black hair"* Horn wasn't that bad nor elderly looking at all – although he might have seemed like that to Clark, a short time newcomer to WFIL-Radio who was, himself, baby faced and 12 years Horn's junior. Too, at that time, everyone I've interviewed who knew him or heard him on the air or saw him on television has said, "Bob Horn was the best broadcasting personality in the entire greater Philadelphia area." A fact was, too, that Bob Horn had more experience and broadcasting knowledge in his little finger than young Clark had in his entire being — or would have for another 15 years. Bob Horn wasn't a pretty boy like Dick Clark but he was a good looking and mature man who dressed well and was business like in his conduct and posture.

At WFIL studios, for radio and TV, Bob Horn wasn't "one of the boys" he wasn't one to chat around the water cooler or the coffee bar as was typical of announcers off duty or between air stints. Bob Horn worked long, hard hours to make his air time tops. He knew the music he played and often he knew the artist or artists who recorded it. He spent hours every day talking to recordings salespeople, listening to fresh selections, and contacting artists around the nation by phone to know what they were up to, what they had new, and when they would be coming to Philadelphia so they could be interviewed on his show. Before coming onto TV from radio Bob worked 12 to sometimes 14 hours a day with probably only 4 to 5 of those hours on the air. After returning to Philadelphia from California Bob didn't have time for bull sessions or coffee talks around a studio. We have to remember he'd done that exercise years before when he was learning broadcasting from the old timers. That, to him in the 1950s, was for kids on the way up and for no longer ambitious oldsters on their way down or just hanging on until retirement. It's no wonder, thus, that Dick Clark said also of Bob Horn, "*Off-camera his personality was abrasive, egotistical, and aggressive. Most people around the station found him less than charming.*" At that point in time and life, Dick Clark was just recently married, with no children, his wife was or would soon be teaching school, and he was making more money than he had ever made before in his life. Not so with Bob Horn, he had a wife and a newly purchased home to keep up. And Horn's literal study of the new wave in rhythm and blues music, along with Alan Freed doing the same thing in Cleveland, didn't leave time for studio bullshitting with people who couldn't teach him anything he hadn't already done in broadcasting or was dong at the time. Sure, Bob seemed aloof to a kid new on the job.

Horn Always Ready To Help A Serious Minded Youth....

But as we see a little here and more further into the book, Horn was always ready to help a kid who wanted to learn. He made time for that and he inspired youngsters who wanted to get into the entertainment or broadcasting business. **Harvey Sheldon**, a dancer, will tell how Bob encouraged him and how Bob wrote the letter that got him into the Columbia University school of broadcasting. **Jerry Blavat**, a dancer, will tell how Bob motivated him to get into the broadcast, entertainment and hospitality businesses. Jerry has by way of compliment added that, "Bob Horn was almost like a father to me and I've been doing things he taught me in the greater Philadelphia area for many years." **Ron Joseph**, another dancer, who has had some success in the field of show production and the making of TV films credits Bob Horn with being his inspiration. Scores of young people of his era remind us, today, of things Horn did to make their lives better than they might have been without his motivation. In this writer's opinion, it is shame that Dick Clark ever took it upon himself to write his impressions of Bob Horn because, as it turns out, **Dick Clark didn't know Bob Horn at all**. What he knew of Horn then (and now), except for working beside Horn for a few minutes a day, was and is only a younger man's opinion of a more mature man, with the personality remarks being repeats of hearsay and newspaper reports — most of which has proven to be erroneous.

Anthony "Tony" Mammarella Could Speak About Bob Horn With Authority...

46

When **Bob Horn's Bandstand** moved from radio to television his work became more complex than when his was strictly a one man radio DJ show. There had to be a set for the show, there had to be cameramen, grips, a makeup person, and a producer to keep everything running smoothly. The man George Koehler assigned to that producer position was Tony Mammarella, a young but experienced TV producer who had come up with WFIL-TV doing most every television job imaginable — including going on the air numerous times for performers who, for whatever reasons, were not available to appear. Tony, God love him, was an even tempered, not easily flustered trouper who could not only get along with Bob Horn (and later with Dick Clark) but would learn to fully understand, appreciate, and love Bob Horn for being the unusual and outstanding individual and creative talent that he was.

School's Back In Session, We Have To Get This Show On The Air....

The decision has been made. The Snaders and Officials are out and WFIL-TV is back to running the old movies in the afternoon for the short time it will take to prepare a version of **Bob Horn's Bandstand** for television that allows teenagers to be dancing in the studio while 'Bob's choice' records are played for dancers and viewers. Neither Clipp or Koehler appreciated Horn's selections of recordings but they can't knock success. On his radio show he's been playing a mix of contemporary standard ASCAP (American Society of Composers, Authors and Publishers) records and BMI (Broadcast Music Industry) records along with small manufacturer rhythm and blues recordings he obtained from all sorts of sources he found on his own. It must be admitted that his DJ audiences apparently like what he's playing and the way he's mixing the records because his audience counts have been growing monthly for near two years. Bob Horn is doing something right, so if we (WFIL-TV) can't have Grady and Hurst we can sure do something like them with people we have - starting with Bob Horn and Lee Stewart. That's pretty much how bosses Clipp and Koehler arrived at maybe, at last, getting the "kid's dance show" the big boss, Annenberg suggested they get on the air for afternoon audiences. Should we allow that **Bob Horn's Bandstand** on TV was Walter Annenberg's idea. Naw, let's not.

Will There Be Enough Kids To Dance? Enough Viewers?

This decision, made on September 28th, 1952, to have the new **Bob Horn Bandstand** for television on TV screens of greater Philadelphia by Tuesday afternoon, October 7th allows exactly eight days and a few hours to have the show ready to go. Not much time when considering that most TV new live TV shows take a month to several months to prepare.

To have enough young dancers and enough viewers to make the show pay, there's a week for promotion. For that WFIL-TV is in a plus position with also and AM and an FM radio station to plug the forthcoming show and the *Philadelphia Inquirer* newspaper to also push the **Bob Horn Bandstand** TV show editorially to people with different interests along with a few trade-out display ads. Ads and news release copy with lines like "TEENAGERS! COME DANCE ON **BOB HORN'S BANDSTAND**! IT'S THE NEW AFTERNOON TV SHOW FROM WFIL-TV, CHANNEL 6 STUDIOS, EVERY WEEKDAY – RIGHT AFTER SCHOOL. CALL PENNYPACKER **6-6666** TO REGISTER FOR YOUR FREE ADMISSION." or, "TUNE IN TO THE FUN, NEW, TEENAGERS DANCING, AFTERNOON TV SHOW, **BOB HORN'S BANDSTAND**! ITS ON CHANNEL 6 EVERY WEEKDAY 2:45 TO 5:00 - THEN STAY TUNED FOR THE NEWS." or, "*YOU CAN'T BEAT THE BEAT ON BOB HORN'S BANDSTAND! EVERY WEEKDAY AFTERNOON, 2:45 TO 5:00, STARTING TUESDAY, OCTOBER 7 ON CHANNEL 6, WFIL-TV.*"

To do everything possible to have enough kids to dance by October 7, and lots of viewers tuning in, WFIL's public relations people sent out news releases every other day to every media outlet in the greater Philadelphia area. Stories sent out spoke about this being the first show like it on TV in the U.S. The stories, accompanied by photos of Bob Horn, of Lee Stewart, of kids dancing, of the interior of the sound stage being converted into a dance hall for two hours and fifteen minutes every weekday, of teenagers dancing, and more photos of Bob Horn – some of Bob with celebrities like Eddie Fisher, Peggy Lee, Nat King Cole or others who he had interviewed earlier on his radio **Bob Horn's Bandstand** to associate Bob, the WFIL radio DJ who thousands of Philadelphians already knew, with nationally known celebrities that everybody knew. And about the news releases sent out, naturally they all ran on all media properties owned by Walter Annenberg (who first suggested a kid's dance music afternoon show for his TV station) and they were also run by his media competitors as a 'professional courtesy.' Every newspaper in the area, every radio station, every TV station (there were 3 TV stations in Philly by then) – they all ran stories and the ones readers and viewers also ran the photos WFIL provided. The new TV show promotional and advertising blitz was a saturation campaign. One would think Bob Horn was in the lead and running for governor with the **Bob Horn's Bandstand** being his campaign platform. News items told viewers about the upcoming teenagers dancing show every other day right up until October 4.

No television show commencing in Philadelphia had previously (and possibly since) ever been given so much publicity in such a short period of time — all in one week. Now, while intent was to make the afternoon show a hoopla success from the start, Bob Horn was personally getting more exposure and publicity than he had ever known before during all of his years in broadcasting, In a matter of a week the number of people who knew who Bob was went, literally, from thousands to millions.

Bob Horn was, in one short week, turned from radio disc jockey to **Bob Horn,**

local celebrity, friend of national celebrities, and **"Maestro" of the new, exciting, and soon to be action packed, Bob Horn's Bandstand.** This new show was Walter Annenberg's vague idea, reluctantly allowed by station managers Roger Clipp and George Koehler, to become 'created on the job' by Bob Horn, who had been doing 40% of the new show's format on radio.

Publicity Is Out. Will The Kids Show Up? Will Viewers Watch?

With all the publicity and promotion prepared and distributed everyone at WFIL knew the people of Philadelphia had to be aware of the new afternoon show's premiere in a matter of days. Response from teenagers to all that exposure, however, wasn't what had been hoped for. A few phone calls had come in to the station and we had reservation names for a dozen or so kids - when we'd hoped to have at least a hundred or so teenagers booked to be there for the opening show. But kids, like adults, often procrastinate. Everyone but Bob seemed worried about 'will we have enough kids?' Bob remained cool, as years in broadcasting had caused him to be, said, "Don't worry. As long as we have a dozen or so kids to dance and we keep the cameras on them we'll be okay. And we're bound to have more than a dozen."

While promotion was going on outside the studio, inside the activity was furious with every person to work the show becoming familiar, as best possible by dry runs, with just what he or she would need to do to make the show click. The people were ready for start day.

A Simple "Get-The-Message-Across" Televising Set Is Ready, Too....

A big step accomplished well ahead of time was preparation, construction and positioning of the set to be used as it was quickly designed and prepared by Nat Elkitz. His set, reportedly now in the Smithsonian Museum (of Americana), depicted the interior of a music store and more specifically, a corner of such a store called the Record Department. The background was made to look, on the right side, like a music store window with the impression of looking out at buildings across the street. To the left of center, appearing to meet the painted window in a corner, was painted a multi-tiered shelves and appearing to be on the shelves were painted spines of lots and lots of record albums. Breaking that left side view up, between the shelves, were musical instruments, some painted to look as if hung on the wall and others actual instruments hung on the set. A 14 inches high stage in front of that scenery was the work area for the **Bob Horn's Bandstand** co-hosts, Horn and Stewart and guests to be up where everybody in the studio could easily see them (especially the cameras). They were pretty much separated from the studio floor dance area and from the gymnasium type, roll-away bleachers at the left side of the studio that could seat about 200 teenagers, by a piece of furniture resembling a record shop sales counter. That big counter look-alike was the work table for Bob Horn when spinning records, interviewing celebrity guests or randomly selected teenagers, talking on the telephone, and chatting with his audience in the studio or, at home, watching on a television set.

That stage was also intended to be the place where co-host and comedian, Lee Stewart and Bob Horn, his intended straight man, would endeavor to add touches of humor to the show – with poor results because Lee wasn't funny, except perhaps in appearance — and Horn was no comedian's straight man. They were just never able to make their attempts at humor come out funny.

Tony Mammarella (Who Was There) Described The First Day Show....
(The First Day of **Bob Horn's Bandstand** on Television, October 7, 1952, a Tuesday)

The show was a first of its kind on television, an original with nothing to copy from except Bob Horn's experience as a DJ on radio and in scores of public events, concerts and dances at which he was often Master of Ceremonies. Well, not quite without something to copy in a way. Joe Grady and Ed Hurst's radio show (the show George Koehler and Roger Clipp tried to get to come to WFIL-TV), the *"950 Club"* had been a popular teenager disc jockey show in Philadelphia for several years with two DJs sharing the hosting. Their studio was big enough and Grady and Hurst played recordings for a live teeneagers' audience. At some time during each days broadcast, Ed Hurst would ask some of the kids their names and let them talk about their high school and say "Hi" to friends over the air. Like Lee Stewart and Bob Horn, Ed Hurst, the supposed funny man was not really funny and Joe Gady was too square to be a good straight man. But for teenagers in the afternoon, the *"950 Club"* was the only young people's show in Philly.

If anything was copied in the evolution of **Bob Horn's Bandstand** to television it was aspects of Grady and Hurst's *"950 Club."* The day after **Bob Horn's Bandstand** went on the air Joe Grady has been reported to have said, "Bob Horn stole our show right out from under us. He's raped us and it's legal." Some months after Bob's Bandstand was on the air, Grady and Hurst paid their way out of their WPEN radio contract and tried a "teenagers dancing on TV" show of their own. It bombed because in those few months they waited to commence their new show, **Bob Horn's Bandstand** was too well established as the Philadelphia and Delaware Valley high school kids favorite program to turn to in the afternoon.

The format and procedural plan for the new **Bob Horn's Bandstand** on TV was so simple as to seem 'it couldn't work on 1952 television.' Bob would control the show and Lee would be his 'buddy' and be the funny one. With Tony Mammarella as producer, a stage manager or floor man, two cameras and that was it — except for a director, a mixer and an engineer in the control booth to decide which camera's coverage viewers would see at any given time, to watch the clock and signal when commercial breaks were due and when it was five o'clock, time to wrap it up for the day.

It's The Day, October 7, 1952 .... And It's The Time, 2:45 p.m.

Tony Mammarella was right there with Horn and Stewart on that eventful day and this is his description of the day and the hour:

Air time was 2:45 p.m. West Catholic High School for Girls was just around the corner from the studio and the girls were let out of school at 2:30 p.m. Fifteen minutes before show time there was not a living soul outside the studio door. By 2:45 p.m., zero hour, the number of kids waiting to "come in and dance" remained a chilling zero.

In the studio: 2:45:00 . . . slide in . . . theme up (Bob Crosby's, Decca Records recording of "High Society" according to Harvey Sheldon, now a California syndication TV producer and then, one of the first dancers to come onto Bob Horn's Bandstand in 1952) . . . **Bandstand with Bob Horn . . . and Lee Stewart . . . Da da Da da, dada Da dadadada . . .** 2:45:30 . . . Horn . . . take camera one.

Hi, I'm Bob Horn and this is Bandstand . . . a new idea for television . . . For the first time teenagers are invited to come to our studio and dance . . . To their favorite records and meet some of the top entertainers in the country . . .

Still no kids Bob . . . keep talking . . . maybe somebody will show up . . . stretch . . . keep talking . . . Lee, say something funny . . . Recite the Bill of Rights . . .

How the heck long can you stretch . . . Bob introduced the first record . . . What in the hell do you do with the camera? . . . pan around the studio . . . take a close-up of Bob talking to Lee . . . take a picture of Lee Stewart falling on his sword . . . do something . . . do anything . . .

51

3:00 p.m. . . . wait . . . two scared little girls, in the back of the studio . . . come in girls, you're just in time . . .

3:10 p.m. . . . five little girls . . . then eleven . . . twenty one kids . . . we're saved . . .

The show was rough around the edges, it was even rough at the core but **Bob Horn's Bandstand** worked. By 4:15 p.m. we had about 50 teenagers , , , 40 girls and 10 boys . . . they were relaxed . . . they were getting the idea and giving Horn ideas about his show. There was a little girl with a cute smile and she was dancing up a storm . . . keep the camera on her . . . what is she doing with her feet? . . . take a close up of her feet . . . darndest thing I ever saw . . . what the heck kind of step is that crazy kid with the crew cut doing . . . stay with him . . . no, wait . . . get a shot of those two girls at the top of the stands . . . whispering to each other . . . back to the dancers . . . roll call . . . lets talk to some of these kids and get a plug in for their high school . . . What is your name . . . Blanche McCleary . . . one of the first dancers on Bandstand . . . a winning smile and perpetual motion on the dance floor . . . A star is born . . .

By the end of the third day we were trying to find a way to get 1,000 kids into a studio that could only hold 250.

During the first hectic days there was hardly time to think of everything. Bob had to be concerned about the records, booking guest artists, preparing the commercials. There was not enough time but Horn knew he had to make enough time, success needs planning.

How are we going to handle the kids? What kind of rules should we have? How do we make sure they have a good time? What happens if it snows and nobody comes?

Bob Horn had the good sense and the experience to go at it slowly. "Let the show evolve," he said, "A little improvement each day. Listen to the kids. Talk to them." A week hadn't yet passed when Bob realized, THE KIDS ARE THE REAL STARS OF THE SHOW!!!

Before the show was a month old, a teenagers committee was formed. Twenty kids were hand picked by Horn to be on the committee and they started referring to themselves as "REGULARS." They weren't all good looking and they didn't all dance well. Some were bold and forward and some were shy. Some came from fairly well to do families and some came from families on welfare. None of the committee members had an identifiable character that came across on television and every one selected wanted desperately to be a "regular" on the show, **"Bob Horn's Bandstand."**

Thirty days or so later, the 'committee' or the 'regulars' membership was increased to 40.

(25 girls and 15 boys) . With forty teenagers committed to be there for the show, rain, sleet, snow or shine, we had a guaranteed audience (group of dancers) for every show.

As with anything new, according to Tony Mammarella, the show's producer, for the first six months it seemed there was a new problem every show day. Most were "wonderful problems," though. We had too many commercials to run and had to struggle to get them all in and still provide an entertaining show for viewers. We ran two 1 minute or one 2 minute commercial after every two dance numbers. We had to squeeze in roll calls, guests, and interviews with kids and our own promotions. Believe me, Tony said, "The show started and ended on a fever pitch." More and more kids were showing up at the studio doors every day. They all wanted to get in — to be on the show. Something had to be done. Not only did the Philadelphia teens want to visit and be on the show, we were getting requests to come to the show from kids from nearly the entire state of Pennsylvania, from Delaware, south New Jersey, and Maryland. This show wasn't just Philly — it was a regional show going out into a population base of well over 8-million people. Kids from far away were begging to come and appear on **Bob Horn's Bandstand**. That was another 'something to be handled,' It was resolved by groups from outside Philadelphia having to write in and we would arrange a day for their group — usually one or two busloads — to visit the show. Swamped with their requests from up to 150 miles distant, we could have had ten to twenty busloads a day.

The out of town kids wanting to come to the show reinforced what Bob Horn knew from our first day telecast, THE KIDS WERE THE STARS OF THE SHOW! Sure, the kids liked meeting Bob Horn but they came to see the kids they'd seen on the show. They hoped to be able to dance with members of the "Regulars." like Tommy De Noble, Jr. or to watch little Blanche McCleary (who was captivating on the show's first day) whirl and twirl. If they could, the out of town kids would attempt to get the autograph of every regular on the show. Then, of course, the possibility of seeing stars like Pat Boone, Bill Haley and the Comets, Little Richard or any of the other scores of famous artists who came to visit the kids on **Bob Horn's Bandstand** from time to time was frosting on the cake.

There was another kind of problem, too, that required more intricate and politically workable handling. It seemed that everybody who worked for the WFIL stations, radio or TV, or for our parent company, Triangle Publications (Walter Annenberg's company), that owned and published the *Philadelphia Inquirer*, each and almost every one wanted us to use their "terrific idea for the show." Once it was known that **Bob Horn's Bandstand** was a real hit, everybody wanted to "improve" the show. These are some of the suggestions that came to Bob through his producer, Tony Mammarella:

53

- Feature some of the big stars of the "thirties." Let the kids know the classy artists that entertained their parents. Let the kids know what they're missing.

- Play a Glen Miller record every day.

- A director at WFIL-TV and who had once worked for Paul Whitman, thought we should feature that "king" of the "twenties."

- It was hearsay around the studio one day that Mrs. Lee Annenberg, wife of the big, big boss (Walter Annenberg) and a Philadelphia socialite, was caused great embarrassment to learn that a TV show her husband owned would allow such shabbily dressed teenagers to be seen in his television show. This rumor went on to include, that she had suggested the boys on the show wear tuxedos and the girls wear party dresses.

- We all know teenagers have pimples. Someone suggested we cover up this unsightly disease by having all the kids wear theatrical make-up.

And, of course early sponsors had to get in their 'wants' on the show, too, mainly that they would like to see the kids using or being seen with their products on every show. Now that wouldn't be too much of a problem with Tastykake Bakery Products, giving samples to the kids at an appropriate time (in sealed packages revealing the Tastykake name and trademark) — but can you imagine the problems with Kissling Saurkraut, Coca Cola, Lem Pudding and Pie Filler, Cherios, or Bosco Chocolate Flavored Syrup. Who would want to see 200 kids slopping those things up on a dance show every afternoon for 2½ hours? We didn't even allow kids to chew gum at or on the show.

It seemed like every idea coming in was to "upgrade the appearance of the kids and the show." Build a fancy ballroom set, dress up the kids, have them wear make-up, get rid of the roll-away bleachers and make the studio look like a night club. It seemed like everything kids aren't, the good ideas people wanted these kids to be.

As for the era's TV critics locally and for hundreds of miles around, they said **Bob Horn's Bandstand** was amateurish. It has no production values and is in very bad taste, The bad taste part was probably objection to the rhythm and blues recordings Bob managed to work into each show — the really rhythmic music the kids enjoyed most for dancing — the music destined to soon herald in "their" rock 'n' roll. Bob Horn knew that and Tony Mammarella quickly learned to know that, too. And as for the critics, the show would for some time remain just a bunch of young teenage savages dancing to inferior mucic in a gymnasium.

While **Bob Horn's Bandstand** was highly successful, with a waiting line for sponsors and high viewer ratings there remained two underlying problems that were with the show from the very first day it was telecast. One of those problems was Bob Horn vs. Lee Stewart and the other was the Roger Clipp, Mr. Annenberg's manager for both the Triangle Publication's two Philadelphia radio stations, WFIL-AM and WFIL-FM, and his TV station, WFIL-TV, who just plain didn't like Bob Horn personally. And because Clipp didn't like Horn, Clipp's TV station manager, George Koehler, appeared (convincingly) not to like Horn either.

As for the first problem, Horn vs. Stewart there wasn't really any contest, particularly when sponsors were waiting to get onto the show and maintaining the 'Mad Man Muntz TVs' account was no longer a great need. Lee Stewart would surely lose. The only question was when. If Horn were to leave the show Stewart surely couldn't carry it alone. On the other hand, if Stewart were off the show it could be better because Horn would have more time to work with kids, THE STARS OF THE SHOW, and not have to play buffoon or straight man to Stewart's daily attempts at comedy – when the poor guy wasn't at all funny on the air. Maybe one on one Lee could tell joke and make a listener laugh – but on radio or TV his humor just wasn't there. Lee Stewart, the pitch man who could sell thousands of Muntz TVs on radio and TV simply couldn't fit in as a constructive or necessary part of **Bob Horn's Bandstand**. With this show part of Lee's life, he was much like the character played by Rodney Dangerfield, "Nobody would show him any respect." People who had business with the show in any way wanted to talk only with Bob Horn or, in his absence, with Tony Mammarella, the producer.

That other problem, built in from the start of the show, and even before, was essentially Roger Clipp's dislike of Bob Horn, and to some degree a similar dislike of Horn by George Koehler, both Bob's bosses — and Bob not being fond of either of them either. The more successful the show became, with Bob Horn getting most of the public's praise, the lion's share of the publicity, and substantial amounts in stipends, tips, finder fees, gifts and per-play commissions (that would later be given the name "payola") — the more Horn's two bosses' animosity toward him increased. Simultaneously, Horn became so valuable to WFIL-TV and to himself that he didn't need, any longer to ask, "How far?," when either of two bosses told him, "Jump!." Truly there seemed to be "unresolvable differences" between Mr. Horn and his two immediate bosses.

Here we must look again at the three men. Clipp and Koehler were both University of Pennsylvania graduates, both had well rounded cultural backgrounds (completely excluding rhythm, blues, and jive, and not much jazz, country or American folk music). Both of these men were in positions of responsibility, and had moved upward in the Annenberg empire, Triangle

55

Publication's, *Philadelphia Inquirer* Broadcast Division. Frankly, I have come to a conclusion that these two men looked down their noses at a guy like Bob Horn; not a college graduate, a man of the streets, of back alleys, pool halls, and cabarets. A man who had merely worked at lots of insignificant radio stations while finding out for himself how to be one of the very best announcers and DJs in a U.S. region where there are hundreds of radio stations seeking broadcast personnel with Horn's learned-the-hard-way talents. Clipp and Koehler were both "move up in the community men." They were joiners and had become pillars in the Philadelphia community, in the area where they will complete their regimented lives, retire and die. Their goals are established and they are on routes of accomplishment. To have to contend with an increasingly independent cuss like Bob Horn — becoming the most popular TV personality in Philadelphia. "My God," they must say between themselves, "have we created a Frankenstein?"

You may note that up to here you author has been using the show name, **Bob Horn's Bandstand**, with very few uses of the word 'Bandstand' without Bob Horn's name in front of the word Bandstand. There is an explicit reason for that choice of wording which will become evident in a later chapter.

Unquestionably, what had developed into an outstanding afternoon television show that was making a star of Bob Horn, the prime host, and stars of the kids who were the 'regulars' on the continuing hit show, in spite of differences between the show's co-hosts and between Mr. Horn and his station bosses, was continuing right along that same winning path Word about the excellent show was getting out all across the nation and Canada. Inquiries from other TV station managers and disc jockeys came pouring in by telephone, through the mail and by some visits by station management and telecast producers wanting to learn "the magic of **Bob Horn's Bandstand**." It looked so simple but there surely had to be some secrets kept hidden that made the show so successful. The secret was, there weren't any secrets. Other DJs across the nation tried a 'same show' but most of them (and all of them in time) failed and usually because of the egos of adults who owned, managed, produced, or emceed the copy-cat shows.

If the people involved had only realized what Bob Horn did on the first day the show was aired, THE KIDS ARE THE STARS; and that to be followed up with the rule of K.I.S.S (Keep It Simple, Stupid). But these other station owners, producers, directors and DJs didn't heed those simple guidelines, so they failed.

About The Names, "Bob Horn's Bandstand" And Plain "Bandstand"....
(Two Slashes with a Sword Can Alter For 50 Years the History of a Music and Dance Masterpiece)

Repeatedly using the full name, "Bob Horn's Bandstand" has been done intentionally to instill that full name in the thoughts of readers of this work before allowing the show's name to suddenly change for no immediately justifiable reason other than salving an irritation — or to prepare a place for a more favored son.

In That Particular Regard....

Earlier, when describing the set for — Bob Horn's Bandstand to arrive on TV a few details were omitted purposely so they could be brought in at this time in the story, when Bob Horn has been made, by publicity and outstanding creativity and performance, "a television king" in the eyes of the citizens of Philadelphia and of people of the entire Delaware Valley.

——This happening in Bob's life, the glory, the glamour, the power and the substantially increased income (mostly from record play gratuities, commissions, and stipends — not salary increases from WFIL-TV — according to information from Mrs. Ann Horn and others who confirmed this information) did effect his ego and did effect his way of living — just as such things wold tend to effect anyone who had never known so much money or glory before to anywhere near the same extent. Bob Horn was, suddenly, a doggoned millionaire (figuratively, not yet literally).

Bob, who always dressed nicely suddenly came to work in even finer threads. He bought some nice things for his wife, Ann, including a station wagon. For himself, Bob bought a fine looking Cadillac, the best looking car seen in the WFIL parking lot. And as mentioned earlier, he bought a little soft top cabin cruiser for himself, his wife, and to keep up with the Joneses. Around the studio people kept saying Bob's boat was a yacht. It wasn't. It was a 27 foot or 31 foot inboard cruiser — good for fishing, relaxing, a picnic on board, and probably too slow to be much of a water ski tow boat. He was better off than he'd been before and he did tend to flaunt it. But Bob Horn worked damned hard for his money. Yet a few people at WFIL radio and TV were envious of him and would delight in putting him down or seeing him put down — even when he was the man earning a sizeable portion of the money that paid these envious peoples' wages. That latter factor was not something the envious ones thought of, or if they did think about, chose to ignore.

The Truth About The Name Of The Teenager's Music and Dance Show....

When I first started researching this historical mystery I was told about and was given some articles and documents statements telling how the TV show, *"BANDSTAND,"* got its name. In these statements were some differences as to when the show was so named and why. In seeking the true chronological history of the show it became evident there can be a lot in a name — especially when conflicting information keeps popping up. The following several paragraphs and several photographs elsewhere in the book are indicative of this truth.

Bob Horn had a DJ show on WFIL-AM radio for two years within the years 1950 and going on into 1952. At some time during those years he gave his radio show a name that stuck with it for as long as he would continue doing the show on WFIL-AM radio. He called his show **Bob Horn's Bandstand** and it became a popular music show among the area's teenagers and forward-watching adults who heard his show, and liked the "new wave" recordings he played. Mingled in among standard music of the time, Bob played the rhythm and blues recordings that would lead to the jive and rock 'n' roll music Americans would learn to accept and adopt. Thousands of people in the regions tuned in to enjoy and dance to the music on **Bob Horn's Bandstand**, heard daily midweek. At that same time this popular DJ was also emceeing "pop" dances and concerts on weekends. He was a busy man, well known and well liked among 'new wave' music fans.

He was also known and written about quite regularly by 'music columnists' who wrote for Philadelphia area newspapers, some pro, some con, pertaining to the records 'of a new trend in pop music' that Bob Horn found and played on his unique-at-the-time DJ show. Like Horn and the music he played, the name of his show and where to find it on the radio dial became almost automatic to thousands of Philadelphia and Delaware Valley listeners.

WFIL-TV Chose To Capitalize On A Good, And Going Thing....

Why not cash in on an already successful, popular and profitable radio show's name with its established following by moving Bob Horn's show onto television? Bob and WFIL-TV management identified the logic of that thought, so when the show moved from WFIL-AM radio to WFIL-TV on October 7, 1952, the name, **Bob Horn's Bandstand**, made the move to television right along with the show, itself.

For Anyone Who Insists The Show's Name Changed To Just "BANDSTAND" Instead Of Remaining "BOB HORN'S BANDSTAND" When The TV Program Premiered On October 7, 1992,

58

The Evidence Is In That Shows That Thought Is A Mistake....

A few pages back the TV set for **Bob Horn's Bandstand** was not completely described, so the description is continued here: On the face of the counter that was the co-hosts' rostrum, in addition to tacked on record jackets and performing artists' photos that were changed frequently for fresh looks, were two permanent displays. One, to the left, looking at the hosts, was a ten slots sign holder for inserted strip signs to reveal the kids' "top ten record choices" for the week. Next to that, to the right, was affixed to the face of the counter an oversize record replica. On the top third of that big record was the word, "BAND." On the bottom third of the big record was the word, "STAND." In the center portion of that big record, where the label would be, was a blown up to proportion white label with the words on top, "BOB HORN'S," and the rest of the label being a picture of Bob Horn. That description of the early set is factual and it can be seen (most of it anyway) in a photo of Bob Horn presenting an award to Pat Boone when Mr. Boone appeared on the show some months after first being telecast daily. That photo may be found in the photos and letters section of this book, on page 101. Just look for Pat Boone and Bob Horn as they appeared in 1954. Bob Horn passed away in 1966 but Pat Boone looks almost the same today as he did then,

Why would anyone change the name of a regionally top ratings TV show that has more sponsors wanting to pay big bucks to get time on the show promote and sell their wares than can be accommodated? Why, unless there is skullduggery and a conspiracy of some sort in the chain of command?

THIS AUTHOR'S SUSPICIONS ARE ALERTED....

Born, raised and educated in Philadelphia and a fan of Bob Horn, his **Bob Horn's Bandstand** on radio, his **Bob Horn's Bandstand** on TV, Channel 6, and fan of the music he was introducing during the inception years of **rock 'n' roll** — your author was there as the Annenberg, Clipp, Koehler, Horn, Mammarella, Steck, Stewart, WFIL-AM and the WFIL-TV's top afternoon TV show of the region, et al, story unfolded.

I was a couple years too young to be a dancer on **Bob Horn's Bandstand** TV show, but as a staunch fan, I followed the show daily midweek, and the Bob Horn defoliating story straight through from 1951 (via radio) into 1952 and on to summer of 1956 (TV years for

Bob Horn) on WFIL-TV. As an astute youngster, many aspects of the 'power figures' railroading of Bob Horn didn't ring true for me then. Some of the buried events and results still seemed wrong to me while attaining adulthood. Upon becoming a successful business man, I started, in 1983, to ferret out the true story, the untold and the erroneously told aspects of early "Bandstand."

Inspiration to dig out the well buried truths of Bandstand history was in part, too, after having read for a second time Dick Clark's autobiography (1976) and [while I was doing my investigating] Mr. Clark's second book, "The History of American Bandstand" (1985). In both books I quickly identified obvious-to-me errors and never verified rumors being repeated in print for the contemporary world and posterity. I realize such writings are not unusual in many books — but within me was a need to find the "truths" of this search to the very best of my ability. To accomplish my goal I have utilized such documentation as I have been able to obtain and I have interviewed many "people who were there when the unconscionable happenings were taking place."

My research has unquestionably opened doorways into an American historical mystery. It is a mystery which I have been able, now, to resolve in my own mind from what information my research has revealed. Given the same information as I have, as it is printed within these pages, a reader may reach the same conclusions I have — or may interpret what I present differently, or even much differently than I have.

And there remains one further mystery solutions element (establishing reason that research should never end). Since word is out about my research efforts among the thousands of dancers who appeared on Bob Horn's Bandstand, there is seldom a day goes by but what I receive a telephone call or a letter, through my publisher, to tell me something more about Bob Horn, or about Bob Horn's status when Bandstand was openly identified as his creation. Believe me, if any information arrives that tells more or tells more accurately about any subject discussed in these pages, such information will definitely be included in a future edition (not necessarily a next printing) of this book.

Now That We Know The Name, "Bob Horn's Bandstand,"
Was Indeed The Show's First Name On Television, Let's Continue....

While the process continues to make the show better every weekday, and while more and more teenagers are seeking to be on the show, and advertisers and potential advertisers, both local and national seek to buy advertising time on the show. The publicity for the show and for Bob Horn, personally, continues on. Too, WFIL is utilizing the interest generated by this show to expound the merits and virtues of the station itself – with even Roger Clipp managing to get his name into the news, too, as in the *Philadelphia Inquirer*, the Annenberg's Triangle

Publication's newspaper that is, via command chain, the parent firm of the WFIL radio and television stations. The following article, somewhat to reflect the underlying 'dignity' of a station that would allow rhythm and blues music and teenage dancers onto its daily telecasting schedule, appeared just six days after the first telecasting of Bob Horn's Bandstand:

THE PHILADELPHIA INQUIRER – October 13, 1952

New Plant Designed for Efficiency
By Roger W. Clipp
General Manger, The Philadelphia Inquirer Stations

WFIL and WFIL-TV are now operating from new quarters which have been designed for top efficiency in our combined radio-television operations. Through 30 years of broadcasting services , WFIL has outgrown three homes and we are proud of this achievement.

Our decision to locate in West Philadelphia was made to provide elboe room for future progress, and to integrate all of our facilities in the interest of better services to our audiences. We have selected the conveniences of a city location without the restrictions of the crowded business district, and we have designed our headquarters for completely coordinated use.

The new WFIL Radio and Television Center is a compact plant for sleek operating efficiency. By getting full value from its operating expenditures, the WFIL organization is in a sound position to provide highest value for the advertiser's budget. The support of national and local advertisers is the keystone of our American system of broadcasting, the finest in the world. It is also the foundation of our industry's impressive record of service to the public.

WFIL has taken a long look at the requirements and potentialities of combined radio-television service and we have equipped our new headquarters to best advantage. Said a top agency executive, whose duties take him through broadcasting plants from Hollywood to New York, "Your new radio-television operation is the most efficient plant in the whole country. You have planned for the future as well as the present."

Actually, we look forward to a future as eventful as the past which saw WFIL grow from one of the nation's first to one of nation's leading stations. We shall continue the forward-looking policies which have made this progress possible.

61

The preceding article is included in this book for a single reason — to provide the level of usual thinking and leanings of Roger Clipp, so totally unlike a Bob Horn, a man of the people who enjoy his DJ and emceeing personality and his choices of standard and new wave music and his radio-TV patter. And that article was published just days after **Bob Horn's Bandstand** was first telecast from the new WFIL-TV's Studio B.

What a tremendous difference in the two men. It's no wonder they have difficulty in tolerating each other – and especially so since Horn is getting awfully big for his britches and is no longer easy to order around. Just reading the above article, and similar articles not included here, about Roger Clipp's being a devotee of classical music, is another clue to me that at some point Clipp and Horn will no doubt clash in one way or another.

Roger Clipp and his WFIL-TV station manager, George Koehler, very much cut by the same cookie cutter as Clipp, will have a tough time when no longer being able to order Bob Horn around. No more meetings purely at the bosses' convenience if Horn feels he has something to do that is more important to the show or to his responsibilities at the station. No more Bob Horn "yes boss" acceptance of show modifications suggested by Clipp or Koehler if they don't make good sense to Horn. At this juncture **Bob Horn's Bandstand** belongs to Bob Horn and he damned well knows it. It's the press and his public that tells him so.

Bob Horn is, by the end of 1952, already **a television shooting star**. Before, when on radio, occasionally on TV, and then during the beginning months of his own television show, Bob was a **bright light** in broadcasting but not a celebrity. Now, wherever he goes, whatever he does, Bob Horn is a 'big shot,' a 'wheel.' It's bound to effect his personality, especially because he earned his way to the top all on his own. No degree to hang on to, no alumni to fall back on, just his own unique abilities as a new wave music guru and an outstanding DJ and master of ceremonies. Good for you Bob Horn. We're pulling for you, and the kids on your show love you. But remember, too, Bob because of your seemingly sudden rise to local super success (and you're tending to flaunt it) you've made a few enemies at WFIL. Stay alert, Bob Horn.

Of course, Bob knows most all of that because he's been around lots of "stars" before and he knows how people kowtow to them. Today, he's one of them. While he can't help enjoying (privately) being in a position to make his bosses kiss his butt for a while — he also knows he has an important job to do for his show sponsors, for his viewers, for the kids and crew members on Bob Horn's Bandstand, for the station and, finally for his two bosses. So he will continue to take the boss's rightful orders, if not necessarily their suggestions. If he's called into a boss's office he'll be there if he believes his being there is important to his show, is important to WFIL-TV, or is important to him personally. If such an 'office call' seems unimportant in any of those three areas he is likely, since becoming a star, to send Lee Stewart or Tony Mammarella to represent him at the meeting.

In The Meanwhile The Publicity Continues On....

Following the first week of performances of **Bob Horn's Bandstand** on WFIL-TV, there was hardly a day that went by without mention of Bob Horn and of Lee Stewart and the dancing teenagers' appearances of Channel 6. The names popped up in greater Philadelphia area newspapers, in shopper publications, on radio and even occasionally on competing TV channels. Names of kids on the show were mentioned in local media — and it seemed like each time such an article or news item came forth, in it somewhere Bob Horn's name would also appear or be heard if it was an audio piece. There is no way that anyone residing in that entire area would not know the name of Bob Horn and what a great guy he was with the kids.

[But by the next two news stories, suspicion looms by a ordinarily minor difference.]

On January 16, 1953 Harry Harris, a writer for the ***Philadelphia Inquirer***, wrote in his column , "Around The Dials:" the following, three months after the show started airing:

Bandstand — Disc Jockey Formula for TV

"*BANDSTAND*," the Channel 6 show which features teen-agers dancing to popular recordings will get under way a half hour earlier beginning Monday.

"To the program's co-emcees, Bob Horn and Lee Stewart, this elongation to two hours and forty-five minutes daily proves they've come up with a successful answer to the problem of transferring that radio staple, the disc jockey show, to TV.

"The question on TV has always been," says Horn, (also) WFIL's director of recorded music, "what to do when the record plays. We were kind of nervous about that when we started. We thought we'd use crowd shots. But ever since the kids first got up and started to dance, there's been no problem."

"Some 5,000 high school students now hold membership cards which admit them to two specific afternoons each week. A volunteer committee of 12 teen-agers is charged with maintaining order and ruling on proper dress.

"No dungarees, pedal pushers or open sport shirts " is the show's rule.

"Several records have zoomed into local popularity because of constant encores on Bandstand, Horn and Stewart claim.

"We introduced Ray Anthony's 'Bunny Hop' just for a short contest," says Stewart, "but now the kids won't let us stop it. Another tune Bandtstanders invariably demand is Dizzy Gillespie's "Oh-Sho-Be-Do-Be."

"The show's A.R.B. (American Radio Broadcasters) rating is impressively high. Channel 3 has inaugurated a similar Saturday morning show. *[The earlier mentioned Grady and Hurst TV show that failed].* And there's talk of network interest in the format.

"It's the show's informality that's appealing," Horn feels. "If it were staged it could be a real bust.

"It's run principally by the kids themselves. We try to intrude as little as possible. Because they're with kids their own age, they're not self-conscious.

"Also, it's a surprise type show. You can never be sure what's going to happen."

"Surprises have included guest appearances by disc celebrities, who offer "lip-synchs" (pantomimed accompaniments to heir latest records) and often dance with the Bandstanders.

"Vocalist Joni James paid a $34 cab fare to keep a date on the show, after missing her train from Atlantic City. Fankie Laine didn't realize until mid-number that he had forgotten to doff his glassses. And Connie Boswell shamefacedly confessed that she didn't know the lyrics of her latest disc.

"Future Bandstand plans, Horn and Stewart report, include fan club meetings on the air, stressing of sectional rivalries, commuting to a tent in warm weather, and for an annual picnic."

(Please note the date of the above article, the paper it appeared in, and the word "**Bandstand**," where it appears. You might note, too, Mr. Harris' words, "talk of network interest in the format" as early as on January 16, 1953. Know, also, that Mr. Harris was an "insider" as a writer for the *Philadelphia Inquirer*.)

*　　*　　*

On March 29, 1953, writer, Rex Polier, in an article he wrote for Philadelphia's *The Sunday Bulletin*, (Philadelphia's non-Annenberg major newspaper) said:

"In Detroit it's the cat dance, Chicago has something it calls the shuffle, but when it comes to dancing, Philadelphia's teen-agers take the jitterbug two to one.

"That's the word from the city's beehive of juvenile jive, the Bob Horn Bandstand at WFIL-TV where the kids cavort each afternoon from 2:45 to 4:30 P.M.

"If you've ever watched these youngsters from Philadelphia and suburban high schools dancing to recorded tunes purveyed by Horn and his hep-mate, Lee Stewart, you've probably wondered if today's children (1953) ever dance anything else but the twisting, twirling, jumping jitterbug.

"Well," says Horn, "they do but when all is said and done, the prefer the jit. Matter of fact, these kids have only two classifications for dancing, the jit and slow. 'Slow' is the word they give to all other forms of dancing.

"A strong bit of evidence to support this statement is the mushrooming of "The Bunny Hop," a step that looks to the adult eye as an offshoot of the danse jitterbug.

"Horn introduced it on his show after Ray Anthony, the band leader, had staged it on the west coast. The bandstand devotees caught it up like a leaf by the wind and now it's definitely the local dance of the hour.

"Horn thinks his bandstand is the long-awaited answer to the problem TV poses for radio's disc jockeys.

"Instead of a solitary character sitting before a turntable and making with the monotonous chatter, the bandstand is animated and varied.

"Horn and Stewart are constantly coming up with new "gimmicks" to maintain the show's fast pace. Big name singers like Frankie Laine, Joni James, and Helen O'Connell appear from time to time in person on the show ....

"All these constant innovations and gimmicks pay off for the bandstand. Its rating is high, its popularity among the teen-agers widespread. It's reached a point now where kids in nearby communities gather in firehouses and the like in the afternoon, tune in the bandstand on TV and dance right along with the bunch in the studio.

"...... Maestro Horn kept putting on platter after platter of what sounded suspiciously like jive . It seemed proof enough for anybody that the youngsters liked it sprinkled with paprika.

[Please note the newspaper name, **The Philadelphia Bulletin**, the article date, and the show name underlined, the Bob Horn Bandstand at WFIL-TV.]

From the two articles, above, we may elect to accept portions of each article as early evidence or clues, pertaining to a WFIL **upper management conspiracy** or calculated plan for in the foreseeable future, removal of Bob Horn from what had been so quickly popularized in the WFIL market area to be **"Bob Horn's Bandstand."** It was the WFIL-TV program merely moved, under Horn's creative guidance and showmanship, from radio to television.

65

- The first article, above, reveals that as early as **mid-January, 1953,** just 3 months after **Bob Horn's Bandstand** was first aired on television, writers at the *Philadelphia Inquirer* newspaper, parent company of WFIL, had already been instructed to use the name, "**Bandstand**" by itself — without further use of the name, **"Bob Horn's Bandstand"** in articles, items or advertising copy for the show.

- In the second article, above, however, published three month after the first article, in the Sunday *Philadelphia Bulletin* — not affiliated in any way with WFIL or Annenberg holdings — as written by Rex Polier, 5 months after **Bob Horn's Bandstand** was first aired on WFIL-TV — feature writer.Mr. Polier, still used the show's original name as **"the Bob Horn Bandstand."** This **can mean for us, 45 years later, that word of the name change, to** *Bandstand,* **without Bob Horn's name in front of it, was apparently being kept "in house" for a while, within the Annenberg, Triangle Publications,** *Philadelphia Inquirer* **and WFIL-AM, WFIL-FM and WFIL-TV organization.** Mr. Polier's article in *The Bulletin* indicates that word of the show's name change wasn't yet out the general media in the greater Philly area.

> Sidenote: With 44 years separtion, we find that besides this author referring to Bob Horn as "Maestro," Temple University archives have allowed us to find and retrieve a published article in which another writer, Rex Polier, in 1953, described Bob Horn as "**Maestro Horn**." Maestro no doubt meaning to both authors, "an extremely capable, talented, creative and innovative disc jockey and TV show host who was in many ways far ahead of his time." This, friend readers was "Maestro" Bob Horn.

- - -

Bob Horn and Bob Horn's Bandstand Were Not The Only Recipients Of Buildup....
Bob's WFIL Boss And Adversary Was Getting His Kudos , Too....

On April 22, 1953 the following 'news release' from WFIL-TV & Radio stations was sent out to every newspaper, magazine, radio station and TV station in New York, Pennsylvania, Washington, DC, Delaware and New Jersey:

NEWS From WFIL

<u>For Immediate Release</u>   4/22/53

<u>ROGER W. CLIPP ELECTED TO BOARD OF DIRECTORS</u>
<u>OF CHAMBER OF COMMERCE OF THE UNITED STATES</u>

PHILADELPHIA, April 22:-- Roger W. Clipp, general
manager of WFIL and WFIL-TV, has been elected to
the board of directors of the Chamber of Commerce
of the United States. Clipp was elected as the
representative of District II, which is composed of
the states of Pennsylvania, New York, New Jersey
and Delaware. He takes office April 28 and his term
is for two years.

Clipp is the first member of the broadcasting
industry to serve on the board. In addition to his
position as general manager of the Philadelphia
Inquirer stations, he is also the President of the
Pennsylvania Association of Broadcasters. Recently
Clipp was also named business manager of TV GUIDE,
nation-wide television fan magazine published each
week by Triangle Publications.

Clipp succeeds George Whitwell, vice president
in charge of sales for the Philadelphia Electric
Company who had served two terms on the board of
directors. He (Clipp) was nominated for the board
of directors by the Chamber of Commerce of Greater
Philadelphia, and his election is as a result of
the votes of the members of the Chamber of Commerce
of the U.S. in the four state area.

As general manager of WFIL & WFIL-TV Clipp has been active in many civic affairs, and has served in an executive capacity with many business and public interest projects. For the past seven years he has been chairman of the Planning and Advisory Committee of the more than 300 stations of the ABC Network. He was appointed by Governor John S. Fine to the Pennsylvania Joint Committee on Educational Television in November 1952, and was names to the Philadelphia Board of Trade by Mayor Joseph S. Clark in that same year.

He is an active member of the U.S. Chamber of Commerce having been a member of the organization's Advertising Committee since 1950. He was Radio-Television Chairman of Philadelphia's successful campaign to bring the 1948 Democratic and Republican National Conventions to this city, and served in an executive capacity on the Mayor's Committee for Convention Arrangements.

Clipp is President of the Philadelphia Chapter of the National Foundation for Infantile Paralysis, and was the general chairman of the 1953 March of Dimes drive in the Philadelphia area for the third consecutive year when the campaign resulted in a record collection of more than $400,000. He is a member of the national board of the United Cerebral Palsy Association, and serves on the Board of Governors of the Philadelphia Heart Association, and the Philadelphia Executive Council of the Boy Scouts of America.

- 0 -

Now, how in the hell could a man described in such a glowing and factually correct news release, as Roger W. Clipp was, above, be concerned with or have time to bother with such proportionally minor things as Bob Horn getting to be too popular, too wealthy and appearing to be flaunting his new position and wealth around too much?

How could a busy man like Clipp allow himself to be overly concerned about, perhaps, Bob Horn being too old to be hosting a TV show with a daily cast of 50 to 200 teenagers?

As far as the "how" Clipp could let himself be involved with the "pulling down to size" of Bob Horn, that wouldn't be too difficult or too time consuming. For that he only needed to mastermind the what to be done — then turn the doing of it over to his "*with him*" employees like George Koehler, his manager of WFIL-TV, and other junior administrative types, like J. D. Scheuer, Jr., who sent the memo to Horn about teenagers not allowed to use the comfort rooms in the basement.

Any "why," of course, is another matter. We know that his first choice to host an afternoon music-dance TV show for kids was not Bob Horn. He would have much preferred the team of Grady and Hurst.

Further, among all the people Clipp knew and dealt with in Greater Philadelphia, some were bound to have said to him, "What's an older man like Horn doing, hosting your TV show with all those teenagers?"

Factors like these were enough to cause Clipp to want a more youthful looking and easier to control replacement for Horn, ASAP.

Those reasons alone, however, wouldn't call for devious actions from a busy executive. Roger Clipp's "why" would have to be stronger than any one or all of those things. Those were things that could be solved by simply not renewing Horn's contract when it came up for renewal. Or, if wanting to remove Horn was more urgent than waiting for his contract to end; tell Horn the reasons for wanting him off of the show, and buy up his contract, along with compensation to cancel out any renewal options — like it's being done today when a company, corporation, organization or team wants to discharge and replace a productive individual. Certainly, that would perhaps cost WFIL-TV a lot of money — and Clipp may have had a difficult time explaining such a large expenditure "to get rid of a star" to his boss, Walter Annenberg.

That latter possibility for "why" the harassment campaign to rid *BANDSTAND* of its creator and host, Bob Horn, hopefully via his resignation, may come closer to the reason for events further downstream than anyone but Clipp, and possibly his associate, Koehler, might have been thinking of as 'workable resort possibilities' on April 22, 1953.

69

In the meanwhile at WFIL-TV is, beyond some ripples of malcontent upon on the water, heading to complete 1953 as a banner year. The show was going great, it was popular with viewers as was its host, Bob Horn. Sponsors were waiting to buy commercials time on the show. The ratings were already high and still climbinng. Everyone connected with WFIL-TV, from its owner Walter Annenberg, right on doen the line to the station's janitors knew they had a real winner at WFIL-TV.

- - -

CHAPTER FIVE

THE POLISHING OF
A TELEVISION MASTERWORK
(WHILE SURROUNDED BY WFIL SKULLDUGGERY)

Moving on with little to no help from the front office of WFIL Radio and TV, meaning manger, Roger Clipp, or from WFIL-TV manager, George Koehler, neither of who were known for contributing much in ways of "includable " ideas for the betterment or improvement of **Bob Horn's Bandstand** — the show was doing absolutely great. This, the show these two managers were already referring to as just plain "*Bandstand*" as early as by mid-January of 1953, a few months after the start of what was already becoming the most consistently profitable 2 hour time slot on WFIL-TV. And as for Mr. Annenberg, he had to be pleased with this program he had suggested some months back to Clipp — and that was in only a few months, a blockbuster for his WFIL-TV .station.

Was, then, the Clipp and Koehler posture a clue of things to happen downstream? This author believes yes. But then, too, we have to recognize that kids jumping up and down and spinning around on a new studio floor was not their idea of fine programming – and Bob Horn was not "their kind of man." To ever find the three of them together socially, away from WFIL studios, and without being commanded to do so by Mr. Annenberg had to be pretty much an impossibility.

The prime movers of the show at this time were:

<u>Bob Horn</u> the principal creative contributor, wise enough to imagine or see something good happen in any given day then figure out a way to try it out on the show. Having worked on so many radio and live stage presentations in the past, many with super-low budgets where improvision was the only way go, Bob had hundreds of entertainment tools and gimmicks to add sparkle to a show already star-studded by the kids and his choices in music for the '60s as early as in 1953.

Lee Stewart, of whom everything I've learned about him and by remarks of everyone I've talked to about him, wanted desperately to make contributions to **Bob Horn's Bandstand,** but simply didn't have that special large audience entertainment knack or talent within his being. Lee's humor, I have learned, was folksy and often slapstick and for small groups, frequently requiring costumes. Lee Stewart's comedy was best suited to a parlor or a family gathering. He certainly tried to bring touches of his brand of humor onto the show but when one time after another time his stunts and jokes failed to entertain, Lee got on Bob's nerves in a negative way and consequently Bob wanted to get Lee Stewart off of **Bob Horn's Bandstand** as quickly as possible.

Tony Mammarella, the show's producer, made most of his contributions to the show by handling the details to allow a Bob Horn idea to work the way Bob had in mind. When Bob came up with his "**Rate a Record**" plan to have teenagers at the show rate the records they liked best each week — it would be Tony Mammarella who would make all of the necessary preparations. If Bob saw fit to change the appearance of their set with new artist's portraits, he would pass his thought on to Tony and Tony would make it happen. Bob had his hands full coming up with "good" new recordings five days a week. It meant meetings with distributors representatives on a near daily basis and listening to hundreds of new recordings every month. Tony listened to records with Bob for some time, until he learned what Bob listened "for." Once Tony knew that he then, alone, could listen to the rep's pitches and records when Bob was overwhelmed by too many records to listen to and too many commercials to become familiar with before show time. Tony would then do Bob's initial listening and make his recommendations to Bob, "thumbs up" or "thumbs down." Bob would suggest, and Tony would work out the details for ideas to work their best. Tony, a fine on-air personality himself, became so familiar with the show and the conduct of it that if Bob had to miss a performance for any reason, he knew Tony Mammarella could and would fill in for him in a masterful manner. Not to be misunderstood, Tony was never a "gopher," and while he was designated the show's producer by Koehler, he was far more than that to the success and continuance of the show. It was more like Tony Mammarella was Bob Horn's "guarantor" to keep the show running smoothly (at least as smoothly as could be) if Bob was away from the microphone, turntable, telephone and cameras — with Tony there in Bob's stead.

"SC," the show's secretary, who worked with and for Bob, Lee and Tony was another major contributor to the show. Not only did she provide ideas for the show (especially with tips for making things work smoothly with the teenage girls who danced on the show) but she was also the sounding board for all three men. "What do you think of this idea, SC?" "How so you think this will go over with the kids, SC?" These were the kind of questions she fielded nearly every work day. The show, many people have said, could not have run nearly so perfectly without "SC."

There were others of the **Bob Horn's Bandstand** crew, cameramen, floorman, engineer, mixer, and even the guard at the door, who came in with workable ideas to help keep the show running excitingly and well. And they were, each and every, one proud of their contributions — but if we were to ask them, any one of them, who made the show click, who made the show run, who created the show, their answers would be, unanimously, "Bob Horn."

Promotion "Bandstand" Was Cut Way Back But Popularity Continued On....

In March of 1953 everything on **Bob Horn's Bandstand** was moving along well. Bob Horn and Lee Stewart, still co-hosts, and Anthony "Tony" Mammarella , the producer who Bob found reasons to introduce to the show's public on almost every show, were by then, after a half-year of doing the show five days a week, household names in almost every home in the greater Philadelphia area — and surely in every home where there were teens and near teens youngsters.

But more than that, **the kids who were the stars**, as Bob had said they would be from the show's very first day, were shining brightly. Fan clubs were formed for the "Regulars" (the committee members, on the show every weekday) and fan letters and gifts for the ones most popular were arriving in the WFIL-TV mail daily.

With Promotional Budget Reductions, The Show's Popularity Surges On....

By mid-1953 advertising dollar expenditures for the show were cut way back, and even "news releases" from the WFIL-TV public relations department were reduced to mostly nothing more than advance announcements of which celebrity vocalists and musicians would be appearing each week. We might note here, too, than any news about the show emanating from WFIL or appearing in the *Philadelphia Inquirer,* or in the newly acquired Triangle Publication's weekly *TV Guide* magazine (First issue out on April 3, 1953) under the executive management of guess who? [And this is almost unbelievable] Walter Annenberg announced as his choice to be business manager of the new-to-the-company *TV Guide* — Mr. Roger Clipp. This new position for Clipp would be in addition to his continuing over-all management of the WFIL radio and television stations. Mr. Annenberg chose Clipp for this added responsibility not because Clipp knew anything about publishing a magazine, but rather because he knew so many people in the television industry. That, Mr. Annenberg

73

thought was a necessary management consideration for *TV Guide* because the cooperation of TV people across the nation would be essential to having TV stations' programs scheduling to publish in the magazine.

The Annenberg appointment to the new magazine was a smart move, but one that made Clipp more powerful than even before within the Annenberg media-entertainment empire. It meant, too, that George Koehler would have more say-so in the running of the WFIL stations, both radio and television.

1953, As Predicted, Was A Very Good Year For Bandstand

As far as the public could see, the remainder of 1953 remained a continuing popularity growth period for what became accepted as *BANDSTAND*. The show, itself, was its best publicity and that was augmented by some news articles in print. Regional celebrity, Bob Horn's photo appeared on a placard used in all the places where *TV Guide* was on sale in the Delaware Valley (hundreds of them) kept his photo in print before his public.

1953 was the first year, too, of a **Bandstand picnic for charity**. Held in Philadelphia's Woodside Park, a park with a huge recreational and picnic area the first annual picnic attracted well over 2,000 teenagers and many parents and siblings. With each attendee paying a moderate admission fee for a picnic meal, the usual daytime BANDSTAND show televised from the park at its usual time, a wonderful time was in store for all. In the evening a shorter version of the show was put on the air so people who couldn't usually see BANDSTAND during its regular daytime schedule could come see it live at the park or on tune it in on their TV screens at home. Various contests and a BANDSTAND softball game were also featured at the picnic. The event, like the show itself, was a huge success. The show and WFIL-TV received a tremendous amount of great publicity (as if it needed it), and a local charity reaped the healthy proceeds. Bob Horn was the event master of ceremonies. Lee Stewart, who wasn't too swift for most things in connection with the show presentations, did a tremendous job of helping organize and conduct the picnics of 1953 and would, again, in 1954.

Under A Beautiful Surface, Are Makings For A Rough Time Ahead....

The animosity between Horn and Stewart remained unchanged, and Bob Horn's being compelled to announce the beginnings and endings of Dick Clark's radio version of Bandstand was driving him nuts. Messrs. Koehler and Horn stayed pretty much out of each other's way, and with his new added responsibility of running *TV Guide*, Roger Clipp was seen less and less around the WFIL offices — but everyone at WFIL still knew Clipp was their number one boss and that he kept himself informed about anything and everything going on at the stations.

With the exceptions of George Koehler, the young announcer-DJ, Dick Clark (according to Mr. Clark), his personal secretary and a very few others around the WFIL facilities who held his unique kind of favor, Roger Clipp, while very much the boss (and everyone knew it) remained an enigma . He was never known to smile, never known to say much of anything to anyone except about work concerns, and from scores of sources this author has learned that Clipp was one of the better "bean counters" and "penny pinchers" of his day. These latter qualities, according to an Annenberg autobiography statement was this: "Walter Annenberg liked about Clipp but simultaneously disliked him because Clipp on some occasions made bad purchases in order to save money." This tightwad characteristic of Roger Clipp has been mentioned before in this work but it is worth a repeat because it may become a factor in a thrust of this story.

Meanwhile, In The Executive Offices, Something Devious Has Been Brewing....

It was four months before **Bob Horn's Bandstand** on WFIL-AM radio would be moved to television. The date must have been somewhere around June 1st of 1952 when Roger Clipp received a phone call from a radio station manager he knew in Utica, New York. The station was WRUN and the man was the father of Dick Clark. Mr. Clark asked Roger if he would arrange an audition for his son at WFIL. He explained to Clipp that his son, then 23, had been working as an announcer at stations WOLF radio in Syracuse, and at WRUN, Utica. The boy had also gained some experience at TV station WKTV, in Utica, Clipp was told.

Apparently Roger liked what Dick Clark's father said about his son. He told Jack Steck, Program Manager, to audition the kid — and probably added, "If he's any good, hire him for WFIL-Radio." Jack did as he was told. He auditioned Dick Clark. Dick did a good audition and Steck hired him.

Young Clark's first work at WFIL was as a relief and fill-in announcer on WFIL-AM. According to Clark, in his autobiography, he finally, one day got to meet Roger Clipp, who usually didn't show kindnesses or friendship to staff people he met. Clark goes on to say, however, that he and Roger Clipp hit it off as compatible right from the start. Soon Clark was doing station IDs, commercials and news. Then he got his own WFIL-AM radio show, **"Dick Clark's Caravan of Stars,"** spinning contemporary pop records.

Between Roger Clipp and George Koehler, it appears that Dick Clark was their choice as a "college boy," baby face, clear skin, youthful announcer with a lot of poise. Clark came across, too, as the nice "boy from next door," the kind of boy every mother wanted for her daughter. Dick Clark was, culturally, the WFIL bosses' kind of "young man" they wanted to be doing air-time on WFIL radio and TV.

In the fall of 1953 the name of "Dick Clark's Caravan of Stars" radio show on WFIL-TV was changed to "***Bandstand***," purportedly to identify with Bob Horn's by then successful TV show. With that single manipulative action the bosses, or perhaps just Clipp – with Koehler simply going along with his boss – saw in this particular programming change an opportunity to make Bob Horn, who might be getting too big for his britches with his own TV show's success, bow down and eat some humble pie.

Adding insult to injury, this was also the time when Bob Horn was ordered (not asked) to pop into Dick Clark's "*Bandstand*" radio booth each day "twice" to announce the openings and closings of Dick's broadcast. Twice a day Bob had to run down the hall to accomplish this mission. Talk about a "come down!" To do this chore at WFIL, came down to Horn strictly as an order – not a suggestion, not a request. Bob knew he had to do it. Twice each day, in Clark's radio booth Bob would say a few opening or closing words, then excuse himself by saying he had to get back to the **Television *Bandstand*,** on Channel 6.

By this devious maneuver (but far fetchedly beneficial), Clipp (or Clipp and Koehler together), were working toward seeing to it that soon the name, "**BOB   HORN'S BANDSTAND"** would become gone from WFIL radio and TV forever. And the managers shared the pleasure of seeing Horn being personally "put down" before his fellow employees and, to some degree, before his public, too.

Look Again To This Public Belittling Of Mr. Horn....

What a blow beneath the belt was dealt to Bob Horn, *the maestro*, when he became compelled to announce the openings and closings of a neophyte, "baby DJ's" radio show. What a miserable slap in the face. With that sort of forced working together, as it can only be called, there was little chance that Bob Horn and Dick Clark could ever genuinely like each other. That was a situation of a master DJ being ordered, not volunteering, to introduce to his own audience (as was the bosses' intent) this baby face kid with a couple of years experience — and who had, then, not an inkling whatsoever about the rhythm and blues kind of music the "Bob Horn's Bandstand" listeners wanted to hear via their radios.

This, what might appear to be but a ridiculous situation, was more likely a viciously conceived and evil act of vindictiveness by Roger Clipp (with possibly George Koehler, too) to bring to his knees and embarrass Bob Horn, a man more creative, as has been overwhelmingly revealed, than either one of those two men or the two of them together. They had to know damned well when they did this unsavory deed that it was Bob Horn's creative genius that had made them look like heroes in the telecasting business and with their boss, and beyond that , was also making WFIL-TV the highest rated daytime TV station of Philadelphia and of the entire Delaware Valley.

And it has to make one sick when thinking about a trusting Bob Horn probably talking

himself into believing his bosses — when they told him, "We're having you start and close the radio "Bandstand" to bring additional attention to your own TV show." S-u-r-r-r-e you are Mr. Horn.....
IT!!

\- \- \-

In 1954 *"Bandstand,"* on Channel 6, kept right on growing in numbers viewers, and in teenagers wanting to be seen on the show. Those teens who were the "Regulars" were becoming downright celebrities, seen not only on *"Bandstand"* but also in photos on the pages of teenager magazines all across America.

And, at the same time, Bob Horn, Tony Mammarella and, to a lesser degree, Lee Stewart, were each growing in public and viewer recognition, too. *"Bandstand"* was a fantastic success, the kids on the show were every bit the stars Bob Horn had predicted them to be — and everybody in town (especially those connected with Triangle Publications and the Annenberg holdings) KNEW IT!!

Of The Earlier Mentioned "Bandstand" Key People, Where Are They Today?

Where are they today, those people close to this story in 1953?. Bob Horn died of a heart attack brought on by a heat stroke in 1966. Roger Clipp is deceased, Tony Mammarella has passed away, Jack Steck is no longer with us, and the only two bosses remaining, who could be defined as bosses over Bob Horn in that year, and who are alive as these words are written, are George Koehler, who moved on in television to become an owner and supervisor of these WFIL stations along with ownership in other stations as well — and Walter H. Annenberg, currently engrossed with his philanthropical interests and his friendships with presidents, kings, queens and international dignitaries, who sometimes come to visit him at his home, "Sunnylands," in Palm Springs, California.

Interestingly though — today when I talk with scores of people in their fifties and sixties who were teenagers dancing on **Bob Horn's Bandstand** (with, incidentally, more among the thousands of former dancers contacting me every week since word of this book's being published is out) — one can only realize that while Bob Horn passed away in 1966, **Bob Horn's Bandstand** is living on into the 21st Century and right on into a new millennium.

And concerning Bob Horn and his Bandstand helping to introduce " the baby boomer era of jitterbug and rock 'n' roll" to America and to the rest of the world — that contribution will live forever because while any style of music might fade for a period of years — music is like MacArthur, it shall return.

78

But This Is Not Particularly A Book Of Nostalgia....

This work is more fittingly <u>a historical mystery</u> from which readers, the jurors, may decide whether or not an unscrupulous, dastardly and self-serving crime was committed by a man, or men, who are today regionally, if not even nationally regarded, or remembered as astute and honorable business leaders in the fields of radio, television and publishing during the second half of the 20th century.

Ann Horn told your author about a network offer Bob had to bring the show to New York. He'd have to change the name, of course, and create another similar show - and buy his way out of his contract. Of course, with Clipp being the "tight with money" man that he was, buying his contract out wouldn't amount to much because Bob, at the time was only being paid about a third of what he should be earning from *"Bandstand,"* In fact, Ann told me, "If it weren't for record play commissions or tips Bob received from recording marketers (the so-called payola), he brought home and his earnings from concerts he emceed or from record hop dances for which he was the DJ, we wouldn't have been well off at all".

As it was Bob was, overall, earning a good income and there were some people at WFIL stations who were very envious of him. And, as indicated earlier, Bob did tend to flaunt his newfound wealth to some degree – but he was earning it and he'd not had so much before in his life so why not live it up a little?

There Were Not Too Subtle Moves Afoot To Encourage Bob Horn To Quit....

①

It started with forcing Bob to have a co-host, Lee Stewart, on the TV **Bob Horn's Bandstand**.

②

It showed up within a few months, again, when "management" (Clipp, Koehler and company), without consulting Mr. Horn, changed the name of the TV show from "**Bob Horn's Bandstand**" to just plain "*BANDSTAND*."

③

It multiplied, when Dick Clark, on WFIL-AM radio doing his DJ thing with a programb called "Dick Clark's Caravan of Stars" was told to change the name of his radio show to "*BANDSTAND*." That is the name Bob had selected for his own radio show three years before.

④

It hit a high note, when "management" demanded that Bob Horn, run down the hall twice a day to make the opening and closing announcements on "fair haired" Dick Clark's "*Bandstand*" on WFIL-AM radio.

⑤

Then, in 1994 commenced a barrage of petty annoyances to extract pleasure from doing one's best for WFIL-TV and continuing to maintain a blockbuster show.

Pettiness....

The two following replicas of "actual WFIL inter-office memos" are a classic example of the unnecessary and disturbing items of pettiness to which Bob, too, (unfortunately) allowed himself to be vacuumed into: .

WFIL

INTER-OFFICE COMMUNICATION

TO: Bob Horn   DATE: February 24, 1954

FROM: J. D. Scheuer, Jr.

SUBJECT:

C O N F I D E N T I A L

I have issued instructions to keep all BANDSTAND youngsters out of the basement effective yesterday.

The reason I have had to take this arbitrary action is because they have defaced the men's room down there and other parts of the building, taken tiles out of the walls, etc.

Actually I don't think this is much of a hardship on anybody but I wanted you to know about it.

Sorry I couldn't reach you yesterday.

JDS

eg

To which Bob Horn felt compelled to reply with the following memo the same day he received the memo the memo from Mr. Scheuer:

WFIL
INTER-OFFICE COMMUNICATION

TO; J. D. Scheuer, Jr.   **DATE:** 2/24/54

FROM: Bob Horn

SUBJECT: A DEAR JOHN LETTER

C O N F I D E N T I A L

You will never know what you have done to me! It is easy to issue an order forbidding people to heed nature's call. But, John, have you ever tried to explain to 200 vigorous young people who have spent a long day in school and some time getting to our studios, that all calls of nature are to be canceled until such time as we permit them to leave our premises.

Not only did I spend a great deal of my show time today (when I should have been being clever and witty) explaining the "no toilet" regulation, but I also learned that getting a drink of water was forbidden. In view of your "no toilet" edict, I can see your thinking on the "no water" rule.

81

However, I might suggest that all advertising pertaining to
natural body functions be excluded from the program -- such
as Espotabs, etc.

Seriously, I think that the "no washroom" or "drink" order
could hurt us if this gets to become common knowledge, as I
believe the Health Department requires places of entertainment, whether admission is charged or not, to maintain
washroom facilities.

Gotta go now!!!

                                            BH____*BH*_____

sc

For a busy man to be drawn into such pettiness when it appears to be another part of a conspiracy to urge him to quit his job is repugnant. — Then again, if he is working for a boss or bosses who utilize psychological warfare or methods to manipulate personnel in an effort to maintain tranquility and keep costs down by retaining only subservient employees — there is method in this madness. At the WFIL stations, if these things indeed happened the way they turn up as evidence-from-the-past, today, an all out conspiracy to rid WFIL of Bob Horn (without having to "pay him off to depart") must have been masterminded by one man, by two men, by three or possibly even four individuals in positions of power in the Annenberg's organization.

Possible 1953-1954 External Motivation To Jettison Bob Horn?

Ann Horn, Bob Horn's widow, and Jack Steck, WFIL's program director and talent scout, told this author that Bob Horn had been approached by a major TV network to come to New York City and to there create for them a nationwide network version of a new show, similar in everything but name to **Bob Horn's Bandstand**. Bob had turned them down because their studios were all too small to accommodate such a show. Tony Mammarella was also aware that Bob had been approached with such an offer and that he's gone to New York on a weekend to discuss the proposal. All he knew, further, was that Bob had turned it down. Tony did not know any of the offer details — or, if he did, chose not to discuss them because it may have involved him, too.

We can be sure that some sort of network offer came to Bob Horn and that, for whatever reason or reasons, nothing materialized. But how do we know whether or not the same or another network had not been in contact with Mr. Annenberg, with Mr. Clipp or with Mr. Koehler (or all three of them) about making *BANDSTAND* a nationally televised, network program. *BANDSTAND* was a hot TV property within a matter of three months after its premiere program in October of 1952. The story was into the early part of 1954 with the show still climbing up, up and up on the ratings charts. National advertisers, like Lever Brothers' *Pepsodent* (toothpaste) Division and *Coca Cola*, via their Philadelphia area bottler, were already or soon would be advertising on *BANDSTAND*.

Word spreads fast when a new TV show is a "super hit." When national advertisers express interest in wanting to buy "commercials time" on a "hot" local or regional show the networks want that show — or want to produce one of their own just like it. That part of TV is no different in the 1990s than it was forty some years ago, in the 1950s. To think for a moment that a network or networks would approach Bob Horn directly, without first (or at the same time) approaching the owners of the show is naive. So when Bob was approached, personally by a network, we might rest assured that the bosses in the front office had been or would be approached by one or more networks, too, about taking a "winner" regional or national on a particular network.

Granted, before even considering Bob Horn (when he was a DJ on WFIL-AM radio) to do an afternoon, kids dancing TV show for WFIL-TV, Messrs. Clipp and Koehler tried first to hire Joe Grady and Ed Hurst to bring their radio show onto WFIL-TV afternoon programming — and were turned down. That, however, would have been a minimal dollars offer to two men who were doing great, but not super great, on radio locally into an afternoon TV time slot of old movies that were simply not attracting enough viewers. That's not even like comparing an orange and an apple, it more like comparing a dried prune with passion fruit.

Yes, we can visualize network executives coming to Roger Clipp and to George Koehler, and maybe even directly to Walter Annenberg, the big boss, with their offers to make *BANDSTAND* a regional or national network program. To think that wouldn't, couldn't or didn't happen would be totally naive. With network scouts having watched the show for three or four telecasts, as co-hosted by Bob Horn and Lee Stewart, network people might have even said to the WFIL bosses, something like this, "If we take it on we'd probably want a younger host (with someone on their payroll in mind) in there with all those teenagers."

Would such an occurrence and conversation be fuel for a "we've got to get Horn out of there before it's too late" deceptive campaign? In 1954 Bob Horn was 38 and the WFIL-AM radio disc jockey, wet behind the ears but drying out fairly fast, as the DJ host of radio *BANDSTAND* was only 26 and could have (dressed the right way) easily passed for 17.

Rationalization, Not Justification, For A Conspiracy Is Becoming Evident....

When the two WFIL station's bosses spoke privately, and with neither of them liking Bob Horn, for some of the same, and some different reasons, they must have discussed at one time or another things like these: "Have we indeed created our own Frankenstein? We put Horn into TV hosting *BANDSTAND* and we've spent thousands of dollars promoting the show and promoting Horn to where, here in our market, he's the hottest name in daytime television. Good God, if we dump him, as hot as he is in television right now, another TV station will pick him up in an instant to for them what *BANDSTAND* is doing for us. We're tops, by golly, and we're got to stay on top! But people are right, our wives, our friend's wives, and some of the men we know say, "You're going to have to replace Horn with a younger host"

And a stiff shirt like Clipp would probably ad thoughts like, "Horn looks like a 'dirty old man' up there with all of those kids. But how do we replace him? How do we get him to go back out to California where he's no threat to WFIL? We might be able to talk Horn into having his own show out at the TV station Mr. Annenberg (Triangle Publications) bought in Fresno, California. That wouldn't be easy, though, because their market isn't even a fifth of the market we have here — and we'd have to pay him a fortune. That's not a solution. We've got ourselves a bull by his horns or his testicles. Either way, any way we can do it, Mr. Horn has to go — and he has to keep right on going out of our market area. He can't be left to compete with WFIL-TV after we've paid out a bundle to help make him a huge celebrity, a king ."

The foregoing fictitious conversation but it is included here, gentle readers, as words that might very well have been part of the impetus for escalating an already going, "bring the star down to subservient employee level" campaign into a far more serious and felonious crime.

Back In TV BANDSTAND Things Continue To Look Up....

On June 17, 1954, a "news release" sent out to all media in the entire WFIL-TV market area, and as made available to sponsors and potential sponsors of TV BANDSTAND, reads precisely as follows:

NEWS FROM WFIL-TV

46th & Market Streets • Philadelphia 39, PA.
ABC AND DUMONT FEATURES • REPRESENTED BY THE KATZ AGENCY

WFIL-TV BIOGRAPHY   6/17/54

BOB HORN
"THE BANDSTAND" ON WFIL-TV

2:30-5:00 PM MON. HRU FRIDAY
11 AM to 1 PM MON. THRU FRI, ON WFIL RADIO

Bob Horn keeps the nation's top tunes spinning musically
Monday through Friday on "The Bandstand" from 2:30 to 5 p,m,
on WFIL-TV. In 3 and a half years Horn has catapulted "The
Bandstand" into a nationally famous show for the teen-agers.
Mixing the best record releases fro the disc companies wit a
blend of informal good humor and chatty interviews with the
top stars, Horn is making headlines all over the record
industry with his novel show.

"Bandstand" has grown into a Philadelphia institution with
the members if the younger set. Each weekday, those who can
hop to the nearest bus, elevated train or car to make their
way to the WFIL-TV studios for the show. Those at home have
their own "Bandstands" in the living room with the rugs
rolled back for the records that Bob plays.

Philadelphia's most popular TV star is a title that Horn
wears lightly. For the Quaker City he's the man to see and
hear for tops in music, and for catching up wit the latest
news from the show business stars visiting Philadelphia.
Patty Page, Tony Martin, Frankie Laine, Tony Bennett, Sunny
Gale, and all of the rest of the singing stars are sue to
drop in for a visit with Horn and his "Bandstand" fans when
they're around town.

It's been that way since 1939 when the versatile Horn
broke loose in Philadelphia radio as special events
commentator and assistant program director. On the side Horn
worked as a public relations specialist and was well on his
way to a major role in that competitive phase of show
business when he caught the spark that was burning in the
disc jockey field, and moved into the newer side of the
broadcasting business.

How he succeeded is a well known story in Philadelphia.
Horn has really carved himself a solid niche in the local

85

disc trade. Through the years he has built up a following
that is as large as it is devoted. Devoted to Horn? Well, in
a way. But also devoted to the best, "the very best" in
modern music. Keenly aware of the demands that a top disc
show can make on the WFIL music library, Horn combs trough
the latest releases - the catalogue of records - and talks to
the disc stars themselves - in order to give his viewers the
tunes they want to hear.

His knowledge of popular music, both new and old, has
resulted in terrific jumps in record sales when Horn has gone
overboard for a new record. Ray Anthony's "The Bunny Hop"
climbed well into the hit class in a few days when Horn
started his kids doing the dance on "Bandstand." Although
sales on the tune went pretty well in the rest of the
country, the "Bunny Hop" sold almost one hundred thousand in
Philadelphia alone. Another that Horn pushed to the top in
Philly was the "Mission Of Old St. Augustine," and there are
countless others that could be added to this continuing list.

His discoveries carry over into the talent field also.
Back in 1945 a velvet voice came up from the stage of the
Academy of Music and headed for stardom. This was the first
modern jazz concert ever given in Philadelphia, and Horn
turned promoter for a while, presented Sarah Vaughn in her
first concert booking. Sitting in on this history making
occasion was a South Philadelphia trumpet player named John
Berks Gillespie. Now, nine years later, [*now 43 years since
this news release was written*] he is famous as "Dizzy"
Gillespie, fronting a band of his own, in the "bop" school.
Elliot Lawrence, another local boy was out in front of the
house orchestra that night, and he, too, is now packing them
in around the country with his dance band, as well as being
musical director of several nationally televised shows.

As a disc jockey Horn didn't have too many ups and downs -
he branched out. In 1946 he received a very attractive offer
from a Hollywood station, and left for the coast.
Philadelphia stations sent him offers on the coast, and
after a year or so away from Philly, Horn decided to move
back and avail himself of the most promising offer.

Once again in Philly, Horn found that his fans were still
anxious to spend a few minutes listening to news of the
latest advances in music, an listening to the disc hits of
the day. He came back to his familiar role as a late evening
platter jockey, and then as time came on, so did television.

Horn came to WFIL in September of 1950 to take over the

microphone chores on WFIL from 11:00 p.m. to midnight. Soon
he added and afternoon stint to the regular schedule, and
when musical films hit television the transition to the new
medium was an easy one for Horn. He began the nation's first
steady afternoon film-disc show on WFIL-TV, Monday through
Friday, and from that first beginning in the spring of 1951,
Horn has been a stedy performer on television.

    His "Bandstand" show has proved a sensation in television
and music circles. Rating-wise the television venture is
topping everything else in sight locally, and is far ahead of
network programs at this 2:30 to 5 p.m. time period.
(On radio also 11 to 1 pm - Mon. through Friday.)

    The kids come in and dance while the cameras pick up human
interest shots that never seem to tire the audience. The new
dance steps, the new records, and daily flow of guest stars
keep the show running along with a fresh outlook every day.

    Bob Horn is leading the way for the TV disc jockey, and
it's one job the guy really enjoys. So does his audience. It
turns our to be a good combination for WFIL-TV and "The
Bandstand."

                    -    0   -

Note: In the above news release the, near the beginning and near the end. words about
(Bandstand) being "On radio 11 to 1 p.m., Mon. through Friday," were both penned onto the
release after it was typed, copied and ready to go out as appears on the copy given to this
author for inclusion in these pages. Whether or not those same written-in lines appeared
on all copies of the release sent out your author presently has no way of knowing.

                    -        -   -

    It's hard to believe that news releases like the one, above, and articles like the one to
follow on the next page, as it appeared in *TV Guide,* on October 9, 1954, were being written
and released to the public — building up the glory of *BANDSTAND* and Bob Horn — while
on those same dates a conspiracy to somehow get Bob off of the show was underway in the
front offices. Hard to believe, but we find more and more indicators saying, "it must be so."
    In reading the following *TV Guide* article, reprinted here in larger type size for easier
reading, we should bear in mind that man who "runs the businesses" at the TV magazine and
at the TV and radio stations is one and the same man. Whether personally involved or not there
was no way Roger Clipp could have avoided knowing that on one hand his operations are
devoting staff time and funds to continually build Bob Horn and *BANDSTAND* up. This, while
on the other hand and at the same time, different staff people at WFIL-TV and radio are doing
things to discourage, to tear down and to coax the resignation of Bob Horn from

87

BANDSTAND, super stellar show that he, alone, created. There is nothing at all in this *TV Guide* article to indicate, in any way; that the ownership and management of WFIL-TV are simultaneously seeking ways to remove Bob Horn from *BANDSTAND* without great cost.

Below, set in larger type, are many of the words from a page in *TV Guide*, as it appeared on October 9, 1954:

TWO DOWN AND EONS TO GO

"It was two years ago, on a Wednesday, Oct. 13, *(Author's note: Sounds good but the wrong date. Show premiered on Tuesday, Oct. 7, 1952.)* that the popular disc jockey, Bob Horn, stood before the WFIL-TV cameras and introduced his new show, *Bandstand*, to the Philadelphia televiewers.

"........In the switch to TV, Horn was introducing a live group of teen-agers who would be seen dancing to the various pop records. Other than this, the video *Bandstand* was the same program Horn had been dishing out so successfully on radio. It didn't take a week for the TV audience to voice its approval and reveal to Horn and the station that her was a "natural" for mid-afternoon televiewing.

"In the past 104 weeks, Horn has tightened up here and there regarding some of the rules and regulations for the teen-age, live audience, introduced a new gimmick now and then, but has kept the same basic format . . . simply spinning records, interviewing guest stars, and having the camera play on the dancing group.

"........On one show the audience may see a million dollars' worth of top name talent (Tony Martin, Kitty Kallen, Georgie Shaw and comedian Phil Silvers is an example of one day's billing).

"Always on the lookout for a special feature, Horn has been responsible for the teen-age craze for Ray Anthony's "Bunny Hop," "Dance of Mexico" by Sammy Kaye, and the current "Sha-Boom."

"........Presented in a studio with approximate 200 seating capacity, *Bandstand* plays to two separate live audiences each day.

"To attend the show, a letter must be sent to WFIL-TV, stating the specific day attendance is desired. Upon approval, a card of admission is then sent to the applicant.

"Having played to live studio audiences totaling more than a quarter million, claiming a cumulative rating of 20.8 (which represents a major portion or the home viewers), *Bandstand*, the people's choice for a 1954 **TV Guide** Award, has grown to be a mighty big baby in the first two years of its TV life.

"Happy birthday, Bob."

Under this October 1954 article in **TV Guide** is a photo of Bob Horn behind his microphones surrounded by thirteen of *Bandstand's* teenage dancers with the caption:

> "Monday is rating day, when Horn and teen-age
> critics give their nod or no to new releases."

In time, however, there would be WFIL-TV management people who, for reasons that fit a devious plan, would change the show title by dropping Bob Horn's name from the show and re-naming it just plain BANDSTAND. Those who removed, naive, Bob Horn's name from the show told him, according to Ann Horn and Jack Steck, they were "doing it because the show had co-hosts on TV, and keeping his name on the show was misleading to the public." What a whopper that was. Nevertheless and reluctantly, while he was making excellent money and enjoying huge regional popularity, Bob Horn, not at all a devious man, accepted the show's name change for the reason he was given.

But worse than the name change to just plain BANDSTAND was an 'in house' concerted effort to create a memory that from the first day the show appeared on television it was BANDSTAND 'in house' until his many months. It was an extremely popular show among young listeners who liked the music Bob played (standards plus a goodly number of 'new wave' rhythm and blues recordings -then still hard to find in record stores but great for dancing — and the forerunner music of rock 'n' roll). because a notification is tantamount to an order when it comes from such disc jockey kingpins. And the distributors and the stars were over the proverbial barrel as the fueding disc jockeys squared off. Today's the day. Watch for this column tomorrow to learn the outcome that I hope will be an amiable solution.

*　　*　　*

PART TWO

UPON REACHING
REGIONAL STARDOM

CHAPTER SIX

REPRINT OF BOB HORN'S PERSONAL COPY OF THE 1955 *BANDSTAND* YEARBOOK
Plus Photographs, Letters & Documents Relating To
Bob Horn's Creating & Hosting Of The **Original** *Bandstand*

Just as 1954 was a banner year for *Bandstand* and for Bob Horn personally, the prospects and the actualities of 1955 were to be of even greater upward progress with show refinements, special events, and creative showmanship in the show itself and in promoting the show and its host to viewing (and more potential sponsors) audiences.

Carrying forward the crowd pleasing memories of things like the 1954 annual picnic, the special Independence Day, Memorial Day, Thanksgiving and Chanukah and Christmas season special shows, and shows for 'fire prevention' and police department recruitment of young women (for which Bob received a special honor from the Philadelphia Police Commissioner), *Bandstand* and Mr. Horn, as principal host had a head start going into 1955, to be the year that Horn's creativity would finish carving marble the format that would remain with *Bandstand*, formerly *Bob Horn's Bandstand,* for as many years as *Bandstand*, by any name, would be presented to viewers around the world.

There Was One Unpleasant Resolve To Accomplish To Ease Internal Animosity....

Because the exact circumstances of an undesirable *Bandstand* situation, that had to come to an end, were best spoken of by a gentleman personally involved with the resolution, this book's author turns here to paragraphs from the personal memoirs of Tony Mammarella, who is deceased, as augmented by conversations with Tony's widow, Agnes Mammarella:

".......Bob (Horn) had worked very hard over the past year and a half (1953-

91

1954) and announced he was taking a three week vacation to Canada. This posed a problem for Bob because he didn't want to be gone and leave *Bandstand* in the hands of Lee Stewart who might do foolish thing in Bob's absence. And he certainly didn't want to give WFIL-TV opportunity to slip Dick Clark in as co-host on *Bandstand*.

"I (Tony Mammarella) had been substitute host at one time or another on most ever show the station carried when some on-air person was on vacation or suffered an illness. Too, at the time I had been made "cowboy" host of the *Hopalong Cassidy Movies Show* that was aired weekdays right after *Bandstand* at 5 p.m. Bob decided to solve both of his worries, Lee Stewart and/or Dick Clark 'moving in,' and named me as his substitute vacation host. He made it clear to everyone at the station that I was the boss in his absence. I would be him and Lee Stewart would be my co-host. I would select the records to play, I would interview the guests (that Bob had lined up before going on vacation), and I would even read the commercials Horn would ordinarily do. For those three weeks I'd be Bob Horn.

"Bob feared, too, losing contact with the show for three weeks. I suggested and he bought the idea that he could telephone in each day during the show, ask for me, and we could have an on-the-air conversation. He could tell the kids on *Bandstand* things about teenagers in Canada and about what he was seeing and doing on his trip.

"Lee Stewart and I had always gotten along okay prior to my taking over hosting the show for three weeks. That changed, however, when I was host and he, co-host. During these weeks Lee did everything he could to embarrass or belittle me in front of our audience or guests. But in trying to hurt Bob, with me being Lee's 'Bob Horn substitute,' Lee truly shot himself down. When Bob returned to the show and had only been back a few day with the animosity between Bob and Lee right back to full pitch — I (Mammarella) was called into the front office to discuss with Jack Steck and George Koehler what I believed was wrong between Stewart and Horn. (As if they didn't already know the animosity between the two during the past two years.) How, the wanted me to suggest as show producer, could the situation be corrected — without jeopardizing the commercially successful show? What was my opinion?

"The show is not a two man show. There is no need for a co-host because Bob already has forty co-hosts in the "regulars" who are there, every day. It's too difficult having two guys picking out two different sets of records to play – or two guys deciding on different guests hen they are not attuned to cooperation. Only one man can produce a show and only one man can properly be the host. Following this meeting at which they still held out for co-hosts, they must have at least soaked up my opinion. Within two weeks Bob Horn did the show solo. That happened early in 1955.

"Reflecting back to the front office meeting, I'd like to do it over again. It was obvious to me after thinking about it in private, that the station management, including those two, wanted to keep *Bandstand* a two man show — but they knew, too, that Lee Stewart had to go. They wanted me to say, "Stewart is the wrong co-host and should be replaced." And they had Dick Clark waiting to be that replacement.

"Lee Stewart was given a morning show of his own on WFIL-TV. It was called *Lee Stewart's Coffeetime* and Lee tried to make if an early morning show, like *Bandstand*, for adults. It did not succeed and a few months later Lee Swewart was gone from WFIL.

"Roger Clipp was the top boss at WFIL radio and TV stations and could have done pretty much whatever he would choose with *Bandstand*. If he had wanted Dick Clark on the show at that time, I don't think there was anything Bob Horn could have done about but accept Clark as his new co-host. But as far as I knew, Mr. Clipp wasn't that way about *Bandstand*. I had argued against changes in *Bandstand* before and probably would again. Somehow Roger Clipp always let me prevail.

"Dick Clark would have to wait nearly two more years."

We Knew Before Tony Mammarella's Words That Lee Stewart Would Have To Leave "Bandstand" But Tony Didn't Know, As We've Already Considered, That Roger Clipp Has A Mental Gymnastics Problem With Bandstand, Too....

Earlier descriptions of Mr. Clipp were presented when introducing the key players to this historical mystery and in more detail by way of a news release about Mr. Clipp in Chapter

Four, Page 67. In those character sketches it was pointed to that all through his life, and after death, Roger Clipp was considered to be a pillar of the community. By these accounts one might assume that Mr. Clipp could do no wrong but then, again, under pressure seemingly perfect people will do strange and out-of-character things. Was this perhaps an occurrence with the Mr. Clipp when he was boss of WFIL radio and television stations?

Such an active and well connected man as Roger Clipp, even though described somewhat differently and in less admirable words by his employer, Walter H. Annenberg, when written about in an excellent Annenberg family biography-autobiography of 1982, should certainly have no trouble disposing of an employee he didn't care for unless —. But that is for later in this story for author and readers to determine, based upon information recovered and presented in these pages .

Because the cultural and socio-economic backgrounds of key people written of in this book vary so dramatically, it is difficult to even envision all of them on a completely level playing field. But then, there is no reason to try scraping the field level beyond knowing that it is differences that make for people doing things in atypical ways — and acting or reacting to same or similar sets of circumstances in, sometimes, significantly different ways.

- - -

While this chapter, with its photos, letters and reproduction of the museum-piece "1955 *Bandstand Yearbook,*" is primarily about how terrific things were going for *Bandstand*, there was also the shadowy, unspoken of but identified "dangling downside" between Bob Horn and WFIL-TV management. As for the show itself, and Bob hosting it, for the entire crew, including the teenage dancers, who presented *Bandstand* to its viewers every weekday afternoon everything with the viewers, sponsors and the press is going great. It will continue to be that way throughout 1955 and on into 1956. But before getting into the glamour side of *Bandstand*, it seemed wise to start this glory chapter by recognizing that internally at WFIL-TV all is not roses and perfume among the show's prime personnel and station management. In simple words, while we keep our eyes open for clues, all may not be quite as perfect as the publicity and news stories might tell.

In 1955 *Bandstand* became in actuality a one host show — which it had been right along, even with a second host on the show set each day doing little to nothing to add to the show. Lee Stewart was gone but Bob Horn remained fearful that his bosses might plan to replace Lee with another co-host because a co-hosted show was what Messrs. Clipp and Koehler had expressed as their "want" ever since the show was first telecast.

Early "Bandstand" Much Bigger And Finer Than Most People Know About....

Because most Americans have little to no idea just how big and influential to American youth _Bandstand_ was in its beginning years it is wonderful now to have on loan from the 1990s Horn family and from the estates of Bob and Ann Horn (with permission to reproduce it for you and the world) **some of Bob Horn's personal photographs** from the early _Bandstand_ years and **his personal copy of the _1955 Bandstand Yearbook_** reprinted (somewhat reduced in page size) into the pages of this book for all of us to look back and enjoy. The Yearbook is now the property of one of Bob Horn's grandsons, Robert Graham , a 1996 graduate from the University of North Florida. Incidentally, while this book was being manufactured one of the photo technicians said, "But it's all in black and white. No color." And he was right, it is all in black and white because in 1952 through 1956 any color on television was still in the experimental stages

**From The Pages Immediately Following This One,**

**Please Enjoy Looking At Photos Of Many**

**Of The People Involved In <u>Bob Horn's Bandstand</u>**

**In The Early Creative Years of "BANDSTAND"**

**And Read About How Much Of It Was Accomplished.**

**Read, Too, Letters From Early Show Dancers,**

**Sponsors, And Community Beneficiaries....**

Lee Stewart, (left) co-host for 2 months of 1952, 1953 and 1954 with
Bob Horn, (right) on "Bob Horn's *Bandstand* " and then on "*Bandstand,*" with
with an unknown dancer (center), in a comedy skit on the show. Lee, the anticipated
provider of comedy for the show lacked the 'right touch' for the audience and, also,
he and Bob didn't get along well together on what should have been a one-host show
to begin with. Lee was let go from *Bandstand* near the end of 1954.

Walter Hubert Annenberg
at "Sunnylands," his home in
Palm Springs, California

Walter Hubert Annenberg
as head of a publishing empire

Walter Annenberg, who his mother always called 'Boy,' took over the reins of Triangle Publications, the parent firm (in the years of this book) of *The Daily Racing Form, The Philadelphia Inquirer, Seventeen Magazine, WFIL Radio and Televisions, and TV GUIDE and a host of other media enterprises.* President Nixon named Mr. Annenberg, Ambassador to Great Britain.

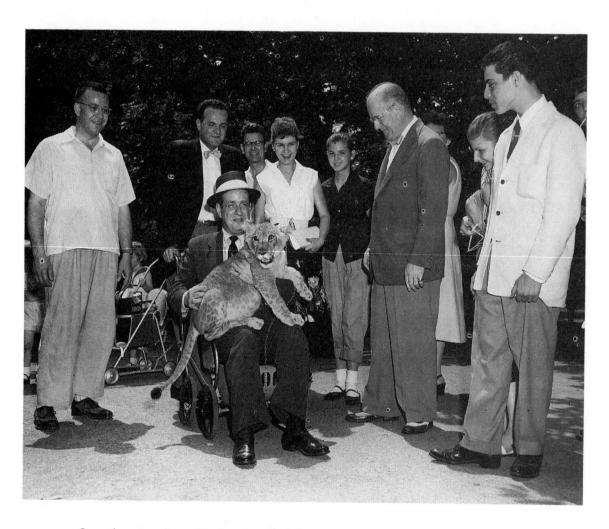

On the occasion of being thanked for giving assistance to a Philadelphia Children's Hospital, Bob Horn and his pet lion '*Whatchamacallum*' (in the wheelchair) are being held in position by **Anthony "Tony Mammarella**, Producer for "*Bob Horn's Bandstand,*" for "*Bandstand,*" and then for "*American Bandstand,*" all the same show as created and first hosted by Bob Horn. Your author doesn't know the others in the photo but the book had to go to press before a solo photo of Tony Mammarella reached our possession — but this photo at least lets readers know that Tony, a man of great importance to this story, was also a handsome man.

George A. Koehler
Manager of WFIL-TV
who would become the
Next General Manager of
WFIL Radio and TV stations
and, ultimately, be a principal
in a corporation to purchase
these stations and other TV
and radio stations from
Walter Annenberg.

Roger W. Clipp
General Manager of WFIL Radio and
Television properties, who would also
become Business Manager of
TV GUIDE and then General
Manager of all Annenberg's
Triangle Publication's radio and
TV stations, nationwide.

Both of these men were considered to be men of highest integrity, forthright,
an pillars of their community. This story puts those beliefs to a test.

Another shot of *Whatchamacallum* being fed by Bob Horn with two young dancers looking on. A purpose of this photo being here is to call readers' attention to the oversize disc to the left of the young man. The wording on that disc, looking closely, reads, **"BAND, BOB HORN'S, STAND."** That name on the *"Bandstand"* set is a clue.

Pat Boone was on "Bob Horn's Bandstand" in 1954. Pat's gone far since then.

Joni James, an outstanding vocalist that Bob Horn helped become a star.

Bob Horn
Dick Clark, wrote in his autobiography, "Bob Horn was an unattractive man."
What do you think?

A young dancer and Bob on the set with **Robert Wagoner** and A *Bandstand* cameraman.

TV GUIDE manager and associate brought Bob an anniversary cake (2nd year) of *Bandstand.* They marked the date as October 13 – but we have the start as Oct. 7th, 1952 from Tony Mammarella and he was there that day.

Jerry Blavat
He was a teenage dancer on Bob Horn's *Bandstand* who discovered his liking and talents for
radio, television, and the hospitality industry. Jerry has stayed with his profession in the
greater Philadelphia area where he is popular today as "The Geater With The Heater."

Frankie Laine accepts a *Bandstand* poll "favorite male vocalist" award from Bob in May of 1953

Tony Bennett was always a favorite guest of the teenagers who were *Bandstand.*

It was a "big deal" and a huge *Bandstand* show in an auditorium when WFIL–TV went "full power"

We've been told *Bandstand* wasn't integrated 'til the show moved west. *Not so by this 1953 photo.*

Sometimes Bandstand went outside of the WFIL-TV studio

Very often dancers came by bus to be on *Bandstand*.

BOB HORN'S GIRLS LOVED THEIR FATHER. TODAY THEY LOVE HIM IN MEMORY

Bob Horn was "at home" at home.

Bob Horn was "at home" at work.

111

Bob's grandson,
Chuck Sturgis and
Bob's youngest
daughter,
Barbara Horn

Barbara Horn
and her friend
Fritz Vandermallie

More of Bob's
grandchildren,
Brooke Sturgis
and **Grant Gay**

Ann Davidow Horn, Bob's wife, when she entertained troops as a USO performer under her stage name, Linda Stevens. (Ann Horn passed away on February 1, 1997.)

Ann Davodow Horn and her sister Helen Davidow Bianchi (1995)

Behold, the mighty fisherpeople. Don't know the man on the right But Bob's behind the fish and Ann is claiming the trophy!

People said Bob's boat, *Bandstand*, was a yacht. It wasn't a yacht but it was a nice cruiser, perfect for fishing.

(Upper left) Bob's eldest daughter, **Marianne Horn Kinsey**

(Upper right) Marianne's son **Robert Graham**

Marianne's daughter, **Alexa**, on the run from gymnastics.

Christine "Pinky" Horn Sanders' son, **John Sanders**, another Bob Horn grandson. Sorry, we didn't have a photo of "Pinky," Bob's middle daughter, at press time but we hope to have her photo for future editions of this book..

(L to R) **Chuck Sturgis, Ann Horn, Barbara Horn, Greg Gay and Grant Gay.**

Alexa Kinsey & Robert Graham at the time of Robert's graduation from U. of North Florida

a.c. Kissling co.

140 EAST RICHMOND STREET
PHILADELPHIA, PA. 19125
Telephone: (215) 423-4700

KRAUT OF THE ONION
Nature Cured

**SAUER
KRAUT**

MAY 8, 1997

MR. STANLEY J BUTZ
16801 N. 49TH ST
SCOTTSDALE, NJ 85254

Dear Stan,

THIS LETTER IS TO CONFIRM THAT BOB HORN
WAS A GOOD HOST, PUSHING KISSLING'S SAUERKRAUT ON
AMERICAN BANDSTAND. HE SPONSORED OUR PRODUCT ON
WFIL TV FROM SEPT 1952 UNTIL AUG 1957

SINCERELY YOURS,
MARK C KISSLING
Mark C Kissling
V.P., A.C. KISSLING CO.

For easier reading, here is the confirming letter typed out:

Dear Stan,   May 8, 1997

This letter is to confirm that Bob Horn was a good host, pushing Kissling's Sauerkraut on American (Bob Horn's) Bandstand. He sponsored (sold) our product on WIFL-TV from about Sept 1952 until Aug. 1957.

Sincerely yours, Mark C. Kissling, VP, A. C. Kissling Co.

116

A SPONSOR

BOB HORN'S *BANDSTAND* had as a sponsor, almost from the very beginning of his creating *Bandstand*, a Philadelphia baking firm known regionally in 1952, when *Bandstand* first started on TV -- and known more and more throughout the nation today. That firm was, and remains, **Tasty Baking Company**. Their product, popular in 1952 and more popular than ever today was and is:

This black and white picture of a colorful TastyKake package
is printed here with permission of Tasty Baking Company.

117

A SPONSOR

"You'll wonder where the yellow went when you brush your teeth with *PEPSODENT.*"

LEVER BROTHERS COMPANY
Pepsodent DIVISION

LEVER HOUSE • 390 PARK AVENUE, NEW YORK 22, N. Y. • MURRAY HILL 8-6000

THOMAS EDWARD HICKS
VICE PRESIDENT

March 22, 1956

Mr. Bob Horn
Station WFIL-TV
Philadelphia
Pennsylvania

Dear Bob:

Congratulations again!

During January and February, competitive activity was
the greatest in the history of the tooth paste business and yet Pepsodent held its own with the consumers.
In certain markets we made substantial gains.

Undoubtedly, your handling of Suzie Q and Billy Brown
and "your public" are the major factors in this success
story. Thanks.

Sincerely

Ed Hicks

In case the, above, 1956 letter is too faded to read, here's what Mr. Hicks said to Bob Horn:
Congratulations again! During January and February, competitive activity was the greatest in the
history of the tooth paste business and yet Pepsodent held its own with the consumers. In certain
markets we made substantial gains.
Undoubtedly, your handling of Suzie Q and Billy Brown and "your public" are the major
factors in this success story.   Sincerely,   /Ed Hicks/

A SPONSOR

On <u>April 19, 1956</u>, Ed Hicks, a Lever Brothers Company, *Pepsodent* Divison, V.P., wrote another letter to Bob Horn. While the copy of this letter is too faded to reproduce on this page, we have that weak copy in our file. Mr. Hicks said:

"Dear Bob: You did it again. Latest report of consumer movement of Pepsodent White Toothpaste shows gains all along the line.

"As I told you in my last letter to you, the competitive situation is extremely keen. Two major producers have launched new products, adn by mail (during January, February and March) have sampled practically every family in the United States. This means that a lot of buyers have been taken out of the market. Notwithstanding all this and special price offers on established brands, you have been able to sell Pepsodent to more and more people.

"Saying thanks to you is apparently becoming a habit with me. I like it. You're a wonderful addition to our "consumer selling department," and our salesmen to the trade love having you with us.

        "Sincerely   /Ed Hicks/

"P.S. Several broadcasters have asked us if we minded their joking about "You'll wonder where the yellow went." Of course we don't mind— we enjoy it and feel that it brings more enjoyment to more people. We're not trying to beat the public over the head with the facts about Pepsodent; we don't even want to argue with the public — we just want them to feel that when they buy and use Pepsodent, they can do no better for themselves. A lot of experience and scientific knowledge go into making Pepsodent the finest product that can be made and used. So play around with the jingle as much as you please, and as much as "your public" will enjoy it.

"It's O.K. with us.   T.E.H."

Mr. Hicks' full name is Thomas Edward Hicks. His first name to friends is "Ed."

FROM WITHIN THE COMMUNITY

THOMAS J. GIBBONS
COMMISSIONER

POLICE DEPARTMENT
ROOM 227 CITY HALL
PHILADELPHIA 7, PA.

November 11, 1954

Mr. Robert Horn
Station WFIL
46th and Market Streets
Philadelphia 39, Pa.

Dear Mr. Horn:

  The Philadelphia Police Department deeply
appreciates the time and effort you are giving to the current
drive to recruit policewomen. As a result of your program, we
are sure to succeed in interesting a large number of Philadelphia's fine young women in this vital work for our community.

  We should like to cite and honor you for the important
part you are playing, and we hope you can attend a ceremony for
that purpose in the Mayor's Reception Room, on the second floor
of City Hall, next Monday, November 15, 1954, at 4 p.m.

Sincerely yours,

Commissioner

The signature on the letter is that of Thomas J. Gibbons, Police Commissioner.

FROM WITHIN THE COMMUNITY

Because the letter on the following page has faded in the years since 1954 (43 years ago), the body of the letter is reprinted here for easier reading:

January 13, 1954

"Dear Mr. Horn:

"The Board of Directors of the Children's Heart Hospital wishes to thank you for the set of Lionel trains which you sent to the hospital.

"The children were thrilled and delighted with the trains. Your continued support has enabled us to bring many more boys and girls back to health. In this twenty-fifth year on these grounds we are seeing our Alumni, young men and women able to carry on normal active lives even thought they once spent many months and years as our patients.

"Christmas is always a very happy time at the Hospital. This year one of our six year old patients said after Santa's visit: "This is the goodest Christmas I ever had."

"Again thank you for the wonderful gift to the children and best wishes for a Happy New Year.

"Sincerely
/Arthur P. Goldsmith/

121

FROM WITHIN THE COMMUNITY

**CHILDREN'S HEART HOSPITAL
OF PHILADELPHIA**

CONSHOHOCKEN AVENUE
PHILADELPHIA 31

January 13, 1954

Mr. Bob Horn
WFIL
46th and Market Streets
Philadelphia, Pennsylvania

Dear Mr. Horn:

The Board of Directors of the Children's Heart
Hospital wishes to thank you for the set of Lionel trains
which you sent to the Hospital.

The children were thrilled and delighted with
the trains. Your continued support has enabled us to bring
many more boys and girls back to health. In this twenty-
fifth year on these grounds we are seeing our Alumni, young
men and women able to carry on active normal lives even
though they once spent many months and years as our patients.

Christmas is always a very happy time at the
Hospital. This year one of our six year old patients said
after Santa's visit: "This is the goodest Christmas I ever
had."

Again thank you for the wonderful gift to the
children and best wishes for a Happy New Year.

Sincerely

Arthur P. Goldsmith

Arthur P. Goldsmith
Secretary

hd

122

FROM WITHIN THE COMMUNITY

ST. CHRISTOPHER'S HOSPITAL FOR CHILDREN
LAWRENCE AND HUNTINGDON STS.
PHILADELPHIA 33, PA.

HENRY G. REIFSNYDER, PRESIDENT
CHARLES C. TOWNSEND, VICE-PRES.
HENRY S. BROMLEY, JR., SECRETARY
PROVIDENT TRUST CO., TREASURER

GA 6-5600

August 2, 1954

Mr. Bob Horn
WFIL-TV
46th and Market Streets
Philadelphia, Penna.

Dear Bob:

All of us here at St. Christopher's want you to know how very much we appreciated your visit to the hospital Festival on Saturday night, July 24. This year's Festival was the most successful the hospital has ever held, both in terms of good-will and pleasure, and in terms of financial return.

There is no question in my mind that the wit and good-humor of our Master of Ceremonies at the end of the evening went a long way toward making the Festival the success that it was.

I hope you had a good time visiting us. I know that everyone enjoyed hearing and seeing you. For all of us here at the hospital, please accept my thanks and an invitation to come and see us again.

Sincerely yours,

Richard H. Warren,
Assistant Administrator
    in Charge of Development

RHW:sg

THE DANCERS   **FRANK SPAGNUOLA'S LETTER TYPED OUT:**

Attn: **Stan Blitz**

    RE: **Book - Untold Story**

    Remembering The Good Old Days - 1955-56-57

    Jerry Blavat and I would leave school early to go to Bandstand. It was always exciting entering the studio before the show started. Bob Horn had a very dry sense of humor - - and a business like attitude.

    I felt very bad when all the problems and publicity started around Bob Horn. Mostly all the kids were very angry when they took Bob Horn off the show and replaced him with Dick Clark

    In my opinion, if it weren't for Bob Horn creating the original Bandstand show which was very popular in the Philadelphia area, Dick Clark would have never went on with his fame and "American Bandstand" as a national show and the rest became "history."

<u>**P.S.**</u>   Copy of me on the cover of Dick's new book with my dance partner, Dottie Horner. Let me know whne the book come out.

                    Sincerely.

                    /Frank Spagnuola/

FRANK SPAGNUOLA
ASID   INTERIOR   DESIGN

8 APRIL 1997

ATTN: STAN BLITZ

RE: BOOK - UNTOLD STORY

REMEMBERING THE GOOD OLD DAYS - 1955-56-57

JERRY BLAVAT AND I WOULD LEAVE SCHOOL EARLY TO GO TO BANDSTAND. IT WAS ALWAYS EXCITING ENTERING THE STUDIO BEFORE THE SHOW STARTED. BOB HORN HAD A VERY DRY SENSE OF ... HUMOR AND A BUSINESS LIKE ATTITUDE.

I FELT VERY ... BAD WHEN ALL THE PROBLEM AND PUBLICITY STARTED AROUND BOB HORN. MOSTLY ALL THE KIDS WERE VERY ANGRY WHEN THEY TOOK BOB HORN OFF THE SHOW AND REPLACED HIM WITH DICK CLARK.

IN MY OPINION, IF IT WEREN'T FOR BOB HORN CREATING THE ORIGINAL BANDSTAND SHOW WHICH WAS VERY POPULAR IN THE PHILADELPHIA AREA, DICK CLARK WOULD HAVE NEVER WENT ON WITH HIS FAME AND "AMERICAN BANDSTAND" AS A NATIONAL SHOW AND THE REST BECAME "HISTORY".

P.S LOPY OF ME ON THE COVER OF DICK'S NEW BOOK WITH MY DANCE PARTNER DOTTIE HORNER. LET ME KNOW WHEN THE BOOK COMES OUT.

Sincerely,

Frank Spagnuola

THE DANCERS

Ralph Gary Brauner
701 City Avenue
Apartment D-302
Merion Station, PA 19066

(1)

In 1954, the year I started going to Bandstand it was primarily a local show which bussed in kids from surrounding towns. The studio was smaller than it looked on TV and the lines outside to get in were long.

To accommodate as many as possible The show was divided into two segments The first was 2:45 PM – 4:00 PM; the second 4:00PM – 5:00PM. The regulars or those on the "committee" which they were called got to stay for both halves. To this day I don't know where that name come from because (to my knowledge) the only decisions made were what song to dance to and with whom.

To get on the "committee" was a dream come true for me at the time These kids were like local stars and some received many letters from fans.

THE DANCERS

I was more interested in being able to stay for the whole show. ~~crossed out~~ ~~crossed out~~.
A few guys I became friendly with and myself started to bug Bob Horn to get on the committee. We told him we came to the show often blah blah blah

Well he finally said yes. "Go see my secretary." What transpired next I'll always remember. She asked me for my membership card and on the back wrote those magic words ~~crossed out~~ in lipstick .... PREFERRED. That was it! Now when I came to the show I didn't have to stand in line. I just flashed my cosmetic card and I was in!
(COSMETIC)

127

THE DANCERS

③

During the early '50's the mcCarthy hearings were broadcast on Channel 6. This, of course, took precedent ~~over~~ a bunch of hormone crazy kids dancing to the hits of the day.

~~They~~

Many of the regulars would still go to the show to see their friends and ~~probably~~ ~~journey~~ prolong the trip home.

We would amuse ourselves by dancing in the studio without music. After doing this for ~~some~~ so many days they took pity on us and would play some music. Were we nuts or what? Once in a while the hearings would end early and we would ~~to~~ have a show. I guess they were paying us for our loyalty.

Those were the days

Ralph Gary
Brauner

128

HARVEY SHELDON PRODUCTIONS

I attended the first telecast of *Bandstand* in October of 1952, and never missed a show through August of 1954.

Because of my dancing talents and instant popularity, Bob Horn chose me and Dimples (my dancing partner) to meet Ray Anthony and ultimately contributed to creating the *Bunny Hop*.

I needed a letter from the broadcasting industry to be admitted to Columbia University in New York. Bob Horn wrote a letter that helped gain my admission.

Bob Horn was my idol in all aspects. In my early years in *Broadcasting*, I tried to sound like him......dress like him. His influence on my programming number one rock stations is totally credited to him.

All of the dancers on his show are totally omitted in books by Dick Clark. We're never invited to any *Bandstand* reunions. The documentary pertaining to *Bandstand* again omitted our existence. Bob Horn was dumped by WFIL and didn't deserve the treatment he was subjected to after his departure from Philadelphia and *Bandstand*.

Bob Horn, without a doubt, deserves to be in the Rock 'N Roll Hall of Fame.

Sincerely,

Harvey Sheldon

7855 E. HORIZON VIEW DRIVE   ANAHEIM HILLS, CA 92808   (714) 281-5929

THE DANCERS

Mr. Stanley J. Blitz
16801 North 49th Street
Scottsdale, AZ   85254

Dear Stanley:

Per our conversation, I was born and raised in South Philadelphia 12th and Wharton.

I went to Barlett Junior High and to Southern High School and danced on Band Stand from 1954 to 1956. Everyday after school I used to jump on the trolly to 46th and Market Street to Band Stand. Then on the way we used to stop in Pop Singers for a coke and then stood in line for Band Stand. I went everyday and became a regular as my name for Band Stand was **Franny with the Bangs**. I always wore my hair with a DA and Bangs. Still wear the DA hair style in the back.

I was a regular on Band Stand the kids from the Philadelphia and suburbs areas used to stop and ask us for our autographs.

I was very popular on the Band Stand Show, when I became 16 they surprized me with a Birthday Party and presented me with a corsage with 16 cubes of sugar and a birthday cake on TV.

When the scandal hit about Robert (Bob) Horn that was never found guilty. I was never permitted to go out per my parents.

Being raised in the neighborhood and allowed to dance on Band Stand there is no doubt in my mind that it helped cultivate my out going personality. This gave me the ability to interact with all cultures and people. It has been beneficial to myself in my present position at Trump's Castle.

My job consist of entertaining, meeting, greeting, bringing new customers and Hosting them at Trump's Castle.

All of my customers who have received knowledge of my greatest experience of being a popular dancer on the famous Bandstand have been and are always very impressed with my with Bandstand and my growth since BANDSTAND spot in Philadelphia.

Your friend,

Fran Saddic
Director of
National Marketing

130

Bandstand Days

I remember my first day on the show. Thrilled to meet Bob Horn, & Lee Stewart, who was his co-host. I was a shy kid who didn't know how to dance. But it didn't take me long to learn all the newest dance steps. The day Bob Horn called me to the side and gave me a Committe card, I could not believe it! It meant no more waiting in the long lines outside and could stay for both sessions.

I started dancing on the show in 1953 and the popular dances were the Bunny hop, the kangeroo, Cha Cha and of course the Jitterbug.

Several times a year, Bob Horn would have a dance Contest & a few times I won for 1st or 2nd place. I still have the trophy for 2nd place, which I treasure.

Bob Horn was a very caring person as was the shows producer, Tony Mamerella. But there were Certain rules you had to follow. No Chewing gum, no swearing, decent attire, and of Course no cutting school, which many of did at the time. One of the shows sponsers I believe was "Tasty Cakes" and every day, Bob would holler "Is everybody ready". He would then throw tasty Cakes to us.

We, the regulars would receive a lot of fan mail and many gifts. It was unbelievable! We were just normal teen-agers who loved to dance. But to be honest, we did like all of the special attention.

The show also gave us the opportunity to meet a lot of the popular singing artists. Such as Jerry Lee Lewis, Fats Domino and many others. Cozy Morley was also an entertainer on his show and we still remain friends. When a guest performer would appear on Bob's show, he would holler "We Have Company".

Some of us regulars still get together & sometimes do shows, which is a lot of fun. I'll name a few, such as, Jo Ann Monte Carlo, Big Dave, Little Roe, Frank Spagnola, Rita and Pete Capobianco, Bobbie Young and Jim Hudson. They are still great dancers and look great.

Some of our dear friends have passed away. Micki Duffy, Carol McCauly, Harvey Robbins, among others.

Bob Horn and Bandstand were a large part of my life and is missed by all of us.

I'm now married and live in S. Jersey, have three grown children. I often tell them how it was growing up in the fifties and Bandstand. It was a very innocent a. We thought so anyway!

Sincerly,
Barbara Marcen Wilston

April 9, 1997

My name is Bobbie Young and I started going to Bandstand in 1954. I had an awful crush on Tommy DeNoble, so that is how I got started going down there. He was the cutest and most popular then.

I was asked to be on the "committee" in 1956. Bob Horn used to take us (committee) to dances, out of town, after the show was over at 5:30 pm. We would stop for dinner on the way and he would treat us. He also had us come to the "Carmen" on Wednesday nights where he was the D.J.

I became friends with Barbra Marcen and Jimmy Hudson. We are still good friends today. I especially became very good friends with Tony Mammarella, the producer of Bandstand. He was like a father to me. Tony and his wife exchanged christmas cards with me, ever year until he died.

Bandstand was the best thing that ever happened to me, in my teeenage years. It kept us "kids" out of trouble and also left wonderful memories.

Sincerely,
Bobbie Young

133A

Dolores Steigrod
4277 N.W. 62nd Road
Boca Raton, FL 33496
561-995-4634

April 15, 1997

Dear Stan:

I've been trying to jog my memory about Bob Horn's Bandstand. I'll give you my best recollection.

As far as I know, the year it started was in 1953 when I was in 10th grade at West Philly High. It was really an exciting time when TV was in it's infancy stage. We used to go after school to 47th & Market, I believe it was WFIL, & line up outside for a few hours. Everybody wanted to get on TV & you always tried to dance in front of the cameras. I don't remember the guests, but just that it was alot of fun & the biggest thing to hit Philly other than Eddie Fisher.

That's about all I can remember. It was a very long time ago.

Hope this helps you out.

Best of luck on the book & if I can help you promote it, please let me know.

Sincerely,
Dolores Steigrod

133B

THE DANCERS

Justine Carrelli

Original Bandstander
BOSCO/CARRELLI Enterprises, Inc.
536 Sierra Vista Suite 9
Las Vegas, Nevada 89109

Telephone 702-737-6969
Fax 702-737-6415
Justine's Web Site: http://www.originalbandstander.com/

It was 1956. I'll never forget the first time I walked into that studio at 46th and Market streets in Philadelphia. My heart was pounding with excitement because a whole new world was opening before me. I was a scrawny kid of twelve although I was supposed to be fourteen to get in. I had gone on a dare that I wouldn't get in which is another story in itself that I have written about my life on Bandstand called: *"IT WASN'T ALL DANCING!"*

I knew from the very first day that I was there to stay! I was going to become a part of this magical place. I was in awe of the dancers out on the dance floor. The way they looked, dressed, and acted was so captivating. I was totally mesmerized. *Bob Horn* was the host at this time and he really had something going with this show that was going to be *"real big,"* I could feel it. I went to the show everyday, faithfully, and soon I became one of the *"regulars."* *I was now an "original Bandstander" and part of a group of teenagers that set the trend for how the entire teenage population across the entire country dressed and danced.* What an experience! How lucky I feel to have been there during those early years of Bandstand and to have been a part of something that took the nation by storm. I am thankful for all the kids I met on the show and how they enriched my life and were such dear friends. They were my *"second family."*

Most of all, I'll never forget the fans that showered me with gifts, letters, and praise. Many of them still write to me today. I'm very lucky... very lucky indeed.

I also met my first love on Bandstand. *"Bob Clayton"* and I became known as America's Sweethearts. The magazine covers and articles, along with the covers of record albums that followed my teen celebrity are in my *personal treasure chest* forever!

And thanks to all the bandstand fans who made me so much a part of their lives. None of us would have been anything without you!

Sincerely,
Justine Carrelli
"Original Bandstander"
1956-1960

Bunny Never Danced on Bob's Bandstand — But She Cares!!
KATHLEEN (BUNNY) GIBSON'S LETTER ABOUT BOB HORN'S BANDSTAND

May 5, 1997   (This letter, in Bunny's own handwriting, appears on the next two pages.)

"I never met Bob Horn, but I wish I did! This man was very much loved by a group of us referred to as "The Regulars." i.e. Those teenagers seen every week on Bandstand and American Bandstand.

"How do I know? Well, last year I went back to Philadelphia to do research on my upcoming book on "The Regulars" called "Behind The Smiles." In the course of my interviews of the other dancers, I was overwhelmed by story after story of the kindness and compassion of this man. They talked about Bob as if it were yesterday. Thy loved him, they respected him, they were protective of him, and they were still angry, after all these years, at his dismissal from the Bandstand show.

"I don't believe the newspaper articles that slandered him; I believe the teenagers that knew him, the teenagers that danced on his show every day, the kids that (in the '50s) had the courage, love and loyalty to picket outside the Bandstand studio in an attempt to bring him back as the Host of Bandstand.

"Pop Singer, our buddy who ran the corner drug store down the street from Bandstand, had a favorite expression. It was, "When we die we leave nothing behind, but a good name." As far as the regulars are concerned, Bob Horn did leave a good name behind.

"In giving us "Bandstand," Bob Horn changed the course of my life, and led me to where I am now – an actress in Los Angeles. When I was 13, I found home in Bandstand and a family of friends that I still have today.

"As a Regular, I honor Bob Horn's creativity and vision as a true pioneer in television. It's time for him to be acknowledged as the man who gave rock 'n' roll a home on television. It's time for him to be honored in the Rock and Roll Hall of Fame, and by the television stations and shows that have profited so much from his teenage dancing show concept.

"It's too late to change the hurt that was done to this man and his family. He was slandered and replaced. He was overlooked and he was forgotten. And what was his real crime? That he was not young enough? Certainly, the teenagers on Bandstand would have disagreed with that. And the teenagers watching Bandstand didn't have any complaints either!

"All that I can do now is to say that I am sorry that this happened to Bob Horn and his family, and to tell his family through this book, that I acknowledge Bob Horn's contribution to television and to the influence he had on my life.

"Thank you, Bob Horn, for giving so much of yourself to so many. Your kindness lives on through the hearts and memories of "The Regulars."

Signed, **Kathleen "Bunny" Gibson**
One of the original "Regulars that danced on Philadelphia's American Bandstand from 1959 to 1969, after Dick Clark became the Host.

Stan, thank you for this opportunity to thank Bob Horn.

135

Bunny Never Danced on Bob's Bandstand!!

"THE REGULARs"

AMERICA'S ORIGINAL
BANDSTAND DANCERS

I never met Bob Horn, but I wish I did! This man was very much loved by a group of us referred to as "The Regulars" i.e. those teenagers seen every week on Bandstand + American Bandstand.

How do I know? Well, last year I went back to Philadelphia to do research on my upcoming book on "The Regulars" called "Behind the Smiles". In the course of my interviews of the other Regulars, I was overwhelmed by story after story of the kindness + compassion of this man. They talked about

"THE REGULARs"

AMERICA'S ORIGINAL
BANDSTAND DANCERS

Bob as if it were yesterday. They loved him, they respected him, they were protective of him, and they were still angry, after all these years, at his dismissal from the Bandstand show!

I don't believe the newspaper articles that slandered him; I believe the teenagers that knew him, the teenagers that danced on his show everyday, the teenagers that (in the 50's) had the courage, love & loyalty to picket outside the Bandstand studio in an attempt to bring him back as the last of Bandstand.

BUNNY PRODUCTIONS

"THE REGULARs"

AMERICA'S ORIGINAL
BANDSTAND DANCERS

Pop Singer, our buddy, who ran the corner drug store down the street from Bandstand, had a favorite expression. It was "When we die, we leave nothing behind, but a good name." As far as "The Regulars" are concerned, Bob Horn did leave a good name behind.

In giving us "Bandstand," Bob Horn changed the course of my life, and led me to where I am now - an actress in Los Angeles. When I was 13 I found a "home" in Bandstand and a family of friends that I still have today.

BUNNY PRODUCTIONS
819 Dickson St.
Marina Del Rey, Ca. 90292
310-306-7254
Fax: 310-821-7375

"THE REGULARs"

AMERICA'S ORIGINAL
BANDSTAND DANCERS

As a "Regular" I honor Bob Horn's creativity and vision as a true pioneer in television. It's time for him to be acknowledged as the man who gave rock 'n' roll a home on television. It's time for him to be honored in the "Rock 'n' Roll Hall of Fame," and by the television stations and shows that have profited so much from his teenage dancing show concept.

It's too late to change the hurt that was done to this man and his family. He was slandered

BUNNY PRODUCTIONS
819 Dickson St.
Marina Del Rey, Ca. 90292
310-306-7254
Fax: 310-821-7375

Bunny Never Danced On Bob's Bandstand!!

"THE REGULARS"

AMERICA'S ORIGINAL
BANDSTAND DANCERS

and replied. "He was overlooked
and he was forgotten". And what
was his real crime? that he was
not young enough? Certainly, the
teenagers on Bandstand would
have disagreed with that. And,
the teenagers watching Bandstand
didn't have any complaints either.
So, why?

All that I can do now is
to say that I'm sorry that this
happened to Bob Horn and his
family, and to tell his family
through Stan Blitz's book
that I acknowledge Bob Horn's

BUNNY PRODUCTIONS
819 Dickson St.
Marina Del Rey, Ca. 90292

310-306-7254
Fax: 310-821-7375

Page 5 of

"THE REGULARS"

AMERICA'S ORIGINAL
BANDSTAND DANCERS

contribution to television and
to the influence he had on
my life.

Thank you Bob Horn, for
giving so much of yourself to so many
your kindness lives on through
the hearts and memories of "The Regulars"

Kathleen (Bunny) Gibson - one of
the original "Regulars" that
danced on Philadelphia's
American Bandstand from
1959 to 1961, when Dick
Clark was the host.

(Stan, thank you for this
opportunity to
thank Bob
Horn!)

BUNNY PRODUCTIONS
819 Dickson St.
Marina Del Rey, Ca. 90292

310-306-7254
Fax: 310-821-7375

Page 6 of

Kathleen "Bunny" Gibson, very much an active player in holding the *Bandstand "Regulars"* together as a going organization, has been most helpful to this book's author in aiding to seek out early days dancers from the **Bob Horn Bandstand**. She, too, is authoring a book about the dancers, titled, *"Behind The Smiles."* It's a great title for a great subject. Look for it soon. I certainly will be. And a special thanks for your help, Bunny.

NOTICE: The "1955 *Bandstand* Yearbook," as reprinted in pages of this book, somewhat reduced size, was originally the property of Bob Horn. It was left in the possession if his wife, Ann, when Bob passed away in 1966, A few years ago Ann gave the Yearbook to Bob's and her grandson, Robert Graham. The Yearbook is on loan to this book's author and to Cornucopia Publications to reprint in these pages so readers, dancers and lovers of rock 'n' roll — in the 1990s and beyond — can see just how terrific **Bob Horn's original** ***Bandstand was*** — way back in 1952, 1953, 1954, 1955 and early 1956 — before the show, lock, stock and barrel, was handed to a new host, in perfect running order, to carry on for some 40 more years.

the Official 1955

"BANDSTAND" YEARBOOK

WFIL-TV

channel 6

PHILADELPHIA

Table of Contents

140

A TYPICAL DAY AT "BANDSTAND"

Most of the fans who come down to visit "BANDSTAND" would hardly call it a "typical" day. For each one it is an exciting event— a real 'behind the scenes' glimpse into televisionland. It's also an opportunity for the folks at home to see them on TV, and maybe even a chance to dance with one of the recording stars, or one of the movie stars whose pictures have given them a thrill. Let's you and I go visit "BANDSTAND."

3

The first sight to meet your eyes as you leave the El at 46th and Market Streets—or your own chartered bus bringing you from out of town—is the line of other eager and cheerful young fans anxiously waiting for the doors of "BANDSTAND" to swing open. For Bob Horn and his co-workers at WFIL-TV the line is a familiar and friendly sight, it's always there, and it's always a friendly group. There are days when the crowds start gathering as early as 12:30 but always by 2:45 when it is time for the doors to open the fans are bubbling with excitement.

Since those who would like to attend the show each day are much more numerous than those who can fit into the "BAND-STAND" studio, membership cards are given to those requesting them. These allow the teenagers into the studio for the show. As a rule the line is so long that the doors are opened twice and two audiences, each attending for half of the program, are admitted.

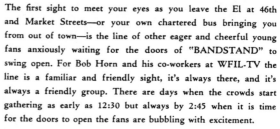

Once inside the studio the first impression you receive is one of activity. Cameras are moving about as the cameramen check their shots before the show—technicians adjust the banks of overhead lights to give viewers at home a well balanced picture—Ed Yates, the director, and Tony Mammarella, the producer, confer about a special effect they may want to use that day. Off to one side a few members of the committee are reading the fan mail that viewers have sent to them.

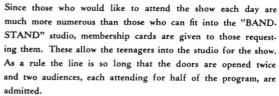

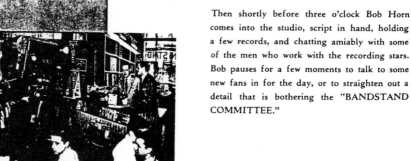

Then shortly before three o'clock Bob Horn comes into the studio, script in hand, holding a few records, and chatting amiably with some of the men who work with the recording stars. Bob pauses for a few moments to talk to some new fans in for the day, or to straighten out a detail that is bothering the "BANDSTAND COMMITTEE."

142

But you shout it out so you're sure the folks at home will hear it even without the microphone.

It's dance time once again, and then after a few numbers you see some of the other fellows and girls joining Bob on the "BAND-STAND" to judge the newest record releases. "Bob, I give that one an eighty-five" (maybe you thought seventy would be better) another record gets ninety-eight "It's bound to be a hit" (you agree—and you know that when they are picked as hits on "BANDSTAND" they usually are). The time is flying past—more guests have come in. "It's Steve Gibson and the Red Caps, with Damita Jo"—they really rock the studio with their music—and you keep it shaking with your applause—back again for their autographs, and then once more over to the dance floor for the finals of the straight dance contest. You join in the applause as the judges pick the winner—and then step out on the dance floor for the closing number.

Too soon it's five o'clock and the studio doors open again. This time, regretfully, it's time to leave. You board your bus—or join the gang at Doc Singer's down the corner near the El for an ice cream sundae to carry you through the ride home. It was fun—you never thought you could crowd so many thrills into two hours. Johnny Ray, the Red Caps, the dance contest, roll call, autographs — Gee, what a day. A "typical" day at "BAND-STAND." Naturally your first question is "Can I come back again?" The answer is easy. You're always welcome. It's your show.

The studio clock ticks off the minutes till three o'clock—over the loud speaker in the studio the "BANDSTAND" audience can hear the announcer "signing off" the previous show. Then a "special message" comes on—the cameramen tense—it won't be long now. Bob is in his place on that familiar "BANDSTAND." It's three o'clock—we hear the theme music—and then "Hello-Hello again — this is Bob Horn with another of our 'BAND-STAND' shows . . ."

The cameras roam over the stands and we're really "on the air." The folks in West Manayunk, Atlantic City, Wilmington, Wilkes-Barre, North, South, East, and West Philadelphia, are seeing you on television. At home you can imagine the excitement as your sis or brother cry out "Hey Mom, there's Joan (or Tommy) on television." You can imagine the questions they're sure to ask

144

you about "BANDSTAND"—But there's the first number—it's dance time. Quick as a flash you start down to the dance floor with dozens of other couples. This is a slow number but you hope Bob plays a fast one next so you can show how well they jitterbug in your neighborhood or town.

The records keep spinning—and every now and then you remember to keep silent while Bob delivers one of his "special messages." Then there is a stir in the back of the studio—Bob looks over and then he calls out that familiar introduction, "We have company." Who is it today? Robert Wagner, Julius LaRosa, Nat "King" Cole, and Red Caps? You see the star—"It's Johnny Ray"—and there he comes striding into the spotlight. Bob chats with him for a few minutes, and then steps out of camera range while Johnny introduces us to his newest record. You hope it will sell as many copies as "The Little White Cloud That Cried" (and he does too.). Perhaps after he finishes you will be one of the lucky ones who have an opportunity to dance with the guest star, just like the girls from school who danced with Jon Hall, or the fellow who jitterbugged with Joni James.

After the music ends the crowd starts forming at the autograph table, and you're right there to get a picture with the signature from one of your favorite stars. Back to your seat, and after a few numbers Bob brings out the hand microphone and you know it's rollcall time. This is your first visit so you join the others in line, and when your time comes you are so excited that you can just about remember your name and school.

6

"WE HAVE COMPANY"

"WE HAVE COMPANY"

"WE HAVE COMPANY"

MARION MARLOWE, formerly one of Arthur Godfrey's "Friends", stops in for a visit with Bob Horn on "THE BANDSTAND" while she was appearing in Philadelphia in May, 1955.

"WE HAVE COMPANY"

AUDREY and **JAYNE MEADOWS** introduce their first recording together on "BANDSTAND".

At least twice each day that well-known cry, "We have company!" rings out on the "BANDSTAND." No matter how often it is heard it always creates a murmur of excitement and expectation. Guest stars visiting in Philadelphia are welcomed to "BAND-STAND" with a spontaneous enthusiasm that is bound to impress them with the friendliness of the fans in Delaware Valley U.S.A.

JOHNNIE RAY has been a "BANDSTAND" guest several times . . .

"WE HAVE COMPANY"

"WE HAVE COMPANY"

"WE HAVE COMPANY"

HAROLD ROME, composer of the score for "Fanny", discusses the hit musical with Bob.

City Representative WALTER M. PHILIPPS and CON-NEE BOSWELL tell Bob about Connee's recording of "The Philadelphia Waltz".

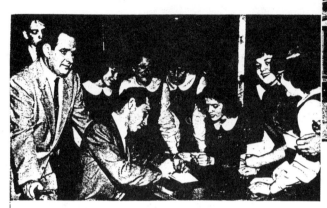

BILL DARNEL is always surrounded by a crowd at the autograph table when he visits "BANDSTAND".

"WE HAVE COMPANY"

Many of these stars have been personal friends of Bob's through the years. He knew them as young hopefuls when they were bringing their first recordings around to him, hoping for a few spins on his radio shows in Philadelphia. Now firmly established as stars, they still come around to spend a few pleasant minutes chatting with Bob and his friends on "BANDSTAND."

PEARL BAILEY pauses for a few seconds to answer that question from Bob, "Pearl, what's your favorite record?"

LES PAUL and MARY FORD tell Bob some of the secrets of their record successes.

FRANKIE LAINE'S "Mule Train" always carries a load of hits . . .

9

147

VAUGHAN MONROE chuckles as he reminisces about his activities as a bandleader—vocalist—and announcer.

ROBERT Q. LEWIS, another star seen on WFIL-TV, gives Bob some highlight stories about his show.

"WE HAVE COMPANY"

"WE HAVE COMPANY"

A roster of the guest stars who have sparkled on "BANDSTAND" might very well be substituted for a "Who's Who" in Show Business. Debbie Reynolds, Julius LaRosa, Jon Hall, Rudy Vallee, Robert Q. Lewis, Vaughan Monroe, are just a few of the famous stars of the entertainment world you have met, and are sure to meet again, on "BANDSTAND."

"WE HAVE COMPANY"

Stage, screen and television star PHIL SILVERS meets a new audience on "THE BANDSTAND".

JON HALL "Ramar of the Jungle" steps into the "BANDSTAND" Spotlight.

10

ALAN DALE

"A Philadelphia Star", SUNNY GAIL.

"WE HAVE COMPANY"
"WE HAVE COMPANY"

One of the newer combos, "The Crew Cuts", takes time out from their schedule to visit "BANDSTAND".

TONY BENNETT . . .

JONI JAMES

"WE HAVE COMPANY"

New stars are discovered every day. In recent years Denise Lor, Joni James, the McGuire Sisters, Bill Haley's Comets, the Crew Cuts, have skyrocketed to the top with "hit" recordings. Perhaps some of the fans who applaud them at "BANDSTAND" will follow in their footsteps. Maybe some day soon they will step into the spotlight as Bob calls "We Have Company!" No one will be happier than Bob when that day comes.

11

149

MEN AT WORK —

BOB and WFIL record librarian GEORGE SMITH discuss music for the show. Getting the latest and the best is no problem—with approximately 40,000 records on file at WFIL, and more arriving every day.

building "BANDSTAND"

Long before the audience forms the well-known line on Market Street, a lot of people are already hard at work on "BAND-STAND." Here's a backstage photo tour:

Guest artists are also an important feature of "BANDSTAND". Everyday, Bob goes through an incoming-outgoing telephone session, arranging appearances for the top recording stars who happen to be, or plan to be, in Philadelphia.

The day's advertising gets a thorough rehearsal, too. Projectionist ELMER (RED) FROELICH lines up the films and slides to assure clockwork operation once the show is on the air.

While music is important to "BANDSTAND", the show itself is important to the music world—because "BANDSTAND" can make a record a hit overnight. Like representatives of practically all recording companies, HARRY FINFER of Gotham Records comes to WFIL to discuss his firm's latest release with Bob and producer TONY MAMMARELLA. As a result, you hear most of the newest records FIRST on "BANDSTAND".

In the minutes just before air time, Bob joins producer TONY MAMMARELLA, director ED YATES, and engineer FRANK KERN in the control room. They've put all of the show's elements in running order so this is a "synchronize your watches" meeting for the lively two hours ahead.

12

150

Once BOB HORN steps to the "BANDSTAND" his view of the show is something like this. Are you in the picture?

Concentration reigns in the control room as Messrs. YATES, MAMMARELLA and KERN keep a watchful eye on the monitors, the assorted dials, the whereabouts of the cameramen. When it's time for a guest to arrive, Tony will be on hand as official greeter. He also makes frequent trips into the studio to discuss changes in plans with Bob.

"BANDSTAND" travels from studio to control room to Master Control where engineer SAM BARBOUR makes sure the picture is properly balanced as he sends it, via cable, to the WFIL-TV transmitter in Roxborough.

When the control room occupants look into the studio, their view of "BANDSTAND" in person is a hodge-podge of mike boom, klieg lights, cameras and props. But none of these things gets into the picture to distract the home audience.

At Roxborough sits engineer ED NEVILLE who, with a seasoned eye and steady hand, mans the controls that put "BANDSTAND" on the air on Channel 6, via Philadelphia's first maximum power TV transmitter. What looks like a peaceful job for Ed Neville could turn into an afternoon nightmare if any of the sensitive and complicated equipment should go tempermental.

Dig this crazy beanpole —it's the WFIL-TV transmitter, rising more than 900 feet above sea level, to send "BANDSTAND" on its way to fans in Pennsylvania, New Jersey, Delaware, Maryland. IT'S THE MOST important part of the show.

13

PERRY COMO says: "It's difficult to pick my favorite record, but I would lean toward 'Because'. This is a wonderful song that carries a beautiful thought. I enjoyed recording it."

PATTI PAGE says: "My favorite Mercury recording, 'Roses Remind Me Of You', was a miss, yet I like the song, the arrangement, and roses do remind me of someone once very dear to me."

AUTOGRAPHS

THE FOUR ACES say: "Our favorite recording is 'Tell Me Why'. This record was our first one with a major recording company (Decca) and became our first record to hit the magic mark of a million seller. With the success of this record we knew we had reached the big time."

LOU MONTE says: "Of all the records I have made, 'Darktown Strutters Ball' is, of course, my favorite and I will be forever indebted to Bob Horn and the 'BANDSTAND' members for their help in making this record a big hit. This one record brought me into national prominence after trying for so many years without success. With 'Darktown Strutters Ball' becoming a hit, I was able to give my wife and three children all the conveniences which I could not give them during the lean years and to provide for their future security.

KITTY KALLEN says: " 'Little Things Mean A Lot' is my favorite recording. After many years in show business as a band vocalist and then a single act, this song and record represents the height of success and a dream come true."

BILL HALEY and THE HALEY COMETS say: "We choose 'Crazy Man, Crazy' as our favorite recording. This was the first song and record to gain national acclaim for us. It was also responsible for getting us a contract with Decca Records. Since then we have had a succession of big selling records, but it all started with 'Crazy Man, Crazy'."

ALAN DALE says: " 'Oh Marie' was the first hit I had in the record business and it's still a steady seller. Guess it will always be my favorite for that reason."

JAYE P. MORGAN says: "My favorite record? Without a doubt that title belongs to my debut disc for RCA Victor, 'That's All I Want From You'. I was very nervous and at first hearing that song just didn't 'reach' me. But Hugo Winterhalter soon changed that. His arrangement was so great that the ballad came to life, and it was love at second hearing."

14

AUTOGRAPHS

EDDIE FISHER says: "I have a lot of favorite records by other artists, but since you ask my own it will have to be 'Oh My Pa-Pa'. I 'felt' this song from the first time I heard it, particularly because of Hugo's arrangement and that trumpet solo. When I heard the playback at the recording session I flipped right off my chair. Anytime I hear that trumpet I still do."

THE McGUIRE SISTERS say: "Our favorite recording is 'Somethin's Gotta Give'. This is the first tune we ever recorded that was written by an established songwriter. As soon as we heard it all of us flipped. We thought it was just great and made sure we cut it on our very next date."

TERESA BREWER says: " 'Music, Music, Music' is my favorite for pretty obvious reasons. This was the tune that established me as a recording star. It also opened the door for lots of other great opportunities as well as other record hits."

SOMETHIN' SMITH AND THE REDHEADS say: " 'It's A Sin To Tell A Lie' is certainly our favorite single record. It was originally released in a long-playing album, and when Epic records decided to release the tune as a single it started a chain reaction, which for us means a promising career in the entertainment field."

DON CORNELL says: "I choose 'I'll Walk Alone' as my favorite recording. This was my first release on Coral and it was a hit! I've been on cloud No. 7 ever since."

MICKI MARLO says: "I am very thrilled with my latest recording, 'I've Got Rythm in My Nursery Rhymes'. I love the DRIVE and the VOCAL background behind the recording, and it is by far the best recording I have made to date and certainly hope that you agree."

DICK LEE says: "I personally like two of my newest releases, 'Daniel Boone' and 'A Touch of Heaven'. Why? Well, I think they are a lot better than any of my previous records, and they are done in what is for me a different vein."

GLORIA MANN says: "My guardian angel certainly must have been with me when I was selected to record 'Earth Angel'. Its success proved to me how fabulous and unpredictable this business really is."

15

"BANDSTAND" GOES TO A PICNIC

1953

Picnics are always fun. But they're even more entertaining when they include two star-studded television shows—the nation's top recording artists—picnic suppers and free rides and games. These are all included in those fabulous "BANDSTAND PICNICS" at Woodside Park. The first, in 1953, was a huge success on at least two counts. First a great crowd had a wonderful time, and secondly, all proceeds were devoted to the benefit of the Philadelphia Children's Heart Hospital.

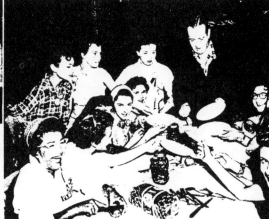

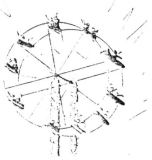

16

"BANDSTAND" GOES TO A PICNIC

1954

BOB HORN'S

From cities and communities all over Delaware Valley U.S.A. thousands of families assembled at Woodside Park for the 1954 "BANDSTAND PICNIC," despite a pouring rain. The regular "BANDSTAND" show was telecast from the Park, and a special nighttime "BANDSTAND" was also televised from the picnic area. Proceeds from the second picnic went toward the purchase of a mobile X-ray unit for Eagleville Sanatorium.

17

HIGH NOTES FROM THE "BANDSTAND"

The annual "BANDSTAND PICNIC"—the thrilling parade of guest stars—and the excitement of a visit to the program aren't the only exciting events at "BANDSTAND." Thousands of "BANDSTAND" fans participated in the "March of Dimes" campaign this year when more than five hundred dollars was presented to combat Infantile Paralysis. George Welsh, secretary of the local chapter, presented Bob with a certificate of appreciation, for this charitable effort . . . Many were present in person, and still thousands more watched on WFIL-TV as Bob received the Krakauer Beneficial Association's annual "Man of the Year" award for 1955 . . . "O Dem Golden Slippers" was the theme on New Year's Day as a special Mummers' float saluted "BAND-STAND" . . . "Happy Birthday" was the password as Gene E. Stout, Philadelphia editor of TV GUIDE presented Bob with a cake marking the second anniversary . . . also on hand adding their best wishes for many more were the local record distributors who bring around the tunes you hear each day . . . Now it's Bob's turn: Bob presents Frankie Laine with a special plaque for his out-

18

standing records, while bandleader Woody Herman looks on . . . "After the show is over . . ." "BANDSTAND" fans spend Wednesday, Friday, and Saturday evenings dancing to top recording selections at the New Carmen, Willow Grove, and at Avalon, New Jersey . . . "Major Maximum Power" tells Bob about the new viewers who are seeing him now that WFIL-TV is telecasting at Maximum Power . . . Some of them were probably in the crowd of eight thousand that packed the Arena last summer for a special "BANDSTAND" telecast . . . And new "High Notes" are heard each day.

19

In the "looks" department, we'll bet Broadway's "guys and dolls" had nothing on this group . . . MARIE DE LULLO, ELAINE BISELLI, PETE STEVENS, ADELINE CATUCCI, MARIE ALLMAN, JERRY BRADLEY.

BUZZIN' ROUND THE "BANDSTAND"

"BANDSTAND" without its guys and gals would be like Tony Bennett without a ballad . . . a wienie roast without the wienies . . . or a Junior Prom without "Stardust." In this section, we would have liked to spotlight *everyone* who ever passed through WFIL-TV's Studio "B" "'BANDSTAND's' home," but to do that would have taken a book, when opened, that would stretch from here to San Francisco. Here are a few of the "'BAND-STAND' regulars" . . . as great a crowd that ever did the Lindy!

DAVID, "Big Dave", FELD-BAUM, a John Bartram alumnus, lived up to his nickname by doing weight-lifting as a hobby. (Mr. America, look out!) "Big Dave" is a strong rooter for MICKI MARLO and GLORIA MANN.

JACKIE CHIRICO really had a bad time one day when she (1) tripped over a shoe one of the other girls had lost while dancing and (2) fell right in front of the TV camera. Apparently undaunted, Jackie wants to be a tap dancer.

PETE CAPOBIANCO has another type of memory . . . the time he "shared the stage" with AUDREY and JAYNE MEAD-OWS when they made a "BANDSTAND" guest appearance. When he's not "co-starring" with recording artists, Pete spends his spare time jitterbugging.

Mention ED CURRY, and BARBARA MARCEN'S eyes light up like a neon sign! She's President of his fan club, and naturally, thinks nobody can put over a song like her boy Ed. A part-time photographer's model, Janet does a bit of singing of her own in Southern High's Glee Club.

20

Owners of the attractive smiles are ANN ("Pudgie") POLIDORE and PAULA ("Snookie") SHARPLESS.

About to glide onto the dance floor are TERRY SCHRIFFER of Ridley Township High, and "Dutch" KRAMER of Central High, both formerly from Frackville, Pa.

BUZZIN' ROUND THE "BANDSTAND"

Enjoying a "break" between dances are MARY ANN COLELLA of Hallahan High, JOE SULLIVAN of Southeast Catholic and SALLY BUNN of West Catholic.

This quartet of cuties includes (l. to r. JUANITA GOMEZ, BOBBIE YOUNG, PEGGY SCARLOTI and BOBBIE MILUZZO.

Yes, perhaps one phrase describes "BANDSTAND'S" guys and gals better than any other . . . "they're the greatest"!

First place in the Carman jitterbug contest was captured by West Catholic's GINNIE O'CALLAHAN. KAY STARR and SAMMY DAVIS, JR., head the list of her favorite recording artists. As for future plans, Ginnie would like to be an actress.

TOM DE NOBLE JR.—Tom hopes to give Eddie Fisher some competition in a few years, and already has several fan clubs. He has sung on WFIL-TV, and in shows at St. Thomas More, where he's a junior.

JO MAZZU—A former cochairman of the "Bandstand Committee", Jo enjoys listening to the new record releases and guessing which ones will be hits. One of her "best" picks was "Sh-boom", a real hit on "BANDSTAND".

BOBBIE MILUZZO is taking Latin-American dance lessons, which includes mambo, tango, rhumba and you-name-it. When it comes to male vocalists, TONY BENNETT is Bobbie's boy.

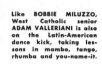

Like BOBBIE MILUZZO, West Catholic senior ADAM VALLERIANI is also on the Latin-American dance kick, taking lessons in mambo, tango, rhumba and you-name-it.

BUZZIN' ROUND THE "BANDSTAN

"BANDSTAND" has been directly responsible for many, many record hits in the Philadelphia area. Here (l. to r.) DELORES DI FELICE, ROBERT AILES and JOAN ARNAUD look through the latest releases, one or more of which might become a "Philly favorite".

JOE TETI is looking towards a career in aeronautical engineering, with eyes on Villanova or Drexel as the college of his choice. Meanwhile, he keeps in practice (though earthbound) by helping to keep auto motors in tip-top shape.

To quote JERRY BLAVAT, a sophomore at Southeast Catholic, "one of the nicest things that ever happened to me at 'BANDSTAND' was meeting JO MAZZU." (So there you are!)

BUNNY PAUL of Capitol Records obliges "BANDSTAND" fans CANDY STOCKBRAND, JOHNNY SACCIOLA, JUANITA GOMEZ and NANCY NEILEY with autographs.

As winner of the Slow Dance Contest, Southern High's ROSALIE BELTRANTE won a lovely evening gown ensemble, including gown, stole, shoes, gloves and jewelry, courtesy of SEVENTEEN magazine. (Her partner was JACKIE STARR.)

Active in more fan clubs than you could shake a camera at, PEGGY SCARLOTI lists dancing as her number one hobby. Among the fan clubs she belongs to are JOHNNIE RAY, the Four Coins, GEORGIE SHAW, JOHNNIE DESMOND, "BANDSTAND'S" TOM DE NOBLE, and the Four Aces.

Whether you watch "BANDSTAND" at home, or from the bleachers in the studio, you probably recognize JANET MURRAY, JOHNNY WILLIAMS and ANDREA ("Andy") KAMENS.

If anyone's interested in joining a Gloria Mann fan club, RONNIE KINGSDORF is the boy to see. Besides boosting his favorite recording star, Ronnie is also active in P.A.L. Boxing.

The graceful ballerina is LUCILLE NAPOLI of Hallahan High. Bent on a show business career, Lucille sings and dances professionally, and has performed at the Varsity Club (a teen-age club), Willow Grove and Town Hall. Equally agile at tap and ballet, Lucille has been studying both singing and dancing for five years.

22

161

HOW A RECORD IS MADE ➤

Nobody knows when a record is made whether it will be a hit or a flop. Only the response of "Bandstandees" and hundreds of thousands like them across the country, when they hear it, will determine whether it climbs to the top of the list or not.

But this is the story of a hit—Rosemary Clooney's version of "Hey There" for Columbia Records.

It all began with a session in the recording studio between ROSEMARY, MITCH MILLER, Director of Artists and Repetoire for Columbia, and orchestra leader PERCY FAITH. Here they talk over the arrangement and the treatment "Hey There" is to be given.

ROSEMARY rehearses, with MITCH and PERCY listening carefully to suggest changes in phrasing or tempo.

Ready for the first waxing, with the orchestra.

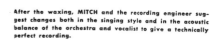

After the waxing, MITCH and the recording engineer suggest changes both in the singing style and in the acoustic balance of the orchestra and vocalist to give a technically perfect recording.

24

ROSEMARY listens carefully as she attempts to remember all the new suggestions and to follow them.

Sometimes it may take a dozen recordings to produce the one perfect version of a song that you hear. But when that final recording is made, it goes on sale, Bob plays it on "BAND-STAND," you like it, and before long everybody knows, "It's a HIT!"

Second take. ROSEMARY belts out the version of "Hey There" that you've heard hundreds of times.

It's good! Everybody, including ROSE-MARY, is pretty sure of that as they hear the tune coming over the loud-speaker.

Waiting for the critical moment—the playback. ROSE-MARY relaxes with only one question in her mind—how will it sound?

25

163

"Put Your right foot forward
Put your left foot out . . .
Do the Bunny Hop
Hop Hop Hop"

Ray Anthony recorded the "Bunny Hop" for Capitol Records. Bob started playing it on "BANDSTAND," and when you heard it that was all you needed. Soon everybody was doing it, and although some recordings become hits and fade in a short time, the "Bunny Hop" is still a favorite in Delaware Valley U.S.A. Ray Anthony was so overwhelmed with the reception you gave the "Bunny Hop" he came down to the "BANDSTAND" himself to join the fun, and express his appreciation to you for making the "Bunny Hop" one of his greatest hits.

BUNNY HOP

26

"Father—Mother—Son
All join in the fun
Do the Bunny Hop
Hop Hop Hop"

It didn't take long for the younger-set to pick up the fun of the "Bunny Hop" and parents too were doing it at parties and dances. On the "BANDSTAND" a contest to select the winners of the "Bunny Hop" dance competition was held. The winners and their parents were the guests of Ray Anthony and his band in New York, and while there they showed Ray and his audience what made the "Bunny Hop" so popular on the "BANDSTAND."

27

BARBARA had breakfast hours ago but she's on hand to make sure Daddy finishes his.

OFF CAMERA

"Look, ma, I'm climbing," but the Horn girls are too busy to watch. ANNE supervises PINKY, 2½, and BARBARA, 1½, on the seesaw, as 7-year-old MARIANNE enjoys a solo flight.

MARIANNE goes for a slide like RICHIE ASHBURN for homeplate— but BOB has to sell the idea to baby BARBARA. MARIANNE'S a third-grader at Pen-Dell School.

What a line! BOB claims he caught this Baracuda himself in Florida and the girls are willing to believe him. PINKY reaches out to make sure it's real.

The Horn girls have their own private disc jockey and put in requests first-hand.

"I guess he knows what he's doing," thinks PINKY, "but I'll hold on tight just in case."

RIN, the Horn boxer, listens to his master's voice . . .

They go for "BANDSTAND"! (And Hoppy and Chief Halftown and Romper Room, too!)

Between shows, Bob Horn performs for his greatest fan club: Anne, Barbara, Pinky, and Marianne Horn. Son Peter is away from home as a member of the Air Corps.

Anne, a native of Springfield, Massachusetts, was a pop singer before she met and married Bob in Mexico. They reside now in Levittown, Pa. One good thing about Bob's afternoon air time—it lets him be home when the kids are rarin' to go (and the grass needs cutting). Here's a pictorial view of a typical day at the Horn household.

. . . and even lets the old man win at wrestling. Smart dog.

"Believe me, it's not loaded." ANNE stands at wary attention as BOB inspects his trusty rifle. He's a better-than-fair marksman and takes to the woods every hunting season.

PETE'S away and lawn-trimming is no job for girls—so Papa Horn furnishes the leg-work behind the power mower. It's good exercise but it will never replace the Bunny Hop.

He's off—for another day at "BANDSTAND", Philadelphia's top-rated daytime television show—and the whole family will keep an eye on him from three to five o'clock.

THE FAMILY ENJOYS "BANDSTAND" AT HOME, TOO

Whether young-in-age or young-at-heart, "BANDSTAND" viewers at home are just as ardent fans of the program as the teen-agers dancing "On camera" in the studio. Few people realize that adults comprise more than one-half of " 'BANDSTAND's' at home" audience. In fact, the program is so popular that Mom finds it difficult to leave the TV set when she's doing the family ironing. So, she moves baggage and baby into the living room and does the ironing, the baby-sitting and enjoys herself all at the same time! Meanwhile, Johnnie and Connie, or Tim and Kim as the case may be, are practicing a new dance step that's being demonstrated in the WFIL-TV studio. Even Dad (if he's lucky) gets to enjoy the show, too, as sign-off isn't until 5 P.M.

My Day at "Bandstand"

Today..I made my first trip to "BANDSTAND," and was it exciting! I left home about............o'clock and met..........................at............................. We arrived at WFIL-TV at................o'clock, and joined the crowd waiting for "BANDSTAND" to begin. Before the show we watched the cameramen preparing for the "BANDSTAND," and I kept hoping that Bob would play my favorite record.................................. by ....

When three o'clock came and "BANDSTAND" was on the air, the first number played was .... by .... I looked around and saw.................... ....and................................., and many other regulars on the "BANDSTAND COMMITTEE." They sure are lucky to be able to come to "BANDSTAND" and help Bob every day.

The dancing, both straight and jitterbug, was a lot of fun. I watched the different styles of jitterburg, and the one I liked best was.................................. I danced with............. ...., ... and .... My favorite was .... After a few numbers the guest stars came in, and we saw........... .... and .... When they finished we went back to the autograph table to meet them in person.

The records I liked best on "BANDSTAND" today were............................. and .... I was sorry when five o'clock came and the show ended. We left the studio with..................................and went to ....where we talked about the great time we had today, my first day at "BANDSTAND."

31

BOB HORN'S "BANDSTAND"

For more than two years I have had the pleasure of being your host on the "BANDSTAND" each weekday over WFIL-TV. It is an exciting experience making new friends with the thousands of fans who join us in person on "BANDSTAND," and with the millions more we meet on television.

From letters and messages we receive we know this enthusiasm is shared by you who have made "BANDSTAND" *your* show. From others now in the Armed Forces or who have moved to new cities, we receive mail telling us how much they miss their friends on "BANDSTAND." When "We have company!" the warm reception our guest stars receive is a personal one that they take away with them and remember for a long while.

"BANDSTAND" is our show—yours and mine—and this feeling is the spark leading us to many new fields. Our annual picnics—with the proceeds devoted to a specific charity—"BANDSTAND" participation in the "March of Dimes,"—the Cerebral Palsy Telethons,—Heart Fund Drives— have demonstrated how eager you have been to help our less fortunate friends.

These have all been highlights of our efforts to bring young men and women together in a friendly atmosphere, and to provide wholesome entertainment for a few hours each afternoon. Any success we may have achieved is due to your participation, at home or in person, in "BANDSTAND."

We hope that this "BANDSTAND YEARBOOK" helps to recall many pleasant moments we have had together on the show. To it I can but add my thanks for your cooperation, and my hopes that we can have many more happy hours of music and fun on "BANDSTAND."

Sincerely,

Bob Horn

1

171

CHAPTER SEVEN

THE MANAGERS BELIEVE
"WE CAN DO BETTER"

By mid-February of 1956, after *"Bandstand"* had completed another full year of outstanding performance in every area of television broadcast scoring as, viewer counts, no overwhelming problems on telecasts, excellent teenager audience-dancer body counts, no known dissatisfied sponsor clients, overall popularity, and more potential sponsors waiting in line to buy "commercials time" on the show. Why then, would the Messrs. Clipp and Koehler, maybe or maybe not egged by their boss, Walter Annenberg, be eager to see Bob Horn removed as host on the show he created?

We can think of many possible reasons for their individually or personally wanting Bob Horn off of the show. We can also think of at least one major and valid reason why, once removed from the show, a same boss or bosses, collectively, might want Bob Horn to relocate far away from Philadelphia.

We are as well that neither of his two bosses at the station cared much for him personally — and this has been made especially a truth since his huge success and his continually increasing income, mostly from recordings salespeople and distributors who gave him cash and gifts rewards when he plays "their firms' records on *Bandstand.* The combination of public acclaim, glory, and more money than he had ever (accumulatively) earned before in a day, a week, a month or for a year was giving Bob Horn motivation to strut his earned and newfound "success status." At the time Bob was still a relatively young man — and his instant wealth and sudden prominence as a luminary was a new and exciting ego trip. His tendency to flaunt his new economic and celebrity status, with no manager handling his affairs, left him much as, today a young athlete or musician "suddenly a multi-millionaire" might tend to flaunt such a marvelous life situation.

To certain envious individuals at and around WFIL-TV Bob's success attitude may have been like waving a red flag in front of a bull. By way of possible examples of envy or quasi-envy could have been either or both of his bosses at WFIL, or other announcers or DJs working for WFIL who discounted the fact that Bob Horn had worked damned hard for a lot of years to finally capture every penny he was receiving. They may, in envy or jealousy, have overlooked, too, that Bob Horn, at the time was the biggest single income producer for the WFIL stations during 1953, 1954 and 1955. But envy, like its companion jealousy, all around them is one of the things that celebrities have to accept and learn to handle quickly, adroitly and with humility. Bob was apparently slow in learning how to cope, in a condition of dignity and humility, with his new success.

This weakness on Bob's part gave individuals like Dick Clark, still wet behind his ears in the field of broadcasting, reason to say things about Bob, as Clark (a kid who didn't know Bob Horn from the proverbial Adam L. Fox) found stimuli to say in his autobiography, "The more I worked with Horn the less I liked him. It was hard for me, in my early twenties, to appreciate that competition can be so fierce." The only way Clark knew Horn at all was that Horn was forced (not by his own desire in any way) to do the introductory and closing announcements for Clark's early afternoons radio show with the management assigned name, *Bandstand,* [a name of Bob Horn's creation when he had a radio DJ show] stolen by management and assigned to Clark's radio show on WFIL-AM radio — while the same name was being used, simultaneously, for Bob's TV show on WFIL-TV. The two men did not ever "work together." When performing his "command assignment" daily, Bob Horn, a long experienced and 100% professional announcer-DJ-show creator and host, he was forced (not asked) to do this flunky radio assignment for some kid in from New York. There was no reason in this scenario for friendship between these two men.

And as for Horn showing jealousy toward Clark? In his book writing implying jealousy by Horn toward Dick Clark, Clark had to be kidding. It is doubtful if these two men ever shared so much together as a cup of coffee or a *Coca Cola*, (one of the sponsors of TV *Bandstand).*

By mid-1955 Bob Horn, with the added earnings of recording salespeople's gifts and tips for playing their records on TV *Bandstand,* beyond his regular salary, he was taking home more money each month than his most immediate boss, George Koehler. Thus, there could have been some envy there, too. This, however, was probably by itself not a 'big deal.'

As for his next higher boss, Roger Clipp, overall manager of WFIL's radio and televison stations, and also business manager of the ***TV Guide*** weekly magazine by this time, Clipp just plain didn't like Bob Horn. The invisible adversarial barrier between these two men seemed to have never disappeared since the first day Horn came to work for WFIL. But that seemed to be a similar situation between Roger Clipp and many of his WFIL employees. Whether real or not, that posture between Clipp and a lot of his employees has been brought to this book author's attention so many times by so many different people as to be truthful.

Walter Annenberg, owner of the stations and of Triangle Publications, and the big boss over the whole shebang had no reason at this time, early in 1956, to have any but good feelings toward Bob Horn, who was doing well for WFIL, well for corporate earnings, and particularly well for WFIL-TV in the ratings systems. Mr. Annenberg had to be hearing and reading good things about the amazing success of 'that little Philadelphia afternoon TV show' that TV stations all across America wanted to copy. After all, a kid's music for dancing show on afternoon TV, was an idea he had suggested to Roger Clipp in the first place. If anyone had a claim to inventing *Bandstand* besides Bob Horn, that individual would have to be Walter Hubert Annenberg. Any negatives he had heard about his TV *Bandstand*, if any had to have come to him from his station managers, Clipp or Koehler, or possibly from some of his cronies asking "what's that older host doing with all those kids?," — or even some similar statement coming to him, second hand through his wife, from ladies at the art museum.

Lee Stewart is out of the picture completely and both Jack Steck, WFIL program director, and Tony Mammarella, producer of *Bandstand*, and fill in host of the show when Bob must be away, get along great with the show's creator and host, Bob Horn. Steck and Mammarella are professionals in their own right and understand and accept Bob's flaunting of his new found celebrity status.

"But We Can Do Better" Is The Word From WFIL Management....

How do you do better than the best? It is usually by coming up with something totally new and superior (if the capacity exists to do so) or, by making some modification and attempting to pass it off as a major improvement, or, finally by making a change desired internally and convincing the public "it could have been no other way."

Henry Ford II tried the first way, something entirely new. He tried it with the "Edsel" and we all know, or can quickly learn from someone a little older, what happened with that costly mistake.

Coca Cola tried improving something already good with a *"New Coca Cola"* only to expensively learn, after a tremendous marketing push, to return marketing efforts to re-selling to the world their proven *"Classic Coca Cola"* — that had never needed the word Classic in front of the name *Coca Cola* to retain worldwide top market shares for most of this century.

In the WFIL-TV front offices, if not indeed even in the parent company, *Philadelphia Inquirer* boardroom, that in order to remove Bob Horn as host (and his name from the position of 'show creator,') and to replace him with another, more youthful host for *Bandstand,* the change would have to be made and then convince the public, the viewers and all the kid dancers on the show, "that it could not have been done any other way!!" This, owner-management members of WFIL-TV, is the only way we can go. Horn and Mammarella have convinced us that *Bandstand* is, indeed a one host show. Horn would not be at all receptive to our bringing in a younger man as his co-host. Yes, we can only make our wanted change then sell it to the

175

viewers, the kids, and the show's production crew.

We Can Do Better. Now, How Do We Go About It....

That's not an easy question to answer. We've been trying for months and months to make things so miserable for Horn at WFIL-TV that he will voluntarily (under such pressure that we don't let up) resign as host of *Bandstand* and possibly remain with WFIL as "musical selections director" with same or maybe a little more pay. But that hasn't worked thus far and we have no indication that it may in the foreseeable future. Horn likes his job with *Bandstand* and it will take more than we've been able to dish out (legally) to make him resign his host position.

Let's review his contract. It has too long to go before we can simply 'just not renew it' when it come up for renewal. Besides, too keep him on the WFIL-TV hook, his contract contains an option for automatic renewal unless he really fouls up badly — which he's not doing and is not the least bit likely to do.

What has he done in the way of not following WFIL employment guidelines in things he's done or said on the air or in front of cameras? Has he done anything wrong in his treatment of or in relationships with other employees? Has he missed any show schedules without due advance notice unless established as 'unavoidable?' Has he related badly with any sponsors or guests on his shows? The answers are a strong, **none of the above**, in any degree of seriousness to justify termination, removal from a show, or even written notices of rules infringements. Unquestionably, Bob Horn is every bit the broadcast professional everybody says he is. No breaking of company rules to throw at him. He doesn't any longer jump when either of his bosses say, like, "Come to a meeting at eleven tomorrow morning," unless he's also given a viable reason to be there – and that being there wouldn't interfere with what he deems to be more important things in connection with (his) *Bandstand.* If he's ordered to be at a meeting he shows up. We have no grounds to even complain seriously pertaining to Bob Horn's compliance with company regulations. Did he ever park in somebody else's assigned parking space? We don't know.

How about the morals clause in his contract? Is there any way we can nail him on an infraction of that clause? We know that he works in dance halls and nightclubs as a DJ or emcee many nights of every month, and he visits the same kind of places lots of other nights in order to see new entertainment acts, to entertain his celebrity guests on *Bandstand* and to hear new music. He's not any tee-totaler so he's bound to come out of such places to drive home after he's 'had a few.' Maybe he's even been picked up a few times for driving after drinking and has maybe even received a few DWI citations. We'll have to look into that. Then, again, why bother, if a cop stops him – most Philadelphia cops know Bob and they like him. Hell, they'd most of them, if they stopped him just say, "Go on home, Bob, but drive carefully."

But we know what we can do about that. Don't we?

Any other morals break throughs beyond what the one guy asked, "What's that dirty old man doing working with all those snazzy little chickens?" Horn may be wide open on that angle, too. Our District Attorney and a couple of judges are going wild on clamping down on pornography this year. Horn's already guilty of that, apparently, in the eyes of some of the dancer's parents – mostly fathers of young girls who envy Horn his position of working with all those cute young things every day. Yeah. There may be something there, too.

Our object, and soon, is to get Bob Horn to relinquish his job as host of TV *Bandstand,* to retain the show intact, and to get an "All American" sort of young man, someone already experienced as an announcer, who is nice looking and who has already had some show hosting or DJ experience on TV or radio to step in as Bob's replacement.

But There's Are Deeper Underlying Problems
Known Only To Roger Clipp And Perhaps To George Koehler....

The first such problem is that literal millions of people of Philadelphia and of the Delaware Valley know and love Bob Horn. If Bob leaves *Bandstand,* they're going to insist upon learning why Bob left, how Bob left, and where is he going to be where they can still see and hear him? Time, of course, can resolve that problem; time coupled with a lot of excellent and prolific publicity for "the new *Bandstand"* and its new host. Some sponsors are going to want answers to the same questions. When Bob leaves – unless he goes far, far away – *Bandstand* will lose some viewers and ratings may decline temporarily but ratings can come right back up when a new host does a good job. After all, it's Bob who has always said, "The kids are the show." And he was right.

Yes, the fickle public can be brought back rather quickly. It's almost like who had the *Tonight* show before Jay Leno? You know the answer to that. Okay, who had the *Tonight* show before Johnny Carson? That's a little tougher. But the viewers are still there. About disgruntled sponsors, most of them are business people who will simply figure Bob's leaving was his or a management's decision. If the show continues well, there is little chance any sponsor will jump ship.

The remaining question is, what will Bob Horn do if he leaves WFIL-TV. He is one of the finest, if not the finest, TV or radio show hosts, announcers and DJ capable individuals of the Delaware Valley and right on into New York. He'd be tough competition should he choose to go with another same area TV station and build there a new show to steal big chunks of the WFIL-TV *Bandstand* viewers.

These, Then, Become Our "Deliver Us From Horn" Choices....

1. Convince him to give up *Bandstand* and have an equal or better pay job at WFIL.

2. Buy out his remaining contract time and buy his continuance option, whatever it will cost. Oh, my God, no. That could cost WFIL-TV hundreds of thousands of dollars (millions in 1990s dollars). Roger Clipp's penny pinching could never let WFIL do that.

3. Frame him for committing a crime or crimes that would violate the morals clause of his contract, then fire him. Following that, hoping for felonies instead of mere misdemeanors, fan the fires of negative publicity his criminal deeds can generate – over a long enough time to prevent him from getting broadcast employment in the area – and cause him to pack up his family and his belongings and leave the Philadelphia area, going to a place far away, for good.

4. Have him assassinated.

Thus: Unless it would be possible to convince Bob Horn to step way from *Bandstand*, as host and accept some other well paying position at WFIL within a short period of time (a time then known and set only by WFIL management), they would need to resort to one of the other three defrocking alternatives — and they definitely didn't want him (physically) assassinated — so that left the other two alternatives:

Either pay him off, whatever the amount, to leave the show and to leave the area. Perhaps, included could be a position at one of the other TV or radio stations by then owned by Triangle Publications (Walter Annenberg), and by then, too, with Roger Clipp being their general manager as representative of the parent corporation.

Or,

Conspire to have Horn arrested in the Philadelphia area for one serious criminal offense or perhaps two or maybe three lesser offenses. A first one arranged could be enough to justify his immediate suspension from hosting or even being connected with *Bandstand* — with, then, exploitation in the media of that offense, perhaps followed by one or two additional offenses, to spoil his popularity and reputation in greater Philadelphia and in the Delaware Valley. That way Horn would be off of the show and looking for somewhere else around the nation for employment. Certainly, under such conditions, no TV or radio station in or near Philly would want to hire him.

178

Next, between the WFIL station managers, would logically come an analysis of probable costs for both ways for deposing King Robert from his *Bandstand* throne, to buy him out or to criminalize him out. One way would be clean but very costly since Horn knows his worth. The other way, causing Horn to become a criminals would mean calling for a few favors from law enforcement people, a moderate cost pretense of wanting to help him out in his time of tribulation, and seeing to it that every charge made, regardless of ultimate outcome, would be vigorously touted in the news by every possible media outlet in the entire WFIL market.

The Die Was Cast. It Would Be Easier To Take "Bandstand" National Without Horn....

PART THREE

*A TRUE STAR
IS SHOT DOWN,
TARRED, FEATHERED,
AND RUN OUT OF TOWN*

*BUT THE STAR
WILL NOT BE FORGOTTEN*

CHAPTER EIGHT

SLAUGHTER THE GOOSE
BUT KEEP THE GOLDEN EGG

The object is to be ready when the offer would come to take TV *Bandstand* nationwide via network television. It's going to happen, it's just a matter of when. The show is a winner, indeed a breakthrough in daytime television. The industry has learned about this mother lode of pure gold and already several TV stations are making efforts to have versions of *Bandstand* of their own. Roger Clipp, George Koehler and possibly Walter Annenberg, too, have heard the word directly — or in combining tidbits of industry conversations and wives' suggestions plus their own prejudices, regarding the drawbacks of a 40 year old man hosting a live show featuring dancing teenagers. The call to take the show nationwide might come any day bcause Roger Clipp, no matter what else he may be, is one of the best known men in the national television industry and a man who knows every key individual in all of the major networks by their first names. Yes, the call will come and now it the time to prepare — to somehow, with out the cost breaking their bank, remove Bob Horn as the host of WFIL-TV's *Bandstand*. In this management dilemma situation we must realize that while we have come to pretty much think of *Bandstand* as Bob Horn's show, which technically it wasn't. True, Bob Horn had created the show and he had done a marvelous job of it — but legally and technically that show, like all live shows on WFIL stations at that time in history, belonged 100% to WFIL-TV to do with as the station owner and management would see fit. And we know, without even giving a second thought, that Clipp and Koehler knew *Bandstand* belonged to the station.

And When Speaking Of Broadcast Industry Contacts, Mr. Clipp Had Them All....

As a reminder of just how powerful Roger Clipp was in the 1950s, let us look quickly, again, to his broadcast credentials — in addition to his responsibilities within WFIL, as general manager of all of the Annenberg radio and television stations proprties, and being business manager of weekly, nationally distributed, Triangle Publication's magazine, *TV Guide*, Clipp

181

also held these other, some functional and some honorary, positions in the radio and television industry during the 1950s: He was **chairman** of the Planning and Advisory Committee of the more than 300 stations ABC Network. He was a member of the Pennsylvania Joint Committee on Educational Television, a member of the Philadelphia Board of Trade, and a member of the U.S. Chamber of Commerce Advertising Committee. To think for one minute that Mr. Clipp didn't have loads of clout in the broadcasting and advertising industries would be most naive. No doubt, too, his contacts nationally, regionally and across the nation had contributed greatly to the success of Walter Annenberg's radio and television holdings, to the almost overnight success of *TV Guide* magazine and very likely, too, to the rapid success of TV *Bandstand* and the recent celebrity status of Bob Horn, personally, as creator and host of TV *Bandstand*. Roger Clipp and his clout in broadcasting is not to be under estimated at all. We must remember, too, that he didn't want to assign Bob Horn to the TV show that would become TV's *Bandstand* — but Mr. Annenberg was waiting the get an afternoon kid's dance music show going on his WFIL-TV, Mr. Clipp's first choice to carry out his boss's request were not available and Bob Horn was. Now Clipp wants Bob Horn off of the show and he suspects (probably correctly) that Horn will not bow to his desire without a fight.

However, as tight as Mr. Clipp is with his boss's purse strings and has been ever since becoming part of the Annenberg empire, it is no way his intent to have to buy up Horn's contract or to pay one red cent to Horn for his (Horn's) option for a contract continuance in another year. Clipp, further, with his long knowledge of the demand among TV stations for people of Horn's professional abilities and caliber, while longing to get Horn the hell out of WFIL, has no desire whatsoever to turn Bob Horn loose in a field of 'stations in need of experienced talent' and to have Bob's very talent returning as a competitor for WFIL advertising income dollars. The author is aware that this paragraph's thrust is redundant but it may be highly meaningful to the rest of the story.

But What's To Do About Bob?

If it were not for the fact that Bob Horn was a true celebrity in the area, a position in the eyes and ears of TV viewers and the public that WFIL-TV money, publicity and community contacts had helped create (the Clipp-Koehler Frankenstein) could go to work building a similar show for a competitor station in a heart beat after departing WFIL, their dilemma would be easy to resolve. Simply trump up some internal charges of Horn's violating company rules or policies — terminate him and let the chips fall where they may. He might take them to court but with their battery of retained lawyers, good Philadelphia lawyers, Horn would be dead and buried before any serious judgments against WFIL-TV could be through trial and appeals and funds to be paid out. And what would that cost WFIL-TV in dollars? Very little because they are feeding the attorneys already. A small amount more legal work wouldn't cost much.

But with Bob Horn's professional abilities, his creative talents and the area public liking him tremendously, imply shoving him out the door is no answer. And there's no way that Horn will simply dry up and blow away. He's going to have to be blasted out with TNT, dynamite or plastic. He must (just maybe and with practically no possibility) either be convinced to take another job at WFIL. Or Mr. Horn must be forced out of WFIL (first) and (secondly), almost in the same breath, also be forced out of the entire WFIL viewing or listening area. Legally, *Bandstand* belongs to the station, but it also belongs to the viewing public and that public likes Bob Horn on the show. And a 1955 penny-pinching manager figures, I'd rot in hell before I'd pay Bob Horn more than $5,000 (1955 dollars that is) to leave the show, leave WFIL and leave our market area - or agree to stay out of on-the-air radio and television in this market area for say, the next five years. I'd do that, $5,000 cash, maybe even $6,000 for fast agreement. But he's too street smart to settle for so little with a hit show in his pocket.

Desperate circumstances call for desperate measures. Are we ready and able to take those measures? Yes, we are. Our backs are in a corner and we are forced to battle our way out. Tomorrow's agenda will include drafting our plan (with nothing in writing, of course.) It will be our plan to take back a TV show we already own. Devious perhaps but a way to accomplish our goal quickly. Actually, we may not even have to complete every phase of a plan we conceive. Our target may collapse and give in to a more subservient work assignment here at WFIL or otherwise allow us to win our goal without our having to use every weapon in the arsenal we establish. Tomorrow (an early March day of 1956) we can set down our plan to commence accomplishment within a few weeks. Tomorrow.

A traffic police officer once told your author that there isn't an auto or truck driver alive who drives more than 55 miles a day who I cannot follow for several hours, during which time that driver will unquestionably violate at least one traffic law or more likely two or three.

In The Meanwhile Keep Supporting Bob To Stave Off Competition....

A mere four months before the managers' planning session another show team on another TV station took a shot at upsetting our *Bandstand* apple cart. Messrs. Grady and Hurst, the team Clipp wanted to hire to do a kids afternoon dance show for WFIL-TV three years before, tried a similar show on another Philadelphia area TV station. Their effort was written somewhat like comparing RC Cola with Coca Cola, by Philadelphia columnist, Frank Brookhouser, in his *Man About Town* column on October 6, 1955. He said:

> "A SHOWDOWN BATTLE BEGAN today in Philadelphia's hottest television feud .

"The participants are, in this corner, WFIL-TV's Bob Horn; and in the othe corner, Ed Hurst and Joe Grady, the veteran radio disc jockeys whose new television show — similar, of course, to Horn's — was inaugurated this afternoon on WPFH.

"And although the geneal public may not have been aware of it, that set the stage for a big struggle for the teen-age audience, with no holds barred.

"The tipoff came last week. First, Hurst and Grady notified all record distributors to have their stars appear on the first show for WPFH today. A short time later, Horn notified the same distributors to have their stars appear on his "Bandsand" to celebrate the "third anniversary" of that show.

"This caused great consternation in the ranks of the distributors — and the recording stars — because a notification is tantamount to an order when it comes from such disc jockey kingpins. And the distributors and the stars were over the proverbial barrel as the feuding disc jockeys squared off."

- end of article -

This feud didn't go on very long before the Hurst and Grady show was pulled for lack of viewers and sponsors. As for the day both recording stars were sought to both shows on the same day, your author doesn't know the except that the stars may have done what was called in vaudeville, "bicycling," between the dance show studios, as vaudevillians used to do when they were booked into two different theaters on a same day. I'm guessing, but that is one way the double requests might have been accommodated. The next time I'm in Philly I will ask Ed Hurst or Joe Grady how the dual requests worked out. They didn't have great luck on television but even today, 47 years later this team still has their weekend radio show reaching listeners in and around Philadelphia.

And In Mid-July Of 1955 TV GUIDE Was Still Printing Praises Of Horn....

On a *TV Guide* page of its July 23 issue of 1955, the praises of Bob Horn and his TV *Bandstand* continue to be sung, in print. On page A-2 of that edition being sold primarily in the WFIL telecast. 8-million viewers, area, appeared this material:

Three photographs with captions: One with celebrities, Mary Small and Mitch Miller, with Bob Horn at the *Bandstand* set podium; another with Bob Horn and Micki Marlo on a carousel horses with the caption, "Bob and Micki Marlo tried a trot onthe merry-go-round." And a third photo of Bob standing at a microphone with his family around him and the caption, "Bob made a family affair by introducing Peter,

Marianne, Mrs. Horn (Ann) and Christine." (Third daughter, Barbara, wasn't in this particular photo.)

The article headline read: "It's Picnic Time Again," with a subhead, "Third Annual "Bandstand" Picnic to be held July 28."

Then came the article about *Bandstand*, supporting the show and its host, Bob Horn, as if he would be with the show forever, it reads:

"Come Thursday, July 28, Philadelphia's Woodside Park once again will be swarming with thousands of record fans. The cry of the barker will be replaced with the strains of Ralph Flanagan, Sauter-Flanagan, etc. How come? This is the date of the third annual "Bob Horn Bandstand Picnic," at which time Ch 6's popular d.j. takes over the park for the day, for the sake of fun and sweet charity.

"From noon until the wee small hours, Horn and his Bandstand fans will be listening to the latest popular records and meeting guest artists, with time out for an open-air picnic supper and the yearly softball fracas. The usual 3-5 *Bandstand* show will emanate from Sylvan Hall and a special *Bandstand from Woodside* show will be telecast from 8-8:30 P.M. (all on Ch. 6, of course).

"Among the stars who have already indicated they'll participate are Gloria Mann, Sunny Gale, Mike Pedicin and his combo, Tony Alamo, Dolores Hawkins and "Somethin' Smith and the Redheads."

"Admission to the soiree is by ticket only, which can be purchased from Ch. 6 (in advance) or at the park. All proceeds will go to the Philadelphia Chapter of the Pennsylvania Chapter of the Pennsylvania Association for Retarded Children. The association is raising a fund for the renovation of a downtown Philadelphia building where retarded youngsters will receive special training.

- end -

On One Hand WFIL-TV Continues To Pump Up The Popularity of Bob Horn While On The Other Hand, Plans Are In The Making To Shoot Bob Horn Down....

Even though this author's description of "what's going on in the front office" and maybe in the Triangle Publication's boardroom, too, may not be hitting the nail exactly on the head, end results point toward what has been stated up to this point hitting close to the center of the bull's eye. On the one hand it's still "blow Bob up" and on the other, "we've got to get rid of

185

this guy" to cover all of our bases — our golden opportunities with one of the big boss's favorite WFIL produced shows, *Bandstand.* With it being almost a certainty that somehow Horn will have to be 'shot down' in order to get him to leave the show he created — as based on the Walter Annenberg elementary suggestion — it's time to start looking for flaws of any and every kind in Bob Horn's character. Let's see what we have for starters?

We know he drinks but we have no evidence at all that he tends to over indulge.

We've heard, like almost everyone else, the stories (whether fact or fiction) about Bob Horn's exploits at the place called Hound Dog Hill. It's supposed to be a lewd, bawdy establishment somewhere on the outskirts of Philadelphia where it is said Bob goes to enjoy watching and to participate in lascivious activities. Maybe that is a weakness in his character we can get to work on.

And there's bound to be more — all we need do is watch and listen — with the word 'wait' left out of the picture because time hs become of the essence.

In Your Knowledge Of Philadelphia, What Do You Know About Hound Dog Hill?

In my early years of researching this untold story of *Bandstand* and was in the process of reading every book I could find that might contain writing about the early years of *Bandstand,* when Bob Horn first used that name for his radio disc jockey show on WFIL in 1950, and when he took 'his' name, *Bandstand,* into TV with him in October of 1952, another name kept popping up. That name referred to a supposed place of ill repute and pornography and it was also supposed to be a place that Bob Horn visited frequently. The name of the place as I read of it and heard of it was "Hound Dog Hill." In those early years of my searching I could only assume from what I read and heard that at one time there may have been such a place in Philly. Among the people I talked with early on, that name came up frequently and I often heard about Bob Horn visiting there and supposedly partaking of the goodies. But it always bothered me that while so many people professed to know about the place, not one of them had ever been there — and not one could tell me exactly where it was located. Dick Clark mentioned Hound Dog Hill in his book but that he'd never been there. It was mentioned, also, in the book, **Bill Haley The Daddy of Rock and Roll**, Haley's autobiography by John Swenson, who tactfully wrote that Bob Horn went to Hound Dog Hill often — but Swenson managed to carefully not use Bob's name in print. When I read his book I couldn't imagine why Bob's name wasn't used when it was so perfectly obvious Bob Horn was who Swenson was writing about. Today, I know why.

When I was in Philadelphia early this year (1997) I wanted to find out for myself why nobody of the right age group, those who so casually yet positively spoke of Hound Dog Hill as being the worst bad spot of the city – had ever been there. Not one among some fifty people who should know, really knew anything beyond a rumor started years ago, that there was such a sporting house. This year on one of my trips to Philadelphia I took the several days necessary to learn for certain that there is no such place today and never was there such a place in Philadelphia. I checked with the Police Department, the City Clerks' offices, Temple University Archives, the city library, with cab drivers who were still, today, or had been driving taxis in Philadelphia since before the end of WWII. On this years first trip to Philly I spoke with well over a hundred people who were knowledgeable about living, working, going to schools or playing in and around Philadelphia all during the 1940s and on through all of the 1950s. Many of these people professed to have heard of Hound Dog Hill but, again, not even one ever visited "HDH" or knew where it is or was.

It's time to put Hound Dog Hill to sleep because it was only someone's dream anyway. It was a Philadelphia rumor that grew to ridiculous proportions, according to some tales, included Swenson's, of super-lewd things supposed to have happened at the non-existent Hound Dog Hill. Farewell, Hound Dog Hill. I would hope not to hear about you any more.

The foregoing research finding is of importance to this work because many of the lewd stories I heard about Hound Dog Hill (and others like Clipp, Annenberg and Koehler must have heard these same stories, or distorted versions of them, too) included Bob Horn right in the middle of the lascivious action described. This author was born, raised and educated in Philadelphia during the 40s, 50s and 60s. I think if there had been such a place as "HDH," I certainly would have heard about it or my older brother would have. Neither of us did.

Management, Or Certain Individuals In Management Have Made Their Expedient And Devious Plan. Bob Horn Is Going To Commit One Or Several Non-Violent Crimes, Soon....

In the meanwhile *Bandstand* is to continue right on as usual. There is no use in rocking the boat before a key part of it is to be scuttled. It's on with the show, and let's start thinking about Bob Horn's replacement. Two possibilities come to mind immediately, Anthony "Tony" Mammarella, who has done the filled in as host on the show repeatedly during days Horn is away, and Dick Clark, the powerful Mr. Clipp's fair haired boy. Of course, this choice is to come later — but soon, too. We're already in the middle of February, 1956.

-    -   -

187

PART FOUR

STARDUST LASTS FOREVER

CHAPTER NINE

THE KING IS EXILED IN DISGRACE, LONG LIVE HIS KINGDOM!!

How To Use "Felonies By Another" As The Perfect Management Crime....

In Chapter Eight it was suggested that a conspiracy to have Bob Horn arrested for a crime that is a felony or perhaps more than one crime all of which are felonies, but not violent crimes, will be sufficient reason to remove him from hosting *Bandstand.*

Too, because of his celebrity status in the region any crime in which he is involved will be "headline news" in local, regional and even in some national news and general readership periodicals. With certainty, what crime is, or what crimes are plotted for Bob Horn's participation – with 'at hand' witnesses and perhaps planted victims to prefer charges, or agents of the law at the scene will definitely make the news. WFIL's parent corporation, the *Philadelphia Inquirer*, Philadelphia's major newspaper will cooperate with bold headlines — and other non-Annenberg media in the region will pick up any such celebrity crime stories to keep up with the *Inquirer.* Similarly, all broadcast media of the region will duplicate news stories of Bob Horn as broadcast or telecast by WFIL-AM radio, WFIL-FM radio and WFIL-TV about Bob Horn's indiscretions – his crimes – his felonies.

Carefully and secretly handled as well conspired, detailed and carried out events, Bob Horn's being involved as the plan's culprit can publically justify removing him as host of *Bandstand* immediately following his act comes out in the news. (Played up in the news, who would want their teenage kids on a TV show with a host that's a criminal? Who wouldn't but laud WFIL management for removing Horn to protect Philadelphia youth - no matter how minor the crime?)

Secondly, Bob Horn's crime charges, designed to be serious enough to make it into the courts, regardless of ultimate outcome during the usual lengthy weeks to months of court appearances for hearings, initial trials and possible appeals, <u>all covered by WFIL and *Inquirer* reporters</u> to repeatedly to "make big headlines" or even lots of "little headlines" in the area's local and regional broadcast and print media — over and over again — can be weapons enough to keep competitor stations from hiring Bob Horn, should he decide not to accept our

WFIL generous, humane and "made-well-known-to-the-public," benevolent offer of an "off the air" management job to a 'former' *Bandstand* host as Music Director at WFIL. We might even include in that consolation offer a radio show of his own fwith no reduction in wages from what he earns for hosting *Bandstand.* That last, a "nice touch" for the public to hear about will come from a caring, forgiving and supportive WFIL.

We (or possibly just "I") have come up with the perfect personnel removal plot, a perfect corporate executive crime, with nobody but the perpetrator and the victim knowing that something is most unusual about how the "Horn crime," or crimes committed were known of to the law in the first place and, in the second place, how so much publicity in connection with an apprehension and charge can make the headlines so quickly. But that's the devious perfection of the plot.

Now For The Major Details....

From management's end it must be kept simple. First, no more than two or possibly three management level people to have any knowledge of this conspiracy. If this knowledge can be held to only two administrators, so much the better for secrecy. In time, right away or 50 years hence there will probably be questions and rumors about a WFIL plot to destroy Bob Horn, but it will always be denied and held to being nothing more than "just a rumor."

Continuing: The first crime can be quite simple, just enough to get that first negative headline about Horn into the media stream of radio, TV and newspapers. It can be as easy as this: It is known that Bob Horn frequents lunch time and dinner time restaurants, nightclubs, and entertainment spots with *Bandstand* guest artists and to seek out new performers and new music. He visits such places five, six or seven times a week. Sometime his wife, Ann, accompanies him but there are also times when she remains at home with their daughters. It is also known that while Bob is in no way an alcoholic, he does imbibe in alcoholic beverages at a sociable level while out for luncheons or evening sojourns. Thus, when he is at one of these establishments and has had a few cocktails or beers (Bob liked good beer), and when Ann is not with him and he'll be driving home alone — a simple "tip-off" to a traffic officer, known to be a firm upholder of the law no matter who he must arrest, that Bob Horn has been seen drinking heavily and he'll be driving away from such-and-such a restaurant or entertainment place in a short time — and a police officer should stop him when he's seen driving — "to protect Bob from a possible accident in which he might hurt himself, or someone else." The law person called must be told, too, that while the call is anonymous, it is from a concerned citizen wanting to help promote safety. Naturally, this will be done with realistic knowledge that most Philadelphia policemen know Bob and they like him. So lots of them, even if they stop him when they see him driving, will merely caution him and send him on his way, telling him to drive carefully. But if tip-off calls are made the right number of times one call will reach officer who will nail Bob for drunk driving. That is newsworthy. A celebrity driving drunk! Here's a headline now, "Local celebrity arrested for drunken driving." That's especially true with Bob Horn because he is a celebrity who works every week day with local teenagers who parents and citizens want to keep from becoming drunken drivers.

The second crime for Bob to become involved in, only if necessary, is more complex and will probably require some payments to appropriate people to make arrangements and "keep their mouths shut forever." Once arranged , this plan, if needed, can will smoothly and most effectively. The plot will be believable among the public because Bob Horn's name has often been linked with alleged lewd activities at the infamous Hound Dog Hill. He's going to be arrested, charged with statutory rape and brought to trial for supposedly having sex with a 12 or 14 year old girl. The girl, a talented little actress, and her guardian or guardians will be well paid for the girl's acting performances in a courtroom. As for security of the plan, the girl and her guardian or guardians will only know that a man or a woman, whose identity and means of locating him or her are unknown, made all the arrangements with them should it ever, ever be proven that the girl lied in court.

This tougher kind of charge against Bob Horn will not only make headlines, lots of headlines — but it will also be the straw that breaks the broadcaster's back as far as Philadelphia, the Delaware Valley, and nearby New Jersey, New York and Delaware States and the rest of Pennsylvania are concerned. No station in these areas will hire a near 40, aging announcer-DJ charged with statutory rape or child molestation. It doesn't matter whether he is found guilty or innocent downstream, the charge and the press coverage it gets will squelch Horn's ever getting on-the-air work in this area again.

Putting The Dirty Deeds To Work....

On the drunken driving charge (the DWI charge), upon finding the just right police officer to issue the citation and get Bob in to court and jail — and get it out to the media fast. That, alone, is all that's needed to justify pulling Bob Horn off of *Bandstand*. After all, what parent could possibly want their teenage kid on a TV show hosted by a dangerous, drunken driver? WFIL will be commended, not criticized, for pulling a drunkard off of a kid's afternoon TV show. PTAs and other parent organizations will respect and honor the WFIL-TV decision to, most unfortunately for the station (not for Bob), be forced to replace the man who did so well on *Bandstand* but couldn't leave the 'sauce' alone before driving his big Cadillac on city streets.

With a DWI bust the first set-up crime, and Bob off of *Bandstand,* the bosses at WFIL-TV can then be really nice, caring and supportive guys by offering Bob Horn that job of Music Director for WFIL at the same (another nice, gentlemanly touch) pay he was earning on *Bandstand.* Then next, if Bob takes that offer, after some months of *Bandstand* continuing to do well with a younger host and possibly going national network, WFIL can dump Bob Horn all together – and who will care? Nobody. A news story about getting rid of Bob some months later on, if mentioned in newspapers at all would be somewhere on a back page, like adjoining the obituaries.

Naturally, if taking Bob Horn off of *Bandstand* works well with only a staged DWI arrest (that isn't totally a set-up because he really will have been drinking) it might not be necessary to continue on with the completing of a Horn's crime number two. After all, there's no need to make getting rid of Bob any nastier or riskier than is necessary to get the job done.

Let Us Reconstruct What Happened With Plot One, The DWI....

Notice: Throughout the next several pages will be presented reproductions of newspaper clippings retrieved from the Urban Archives of Temple University in Philadelphia. Attempts were made to obtain same or paralleling clippings from other sources as from microfilm but the results were so poor as to not be readily reproducible in this book. While the Urban Archives do not have the names of the source newspapers for most articles here reproduced, all were from one of these three Philadelphia newspapers: The *Philadelphia Evening Bulletin*, the *Philadelphia Daily News, or the Philadelphia Inquirer.*

With the date of Bob Horn's arrest (June 21, 1956) substantiated by this small article printed after Bob had been out of jail on bail prior to July 16, 1956, his day of indictment, and from interviews with individuals who were there, as Tony Mammarella, *Bandstand* producer and interim host, Jack Steck, WFIL Program Director and Ann Horn, it all fits together. The article reads:

Bob Horn Indicted On Driving Charge

Bob Horn, of Sweetgum Rd., Levittown, WFIL-TV and radio personality, has been indicted by the grand jury on a drunken driving charge.

Horn remains free in $500 bail after his indictment yesterday. He was arrested June 21 when police said he passed a red light at Rising Sun and Erie Aves. A police surgeon pronounced him intoxicated.

Horn, who conducted the TV "Bandstand" dancing - record show for teen-agers, has been reported "on vacation" since his arrest.

JUL 17 1956

Bob Horn Indicted On Driving Charge (7/17/1956)

Bob Horn, of Sweetgum Rd., Levittown, WFIL-TV and radio personality, has been indicted by the grand jury on a drunken driving charge.

Horn remains free in $500 bail after his indictment yesterday. He was arrested Jun 21 when police said he passed a red light at Rising Sun and Erie Aves. A police surgeon pronounced him intoxicated.

Horn, who conducted the TV "Bandstand" dancing – record show for teen-agers, has been reported "on vacation" since his arrest.

194

FACT 1.   Bob Horn, was arrested on June 21, 1956 for driving while intoxicated and violating a traffic ordinance. Patrolman Russell Firesinger, one of the arresting officers, said Horn drove his 1955 green Cadillac sedan through a red light on Rising Sun Avenue at Erie Avenue. Dr. Maxwell Cherner, the police surgeon who examined Horn said that the disc jockey was under the influence of alcohol and not fit to drive when he was arrested. This occurred, apparently, at mid-day, after luncheon in a restaurant before *Bandstand*'s air time.

FACT 2.   George Koehler, General Manager of WFIL-TV, received a telephone call well before *Bandstand* air time and he asked Tony Mammarella to host the show that day, telling Tony that Bob would not be in to handle the show. Whether or not Koehler told Tony that Bob had been arrested this author has yet to learn for sure.

SPECULATION OF A POSSIBILITY: George Koehler telephoned Roger Clipp, his boss, who, in turn telephoned his boss, Mr. Annenberg, at his newspaper building office, to let him know that Bob Horn — who it is believed Mr. Annenberg liked — had been arrested for drunken driving and wouldn't be in to host *Bandstand* that day. At which point Walter Annenberg, known to have a strong temper, could have easily become 'high test' and said, **"Get that SOB off of the show!!!"** If that speculation did occur, it would have been like music to Messrs. Clipp and Koehler's ears because under that circumstance it would be Mr. Annenberg, the big, big boss, and not them removing Bob Horn from the show.

FACT 3.   Regardless of who told Bob Horn he was no longer to be on *Bandstand* for his violation of the morals clause in his contract, he was notified within 24 hours that he was on suspension from the show and that Tony Mammarella would be host of the show in his place.

FACT 4.   Apparently Bob Horn had a goodly amount of paid vacation time coming to him because after being pulled off of *Bandstand* he immediately went on an extended vacation but remained in the Philadelphia area where he continued doing his moonlighting work (which for the moment became his vocation as well) running Bandstand Dances in Wildwood, New Jersey and serving as emcee for various other events in the area.

FACT 5.   At some point in time after June 21, 1956 and August 14, 1956, and after Dick Clark had been named the new host of *Bandstand* in, according to Dick Clark in his autobiography, the first week of July, 1956, [and in his most recent book, the date pinned down to July 9, 1956] Bob Horn had been offered the opportunity to stay with WFIL in the capacity of "music director." (All according to plot thus far. In fact, the plot is going even easier than anticipated) until:

FACT 6.   On August 14, 1956 this one paragraph article appeared in one of the major Philadelphia newspapers. Part of the left side of the article was cut off when it was placed in the Urban Archives at Temple University. But even so it helps tell the story today:

> **Bob Horn**, who is running his "Bandstand" dances in Wildwood, personally severed continuations with WFIL-TV. Horn said he was taken of his television "Bandstand " show because of "embarrassment to the station." At the end of his vacation the disc jockey was asked to continue in his capacity as music director at WFIL and was given a radio program. He turned the offer down.

People Are Still Saying "Bob Horn Was Fired."

But That's Not So.   He Turned Down A Belittling Offer And Resigned....

By way of example of people who should know – not knowing, the following words are the way Dick Clark, in his autobiography, described Bob Horn's leaving *Bandstand* and WFIL.
It appears that Mr. Clark wrote only what he heard from the grapevine:

"About <u>five o'clock one afternoon</u> in the summer of 1956, George Koehler got a call that Bob Horn had been arrested for drunken driving and was in jail.
"At the time, the Philadelphia *Inquirer*, WFIL's owner, was conducting <u>a campaign against drunken driving</u>. <u>Horn was fired immediately</u>. (?) It's my impression that somewhere in the back of management's minds they had been looking forward to the day they could get rid of Horn. There was always an unspoken feeling that they wanted to see someone younger and better-looking do the show."
He was right about one thing, Koehler and Clipp wanted to get rid of Horn.

Your author has heard from several sources that the *Philadelphia Inquirer* was conducting a campaign against drunken driving at the time Bob Horn was arrested for a DWI. He has not thus far, however, has been unable to find any evidence whatsoever, via news clippings microfilm or any other substantiating information to say such a campaign was under way on June 21, 1956.
We do know, however, from news items from 1956 that Bob Horn was not fired at all, let alone being fired immediately. He was suspended from *Bandstand* and offered the job of musical director for the stations (which he already had with other duties) and a radio show.

196

These news clippings, obtained from Urban Archives of Temple University reveal some of what transpired from a not uncommon DWI arrest on June 21, 1956:

OCT 1 1953
J   3

Bob Horn Trial Hears Doctor

He Says Disc Jockey Drove While Drunk

A physician testified today that Bob Horn was under the influence of liquor and not fit to drive safely when the disc jockey was arrested for drunken driving in June, 1956.

Dr. Maxwell Cherner, the police surgeon who examined Horn, testified at the first of two drunken-driving trials facing the entertainer, who is 41.

Horn took the stand today to deny the charges.

His trial before Judge Peter F. Hagan and a jury of eight women and four men involves his arrest at Erie and Rising Sun avs. on June 21, 1956.

Drunk in Third Degree

Dr. Cherner, who retired as a police surgeon last August 30, said he examined Horn at the Front and Westmoreland sts. station at 2.30 A. M. Horn was arrested at 1.45 A. M.

Dr. Cherner said there are four degrees of intoxication and Horn was in the third degree. He described them as: first, stimulation; second, depression; third, impairment of co-ordination, and fourth, unconsciousness.

The doctor said Horn's balance was impaired, his face pale and dull, his expression fixed and his pulse rapid. He said Horn staggered and had the odor of alcohol on his breath.

Went Through Light

One of the arresting officers, Patrolman Russell Firesinger, said Horn drove his 1955 green Cadillac sedan through a red light on Rising Sun av. at Erie.

He said Horn swayed as he got out of his car.

Firesinger testified that when he said he was taking Horn to the police station Horn replied: "Go ahead. I know Gibbons."

Firesinger said that Horn, who was wearing dark glasses, identified himself to the desk sergeant by saying, "I'm Bob Horn, Bandstand."

Horn at that time conducted a television dance program of that name over Channel 6.

Working in Texas

He is now working for a radio station in Houston, Tex.

The other officer, Patrolman Joseph F. Gordon, Sr., testified that Horn's son, Peter, now 21, who accompanied his father, told Horn not to argue with police after they stopped him. He quoted the son as saying, "Come on, Dad. You went through the light."

Horn, however, denied that his son said this. He also denied all other points made by the prosecution.

He said he was not drunk or unfit to drive, having had only two beers with two sandwiches in a two-hour period before getting into his auto.

Horn said he set out to drive his son, then and now serving in the Air Force, to Stone Harbor, N. J., where the family was staying.

Then he planned to drive alone to the family's home on Sweetgum lane, Levittown, to get some sleep before returning to work, said Horn.

He said the traffic light was green when he started across Erie av. but that it turned red before he completed crossing it.

Didn't Stagger, He Says

Horn denied staggering, being flushed or having liquor on his breath.

Peter Horn substantiated his father's story. He denied that his father was intoxicated. He also denied saying that his father had driven through the red light.

Horn's account of what he had to drink before his arrest was confirmed by Furey Campellone, 35, bartender at a taproom at Germantown av. and Roy st. where Horn was said to have been.

Four friends of Horn said he was sober and talking business with them in the taproom.

2d Trial Next Week

Horn is listed for trial next Tuesday on a charge of driving while drunk last January 22 at A and Clearfield sts.

He was arrested following an accident there in which a man and his wife and three children were injured.

Last June 26, Horn was cleared of morals charges involving a 17-year-old girl. He was acquitted at his second trial. The first ended in a hung jury.

197

14 F **The Evening Bulletin** Wed., Oct. 2, 1957

Bob Horn Convicted, Fined On Drunken Driving Charge

A jury of eight women and four men took less than 15 minutes yesterday to convict Bob Horn of driving while intoxicated in June, 1956.

He was fined $300 and put on probation for one year.

The one-day trial ended at 5.40 P. M. when the jury went out to deliberate. It was back in the courtroom at 5.55 P. M. with the verdict.

Horn, a former television disc jockey here, stood at the bar as Judge Peter F. Hagan asked for the verdict. His face paled and his hands clutched the bar when the guilty verdict was announced.

Horn's attorney, Louis Lipschitz, immediately asked that the jury be polled. After each juror indicated a guilty vote, Lipschitz turned to the judge and asked for the usual four days to file motion for a new trial.

Judge Hagan denied the motion, saying that he could see no purpose and that the case had been well tried.

The judge then asked Lipschitz if he had anything to say on behalf of the defendant before he passed sentence.

Lipschitz brought Horn's wife, Anne, to the bar.

Mrs. Horn said she had been married to Horn for 11 and a half years and they have four children, aged three to nine.

She said her husband was now working in Houston, Tex.

"At a greatly reduced salary," Lipschitz interjected.

Lipschitz then said that the publicity attached to Horn's other prosecution (last June 26 when he was cleared of a morals charge involving a 17-year-old girl) had deprived him of the opportunity to earn a living here.

Horn had been punished severely, though acquitted, the attorney declared.

The judge then fined Horn $300 plus costs and put him on probation for one year.

Lipschitz pleaded that Horn was financially hard-pressed, but Judge Hagan said that some punishment must be given for the offense of drunken driving.

During the trial, Dr. Maxwell Cherner, the police surgeon who examined Horn, testified that the disc jockey was under the influence of liquor and not fit to drive when he was arrested for drunken driving.

One of the arresting officers, Patrolman Russell Firesinger, said Horn drove his 1955 green Cadillac sedan through a red light on Rising Sun av. at Erie.

Horn formerly conducted the television dance program, Bandstand, over Channel 6.

Bob Horn Guilty Of Tipsy Driving, Gets $300 Fine

OCT 2 1957

Bob Horn, former disk jockey and promoter of teen-agers' dance programs, was found guilty last night of drunken driving by a jury of eight women and four men after 15 minutes deliberation.

The verdict was returned to Judge Peter F. Hagan at 6 P.M. He overruled a motion of the defendant's attorney, Louis Lipschitz, for a new trial and fined Horn $300 and costs and placed him on probation for one year. The judge allowed 45 days in which to pay the fine.

MAINTAINS INNOCENCE

Judge Hagan also overruled a defense objection that the fine be suspending saying the fine "was intended to be harsh and was a deterrent not only to the defendant but to others."

The case went to the jury after Horn, who now is working in Texas, denied he was under the influence of liquor when he was arrested June 21, 1956, at Rising Sun and Erie aves.

Horn, 41, testified he had had "only two beers" at a nearby cafe late the previous evening after conducting a program at the Carman Skating Rink, Germantown ave. above Allegheny av.

SON TESTIFIES

Defense witnesses included Horn's son, Peter, 21, an Air Force enlisted man; Ray Jackson, a business associate; William A. Layne, of Ridley Park, and Don Hines, members of a comedy team, and Furey Campellone, a bartender in the cafe.

Prosecution witnesses were Dr. Maxwell Cherner, a police surgeon who retired from that post last Aug. 30, and Patrolmen Russell Firesinger and Joseph Gordon, who arrested Horn after he assertedly went through a red light and who charged him with drunken-driving.

The DWI Would Be Spasmodic News All Through Jury Trials....
These News Items Are Not Enough To Run Horn Out Of Town....
The Statutory Rape Or Morals Charge Will Do More. Time For Plan Two...

The continuing WFIL employment plan for Bob Horn could have worked out quite well if he had accepted the offer. But since he didn't more powerful medicine is necessary to get him to move out of WFIL territory. We have contacts, maybe it can become a part of another major courts action with Horn as one of several defendants. That would surely get the whole thing further away from WFIL and its management. And it should happen pretty fast.

Such offers of continuing employment as was made to Horn fit perfectly with a conspiracy to, as gracefully as possible (on the surface), eliminate Bob Horn from WFIL. Not willing to accept such a step-down offer, Bob resigned rather than bow to such treatment. No doubt, at the time, he was thinking he would have no difficulty in finding another good radio or TV air-time position with another nearby station. The WFIL "get rid of Bob" conspiracy was too well calculated for that, however.

The statutory rape charge and the trials and hearings that would accompany it would leave Bob 'dead in the water' so far as finding work at another station in the greater Philadelphia area.

A Plotted Time Line Was Well Ahead Of Ordinary Circumstance....

Earlier it was mentioned that there might be another crime in which Bob Horn would be involved to remain "heavily and negatively named in the news." It's interesting to note that the statutory rape charges didn't occur <u>until</u> **after** Bob Horn (in August of 1956) turned down the WFIL management offer to remain with the stations. Then, once he had turned the WFIL offer down, this came up:

FACT 7. From old news clippings we learn that on November 8, 1956 Bob Horn was indicted on four statutory charges and four charging corruption of the morals of a minor.

FACT 8.   On December 11, 1956 the morning paper read:

Bob Horn's Trial Slated for Today

199

Bob Horn, former TV personality, goes on trial today on eight morals charges. Horn was slated for trial yesterday before Judge Joseph L. Kun. But a delay had been granted last week by Judge Charles A. Waters. This was unknown to Judge Kun, who issued a bench warrant for Horn when he failed to appear. Louis Lipschitz, Horn's counsel, advised Judge Kun of Judge Water's action and agreed to produce his client for trial today.

Judge OKs Delay In Horn Vice Trial

DEC 11 195_

Judge Joseph L. Kun finally agreed today to postpone Bob Horn's vice trial. It will start Jan. 2.

That was the new date approved last Friday by Judge Charles A. Waters at Horn's request. Not knowing of the change, Judge Kun had called the ex-disc jockey to trial yesterday. When he found that Horn was not there, he issued a bench warrant for Horn's arrest.

HORN WAS in court today. His lawyer, Louis Lipschitz, asked Judge Kun to grant a postponement. Lipschitz said he has talked so far with only 10 of the 40 defense witnesses he may need. He also wants to take his ailing daughter on a trip this month, the lawyer said.

Judge Kun said he saw no attempt to dodge a trial in his court and agreed to the Jan. 2 starting date. Horn faces eight morals charges. His trial is one of several growing out of a major probe of a vice ring using teenage girls.

STEVE ALLISON, suspended late night radio disc jockey, also was granted a delay in his trial by Judge Waters.

Allison, snared in the investigation of the tri-state vice ring, was scheduled to go on trial next Monday. Judge Waters delayed the trial until Dec. 26.

THE DEFENSE rested its case today in the trial of three persons allegedly involved in an abortion. Defendants are crooner Joe Valino; his manager, Nick Bussillo, and Mrs. Rachel White. The woman allegedly performed the illegal operation on Marion Melet, 20, on Aug. 22, 1955. Miss Melet said the crooner made her pregnant.

In his closing speech today, Asst. Dist. Atty. F. Emmett Fitzpatrick said abortion is "the most defenseless type of homicide."

He called the operation a "butcher job."

Irate Judge Orders Bob Horn's Arrest

12.10.

Judge Joseph L. Kun today issued a bench warrant for one vice defendant and quickly convicted another.

The warrant was for disc jockey Bob Horn. Judge Kun was plainly angry on hearing that Horn's morals case had been postponed from today until Jan. 2.

He ordered county detectives to seize Horn and bring him to City Hall at once. Last Friday Judge Charles A. Waters had set the trial back at the request of Horn's counsel. Judge Kun, to whom the case is assigned, did not learn of the change in date until today.

HORN IS ACCUSED of leading eight girls into acts of immorality. He is 40 and lives at 66 Sweetgum Rd., Levittown.

The no-jury trial of another vice figure, photographer Jerry Clarkson, was swift. He had pleaded innocent to four morals charges. Maxine Milder, 18, formerly of the Garden Court Apartments, 47th and Pine Sts., is the girl in the case. She told of committing immoral acts with Clarkson and of posing in the nude for him.

IN ANOTHER TRIAL, Mrs. Rachel White swore today she was in North Carolina the day she is accused of committing an abortion.

It was the first day on the stand for Mrs. White. She is 43 and lives at 3039 W. Dauphin St. Marian Melet, now 20, has said she had the illegal operation at the suggestion of crooner Joe Valino. Mrs. White did it, Marian has said.

VALINO and Nicholas Busillo, 35, of 1023 N. 67th St., his manager, are on trial with Mrs. White in the abortion case. It is one of a series of trials growing out of a major probe into a teen-age vice ring.

Mrs. White said she and her son drove to Mount Olive, N. C., Aug. 19, 1955, and returned here Aug. 23. The abortion allegedly took place at Mrs. White's home Aug. 22, Miss Melet's 19th birthday.

...after his arrest for drunken driving last June.

Horn, heavy set and with graying black hair, described his daily routine while he was connected with "Bandstand."

Horn said he usually was at a bar between 6 and 8 P. M. with song pluggers and music publishers, and then went to a restaurant at 62d and Walnut sts. for dinner.

Finally, Lipschitz asked him if he knew Lois Gardner.

"Yes," Horn replied, "I've known her at least two-and-a-half years, and I had known her by sight even before that."

Tells of Meeting Girl

He said he first spoke to her when she entered his office around 6 one evening in 1954. Horn said she introduced herself saying she wanted to appear and take part in the "Bandstand" program.

Horn testified that he told her that was not possible. He said he did not offer to take her home and did not take her to dinner.

He said he saw her around the studio after that from time to time and spoke to her on occasion.

Saw Her at Restaurant

Horn said he saw Miss Gardner frequently at the restaurant where he ate dinner.

He was asked by Lipschitz: "Did you have relations with her in 1954?"

"No, I did not," he answered.

He was asked if he had relations with her in 1955 and again answered no.

Judge Edwin O. Lewis, presiding, asked: "Have you ever had relations with her?"

"I have not," the defendant answered.

Never Went to Dinner

Horn said he never took the girl to dinner and never kept any apartments in Philadelphia. He denied ever living at apartments at 47th and Walnuts sts. or at Hicks st. near Pine—locations cited by Miss Gardner as places where Horn took her.

He said he went to the Gardner home twice, once for an anniversary party and once at the girl's mother's request to cheer up Lois, who was sick.

Horn said the girl got to know many of his friends and "drifted into the same pattern as I did."

"She has an uncanny way of getting to know people," he said. "She isn't reluctant or shy. She just walks up and introduces herself. I'll bet she knows more artists in the business than I do."

Character Witnesses

Four character witnesses testified for Horn before the noon recess. They were singer Gloria Mann; Samuel H. Kipp, of Lebanon, N. J.; John J. Kelly, public relations man here, and Joseph Sullivan, 16, a fan of "Bandstand."

All said that Horn's reputation and character were good.

"Bandstand," a teenage dance program, was tried on four bills charging statutory offenses.

Miss Gardner testified that she and Horn had illicit relations over a period of two and a half years, starting in 1953, when she was 13. Horn denied all her allegations. He said he knew the girl but denied dating her and said he never entertained her in either of two apartments she said he had in the city.

Denied Having Apartments

He denied having the apartments.

Horn, 40, of Sweetgum road, Levittown, is the last of 18 defendants to be tried in the vice investigation launched last fall by District Attorney Victor H. Blanc's office. Today was the fourth day of Horn's trial in Room 296, City Hall.

The maximum sentence on conviction for the statutory offense of which he was accused is 15 years in jail and $7,000 fine.

The summations were delivered earlier by Assistant District Attorney F. Emmett Fitzpatrick, the prosecutor, and Horn's lawyer, Louis Lipschitz.

Accused of Lying

Fitzpatrick accused Horn of lying; Lipschitz accused Miss Gardner of making "baseless and dastardly" accusations.

Fitzpatrick, speaking for 48 minutes, told the jury that these two stories could not be reconciled.

"One must be the truth; the other must be a lie," he said.

He said the fact that Miss Gardner was not entirely sure of the four dates of meeting alleged in the bills of indictment indicated that her story was truthful.

'He Was Lying'

He noted that Horn testified as to exactly what he was doing on the four dates.

"He was lying to you," Fitzpatrick said. "His reason for lying was that he doesn't want to be convicted. Miss Gardner had no reason to lie. In fact, it took courage for her to tell the story as she did."

Fitzpatrick said another sign of the girl's veracity was that she did not claim that Horn forced her into the relationship but said she submitted voluntarily.

Lipschitz told the panel that the defense "bared our soul to you." He said he had never seen a more courageous woman than Horn's wife, Ann, who corroborated his alibis on the four dates.

'Dastardly Thing'

He asked the jurors whether they could believe the girl's story of the four meetings.

"I put it to you that she or someone else thought Mr. Horn would have difficulty in getting an alibi for these four days," he said. "It was a scheme conjured up by her or by someone else.

"It seems unreasonable that no one had ever seen Horn with her in either one of the apartment buildings. The reason no one saw them is that they were never there.

"It is a dastardly thing that is being done here. I ask you not to allow it."

Before the lawyers spoke, Miss Gardner testified briefly about the first date alleged in the indictments, Thanksgiving Day, 1954. She said she saw Horn between 1 or 1.30 P. M. and 2.30 P. M. that day after he had seen a high school football game here.

Horn testified earlier that he went directly home for Thanksgiving dinner after watching the game.

About a week later, she said she watched Horn do a radio show and that, on that occasion, he asked her to wait and he'd take her home.

She testified that Horn took her to his apartment near 47th and Walnut sts. She answered "no" to the question: "Did anything go on there?"

She said they had a discussion and Horn gave her $20 explaining it was for taxi fare.

The witness said Horn asked her not to tell anyone she had been at his apartment. She said he drove her to center city and she took a cab home.

Taken Out to Dinner

She said she had given Horn her telephone number and that the following week he took her out to dinner but "nothing happened."

Miss Gardner then testified that she saw Horn once or twice weekly until the end of 1955. She said they had improper relations on nearly every occasion.

"Why did you stop?" Judge Lewis asked.

"I guess we both realized it was wrong," she replied.

In the course of her testimony, the witness broke down in tears. Louis Lipschitz, Horn's attorney, asked the judge to instruct her to pull herself together as he did not want her tears to influence the jury. The judge did this.

She said that she first had relations with Horn in his West Philadelphia apartment just before her 14th birthday, which fell on November 18, 1953.

Pleads Surprise

Lipschitz objected to this. Pleading surprise, he asked for a continuance on the grounds that the illegal acts alleged in the indictments did not occur until November, 1954, and later.

Fitzpatrick said the testimony about earlier meetings was meant only as background.

Judge Lewis then ordered Fitzpatrick to question the witness about the offenses charged in the indictments.

Miss Gardner testified that the four offenses mentioned in the indictment occurred in Horn's other apartment on Hicks st. near Pine. She named the dates as November 25, 1954, which was Thanksgiving Day; about January 15, 1955; February 17, 1955, and March 10, 1955.

Gave Her Record Player

Asked if Horn ever gave her presents, she said that he gave her $100 as a birthday present one year and another time gave her a record player.

She said they made a trip to Stone Harbor, N. J., for two and a half days in August, 1955. They went out in Horn's boat, she said.

Horn was indicted last November 8 on four statutory charges and four charging corruption of the morals of a minor.

Objections From Attorney

In preliminaries this morning, Fitzpatrick announced that the state wanted to proceed only on the statutory bills. Lipschitz objected.

"We don't want to come back here again," he said.

Fitzpatrick said he did not think this would be necessary. Then, although the four bills charging corrupting the morals of a minor were not nol-prossed, it was agreed that Horn would be tried only on the other four bills.

Horn, of Sweetgum road, Levittown, formerly headed "Bandstand," a teenage dance program on WFIL-TV.

He is the last of 18 defendants in the vice investigation to stand trial. One of the others, Steve Allison, former disc jockey for WPEN, will be tried a second time. His first trial ended in a hung jury.

Bob Horn Trial Goes to Jury

JAN 31 1957 F4

Judge's Charge Nearly Hour and Half

The vice trial of former television personality Bob Horn went to the jury at 3.40 P. M. today.

The panel of nine women and three men began its deliberations after receiving a one-hour-and-25-minute charge from Judge Edwin O. Lewis.

Judge Lewis, speaking after the prosecution and defense made their closing arguments, briefly reviewed the testimony produced by both sides.

Reputation Brought Up

He told the jury that it should decide whether the girl in the case, Lois Gardner, 17, of Sheridan st. near Shunk, had a bad reputation and if so whether Horn was to blame for this.

If it decided that Horn was not to blame then it might convict him of adultery, instead of a statutory offense, Judge Lewis said.

Horn, dismissed last summer as conductor of WFIL-TV's "Bandstand," a teenage dance program, was tried on four bills charging statutory offenses.

Miss Gardner testified that she and Horn had illicit relations over a period of two and a half years, starting in 1953, when she was 13. Horn denied all her allegations. He said he knew the girl but denied dating her and said he never entertained her in either of two apartments she said he had in the city.

Horn Denies Girl's Charges

JUN 25 1957 E4

Takes Stand as Trial Nears End

Bob Horn, 41-year-old former TV and radio performer, took the witness stand this afternoon and denied charges brought against him by a 17-year-old girl.

In a short, 20-minute examination by his attorney, Louis Lipschitz, Horn admitted he knew the Commonwealth's chief witness, Lois Gardner, but denied having relations with her on four occasions charged in the bills of indictment.

For each of those occasions—Thanksgiving Day, 1954, and January 15, February 17 and March 10, 1955—he gave explicit alibis.

He said he was at home with his wife and four children Thanksgiving afternoon, when he is charged with being with Miss Gardner at an apartment at 345 S. Hicks st.

He said he was hunting with friends in New Jersey on January 15, and was at a New Jersey night spot all during the evening of February 17. On March 10, he testified, he spent the evening in a midcity night club.

His testimony didn't last half as long as it did at his first trial, last February, which ended with a hung jury.

The defense concluded its case at 3.30 P. M. Attorneys for both sides agreed to dispense with final arguments and summations because "the case is so fresh that it would amount to belaboring the issue."

Judge Cyrus M. Palmer, of Pottsville, who is hearing the case without a jury, said he would make an adjudication at 10 A. M. tomorrow.

State Rests Case

The Commonwealth rested its case this morning. Lipschitz then urged that Horn be freed immediately because of insufficient evidence.

Judge Palmer listened to argument, and then called the opposing attorneys into chambers, but finally — after more than an hour — turned down the defense motion.

Defense Case Begins

The defense then began its case. Character witnesses were called to the stand, as well as several alibi witnesses, who said that Horn was at home or somewhere else on the dates when he allegedly was with Miss Lois Gardner, the state's star witness.

The Commonwealth at this trial has been restricted to testimony about the relations between Miss Gardner on four occasions mentioned in the indictment. At the first trial, there was also testimony about numerous other occasions when the pair allegedly had relations. The association between Horn and Miss Gardner was reported to have started when the girl was 13.

Horn was formerly director of a teenage dance program. His first trial ended in a hung jury last February.

Bob Horn Jury Released After 6-6 Deadlock

FEB 1 1957 F4

Locked Up

Had Reached 10-2 Vote for Acquittal

The jury that tried Bob Horn, former TV performer, on morals charges, was split right down the middle—six for conviction and six for acquittal—several members said today.

The jury, after seven hours deliberation, reached an impasse and Judge Edwin O. Lewis dismissed it—by telephone—at 11.25 last night. They had heard testimony for four days.

Some of the jurors said that the tally was even most of the time but at one time it was as high as 10 to 2 for acquittal.

This morning just before court convened, the jurors were ushered into an anteroom, where they conferred for about ten minutes with the judge.

Confers With Counsel

Afterward the jurors took their places in the jury box while Judge Lewis held a sidebar conference with Assistant District Attorney F. Emmett Fitzpatrick and Louis Lipschitz, defense attorney.

When the sidebar conference was over, Judge Lewis told the jury:

"I just commended the assistant district attorney. I think he tried the case very, very well. It was not any deficiency on his part that has brought about this disagreement, nor any deficiency on the part of Mr Lipschitz.

"It was a lack of evidence to convince you beyond a reasonable doubt. The case was tried well by both counsel."

Lewis Addresses Press

After Horn and his attorney left the courtroom, Judge Lewis turned to the press table and said:

"I have ascertained from discussions with the jurors this morning that there was no possibility of an agreement. Last night I thought of sending them to a hotel, and I had Mr. Shanahan (John Shanahan, court crier) prepare rooms for them.

"However, I was informed by phone that there was no possibility of an agreement, and that is confirmed this morning.

"The jurors agree with me in regretting the waste of time, but they were under oath and they did not feel the case was proved beyond a reasonable doubt. The public ought to know about these things."

Four-Day Trial Of Horn Ends In Hung Jury

Panel of 9 Women, 3 Men Deliberate For Nearly 7 Hours

The four-day morals trial of Bob Horn, former television performer, ended in no decision last night.

Judge Edwin O. Lewis announced from the bench today that the nine women and three men jurors were so hopelessly deadlocked after nearly seven hours of deliberation that there was "no possibility of an agreement."

The jury announced its deadlock at 11.25 P.M. Judge Lewis, in an unusual action, dismissed the jury by telephone from his home.

This morning just before court convened, the jurors were ushered into an anteroom, where they conferred for about ten minutes with the judge.

Confers With Counsel

Afterward the jurors took their places in the jury box while Judge Lewis held a sidebar conference with Assistant District Attorney F. Emmett Fitzpatrick and Louis Lipschitz, defense attorney.

When the sidebar conference was over, Judge Lewis told the jury:

"I just commended the assistant district attorney. I think he tried the case very, very well. It was not any deficiency on his part that has brought about this disagreement, nor any deficiency on the part of Mr. Lipschitz.

"It was a lack of evidence to convince you beyond a reasonable doubt. The case was tried well by both counsel."

Lewis Addresses Press

After Horn and his attorney left the courtroom, Judge Lewis turned to the press table and said:

"I have ascertained from discussions with the jurors this morning that there was no possibility of an agreement. Last night I thought of sending them to a hotel, and I had Mr. Shanahan (John Shanahan, court crier) prepare rooms for them.

"However, I was informed by phone that there was no possibility of an agreement, and that is confirmed this morning.

"The jurors agree with me in regretting the waste of time, but they were under oath and they did not feel the case was proved beyond a reasonable doubt. The public ought to know about these things."

District Attorney Victor H. Blanc, when informed that the jury was unable to reach a decision, said "there is no question but that the case will be retried," possibly in about two months.

2d Awaiting Retrial

Also awaiting retrial under similar circumstances is former disc jockey, Steve Allison. His trial on morals charges ended in a hung jury on December 27. It was reported that in his trial the jury was 10 to 2 for acquittal.

Horn, 40, was fired last summer as director of WFIL-TV teenage dance program, "Bandstand." He was tried on four bills charging statutory offense growing out of accusations by Lois Gardner, 17, of Sheridan st.

Four-Day Trial Of Horn Ends In Hung Jury

Panel of 9 Women, 3 Men Deliberate For Nearly 7 Hours

2-1-57 B

A jury of nine women and three men, who for four days heard testimony on morals charges against Bob Horn, former television performer, deliberated for almost seven hours last night.

Then they announced that they could not agree on a verdict.

At 11.25—in an unusual action —Judge Edwin O. Lewis dismissed the jury by telephone.

The jury was actually dismissed by John Shanahan, court crier, who acted after conversing with the judge and telling him that the jurors were unable to come to a decision.

District Attorney Victor H. Blanc, when informed that the jury was unable to reach a decision, said "there is no question but that the case will be retried," possibly in about two months.

2d Awaiting Retrial

Also awaiting retrial under similar circumstances is former disc jockey, Steve Allison. His trial on morals charges ended in a hung jury on December 27.

Horn, 40, was fired last summer as director of WFIL-TV's teenage dance program, "Bandstand." He was tried on four bills charging statutory offense growing out of accusations by Lois Gardner, 17, of Sheridan st. near Shunk.

His trial went to the jury at 3.40 P. M. after a one-hour-and-25-minute charge from Judge Lewis.

The judge told the jurors they would have to decide if Miss Gardner had a bad reputation and if so whether Horn was to blame for this. If it was decided that Horn was not to blame, then the jury might convict him of adultery instead of statutory offense, he said.

Horn Jury Disagrees

The morals trial of former radio and TV disc jockey Bob Horn ended last night with a hung jury.

Judge Edwin O. Lewis dismissed the panel of nine women and three men at 11.22 p.m. when they announced they were unable to reach agreement on a verdict. The trial began on Monday.

There was no indication of what caused the disagreement.

Horn was accused of immoral acts with Miss Lois Gardner, 17, beginning in 1954.

THIS IS the second hung jury in the 18 trials resulting from a teen-age vice probe last fall. On Dec. 26., a jury was unable to agree on a verdict in the case of former radio commentator Steve Allison. He will get a new trial Feb. 19.

THE CASE went to the jury at 3.30 yesterday after a one hour and 25-minute charge by Judge Edwin O. Lewis. At 6 the jury was given two hours for supper.

Judge Lewis told the jury that it should decide whether Miss Gardner had a bad reputation and whether Horn was responsible for it. If he were not, Judge Lewis said, the jury might convict him of adultery instead of statutory rape.

IN HIS summation, Asst. Dist. Atty. F. Emmett Fitzpatrick said Horn had lied to the jury. He said Miss Gardner "had no reason to lie. In fact, it took courage for her to tell the story as she did."

Defense counsel Louis Lipschitz claimed Miss Gardner made "baseless and dastardly" accusations. He told the jury the defense "bared our soul to you."

PHILADELPHIA DAILY NEWS, FRIDAY, FEBRUARY 1, 1957

BOB HORN
... free in bail

Bob Horn Jurors Divided, 6 to 6

By ROBERT GOODWIN

The jury of three men and nine women trying former disc jockey Bob Horn on morals charges was divided, 6-6, it was learned today. Judge Edwin O. Lewis formally dismissed the jurrors this morning after announcing they were deadlocked.

BobHornWaivesRight To Jury Trial as Case Gets Its 2d Hearing

JUN 25 1957

Bob Horn, former television disc jockey, whose first trial in January on morals charges ended in a hung jury, pleaded not guilty yesterday and, unexpectedly, waived a jury trial as visiting Judge Cyrus M. Palmer began a rehearing of his case in Room 483, City Hall.

Opening of the new trial was delayed 10 minutes as Horn's attorney, Louis Lipschitz, and Assistant District Attorney F. Emmett Fitzpatrick, Jr., held a sidebar conference at the former's request with Judge Palmer.

SATURDAY INCIDENT

"I want to discuss with you something that happened on Saturday involving an incident that may be pertinent to this case," Lipschitz told the jurist, who is from Pottsville.

After the parley ended, the bench made no statement and the Commonwealth's star witness against Horn, Lois Gardner, 17, of Sheridan st. near Shunk, was called as the first witness.

The conference presumably concerned the handing over of $2500 by a friend of Horn to a friend of the young woman at her home on Saturday, reportedly to enable her to "get out of town" and not testify against Horn. She denied at the time to Fitzpatrick and county detectives, who came to her home a short time later and with whose knowledge the money had been offered, that she had asked for any money.

TESTIMONY GIVEN

Miss Gardner testified yesterday that she and Horn, formerly employed by WFIL-TV, had had illicit relations in an apartment on Hicks st. near Pine on four different dates—Thanksgiving Day, 1954, Jan. 15, 1955, March 10, 1955, and Feb. 17, 1955.

At the first trial, the girl had stated, in the face of Horn's denials, that the relations had started in 1953, when she was 13, and had continued for two years. Judge Palmer ruled yesterday that her testimony must be confined to the four specific dates she mentioned.

PARKING ATTENDANT

Yesterday's second witness, Roosevelt Tyler, of 17th st. near Sansom, an attendant on a parking lot at Hicks and Pine sts., testified that on Thanksgiving Day of 1954 he saw Horn park his car there and go into the Hicks st. apartment nearby.

At that point—it was then 3:15 P. M.—lawyer Lipschitz asked for an adjournment because of the "oppressive heat" in the courtroom. Palmer agreed the case should be resumed at 10 A. M. today and granted the request.

Horn Denies Girl's Story

JAN 29 1957

TV Personality Takes Stand in Vice Case

Bob Horn took the stand in his own defense this afternoon and denied the charges against him in his vice trial.

Yesterday and again this morning, his accuser, 17-year-old Lois Gardner, told the jury that she and the former television entertainer had had improper relations over a period of more than two-and-a-half years, starting just before her 14th birthday in November, 1953.

Horn is specifically charged with four statutory offenses which allegedly occurred on November 25, which was Thanksgiving Day, 1954, and on dates in January, February and March, 1955.

Horn, 40, of Sweetgum road, Levittown, was called to the stand by his attorney, Louis Lipschitz, after the Commonwealth concluded its case.

Tells of TV Show

He began in a clear voice by describing his former duties in conducting "Bandstand," a teenage dance program over WFIL-TV. He said he was one of the program's originators in 1952 and was its master of ceremonies and senior producer.

He said he also was director of recorded music for WFIL and WFIL-TV before being fired from the station after his arrest for drunken driving last June.

Horn, heavy set and with graying black hair, described his daily routine while he was connected with "Bandstand."

Horn said he usually was at a bar between 6 and 8 P. M. with song pluggers and music publishers, and then went to a restaurant at 62d and Walnut sts. for dinner.

Verdict Due Today In 2d Horn Trial

A verdict in the second morals trial of Bob Horn, former TV star, was due today. It will be given by visiting Judge Cyrus M. Palmer of Pottsville.

Attorneys for both sides agreed yesterday to dispense with final arguments and summations.

The defense rested yesterday, in the second day of the jury-less trial, after presenting testimony by Horn and some character witnesses.

HORN DENIED having intimacies with Lois Gardner, 17, of Sheridan St. near Shunk. He said he had been in different places on each of four occasions he was charged with having been with her.

Defense witnesses attested to Horn's character. They also backed up his statements of where he was on the dates he had been accused of being with Miss Gardner.

Some half dozen teen-age witnesses described Horn's conduct on his "Bandstand" program. One sparked a brief exchange between Judge Palmer and Asst. Dist. Atty. E. Emmett Fitzpatrick Jr.

MARY MURPHY, 18, said she and a number of other boys and girls had attended the programs frequently. She called herself and the other regulars "bandstanders."

At this point, Fitzpatrick interrupted to ask: "You mean that you are another one of those bandstand girls?"

Before Miss Murphy could answer, Judge Palmer turned to Fitzpatrick and asked him: "Are you being contemptuous?"

"No, the prosecuting lawyer said. "I am not being contemptuous, your honor."

"Well," the judge then said, "I am just as contemptuous of you as you are of me." With that, he recessed the court for lunch.

AFTERWARDS Judge Palmer said, "I guess I lost my temper. I felt Fitzpatrick was trying to derogate the witness."

Fitzpatrick said he had not meant anything derogatory. He said he had only "meant to clarify what the witness had meant."

Horn's first trial ended in a hung jury last February.

Horn's trial on the same charges last January resulted in a hung jury.

In announcing the verdict, Judge Palmer noted that the Commonwealth had failed to indicate in the four bills of indictment that the complainant, Lois Gardner, of Sheridan st. near Shunk, was 16 years old or under at the time of the alleged illicit relations.

A NECESSARY POINT

The jurist said this was a necessary point to make out a charge of statutory rape and was a matter of proof that the Commonwealth failed to produce.

But beyond that, he said that he believed a motion in arrest of judgment would have had to be sustained.

Horn, 41, formerly with WFIL-TV, standing at the bar of the court with his attorneys, Louis Lipschitz and Albert S. Oliensis, smiled as Judge Palmer announced the verdict.

OTHER CHARGES CLEARED

First Assistant District Attorney F. Emmett Fitzpatrick asked the court to dispose of four companion bills of corrupting the morals of a minor which still remained against Horn.

"The evidence on these is exactly the same, he said, and we therefore submit these bills for disposition."

The court asked whether the Commonwealth was seeking a nolpros on the bills and, when Fitzpatrick replied in the affirmative, Horn's counsel urged that a not guilty verdict also be found on these.

Judge Palmer then announced acquittal on the four charges after Fitzpatrick said the Commonwealth had no objections.

TESTIMONY CONFINED

At Horn's first trial Miss Gardner had testified the illicit relationship began in 1953 when she was only 13 but at the second trial Judge Palmer ruled that her testimony be confined only to the four dates mentioned in the bills of indictment.

These were Thanksgiving Day, 1954; Jan. 15, 1955; Feb. 17, 1955, and March 10, 1955. The girl testified to immoral acts with Horn on these dates in an apartment on Hicks st. near Pine.

Horn on the stand denied the charges and defense witnesses testified he had been elsewhere on those dates.

Ex-Disc Jockey Horn Cleared of Morals Charges

JUN 27 1957

Bob Horn, former television disc jockey, was acquitted of morals charges yesterday by visiting Judge Cyrus M. Palmer, of Pottsville, who presided at the two-day trial without jury.

207

With the morals charges in place....
Negative Fate Stepped Into The Bob Horn Picture, Too....

Also in 1956, on November 8, the very day of his indictments on the eight morals charges, when Bob's son, Peter, was home on furlough from his Air Force duties, the two of them went out on the town celebrating Peter's being there. When it came time for them to go home night-time had filled with a dense fog. Not being in a familiar part of the city, Bob, driving his heavy car, turned the wrong down a one way narrow street after continuing on that street for several blocks he collided with a smaller, lighter car in which a man was driving with his wife and three children. (This, incidentally, could not have been any part of a conspiracy. This was definitely an accident in which Bob Horn was the driver at fault. One of the little girls in the car he hit was quite seriously injured and the other young girl painfully injured, too. The parents and the other child were also injured but not seriously. When police officers arrived at the accident scene, and after the injured girls were on their way to a hospital, they arrested Bob and cited him as being drunk. Upon taking him to their police precinct office, approximately one and a half hours after the accident, the police surgeon on duty tested Bob for intoxication and found him to be somewhat intoxicated, but not enough so to prevent him from driving safely. Bob, during dinner with his son had apparently had several beers (he told the police two beers). Later, in court, the police surgeon's testimony would be pretty much discounted by the judge, apparently because of Bob's other DWI case still pending in court from June without, yet, any court findings in the case. In this case, however, Bob was to be found guilty and his insurance company was reported to have paid an approximate $100,000 in claims to the family in the auto Bob hit, and to the owners of two other parked autos struck by the family auto driver's car as result of Bob's heavy car striking his light one and pushing it into two parked autos.

The newspaper, TV and radio news coverage of this accident over an approximate eight month period, in and out of courtrooms until damage and fault driver rulings were handed down gained a lot of negative press coverage for Bob and helped solidify the WFIL-TV decision to remove Bob from *Bandstand* and ultimately from WFIL and from Philadelphia and Pennsylvania. On the following page are photostats of old newspaper clippings which represent but a small portion of all of the newspaper space devoted to telling Philadelphia, the Delaware Valley and most of all Pennsylvania about Bob being a drunken driver in this accident, which the police surgeon said he was not. This incident, however, following on the heels of the first drunk driving (DWI) offense, still unresolved in November of 1956, and the statutory rape charges against Bob Horn were collectively enough to turn many of Bob's former fans, viewers and supporters away from him, against him. By this time with the individual cases against Bob still pending there was very little to zero hope of his ever again being able to find on-the-air broadcast or telecast employment with and station or stations in the Philadelphia area.

But let us look here for a moment or so at the unfortunate accident in which Bob Horn was definitely at fault. As to whether or not he was intoxicated at the time of the accident, that had to be a matter of degree. He said he had finished two beers, the police surgeon said he was not too intoxicated to drive safely, the judge said, "you're guilty." All three were probably part right and part wrong. Nevertheless, the accident occurred at a most unfortunate time in Bob's life and between this accident, the first DWI case, drug out for months and months, and the statutory rape charge (whether guilty or innocent – and just like your author has come to believe WFIL managers called the shots) were enough to force Bob Horn out of Philadelphia.

The next few pages of clippings are with regard to the accident:

Gail, 5, Wins Fight for Life

By MIKI MAHONEY

Over and over. Again and again. That gentle mumble.

"I'm going home, I'm going home."

All day yesterday it haunted the children's ward of Episcopal Hospital. And finally, at 4 p.m., five-year-old Gail McKnight went home with her parents, her older brother and younger sister.

Gail had been a long time at Episcopal Hospital. Since Jan. 22. She doesn't remember the first six weeks when she lay unconscious and near death.

IN FACT, she doesn't remember the accident. It happened shortly after midnight as they were returning home from a visit with relatives.

The collision occured at the intersection of A and Clearfield Sts., near the home of Mr. and Mrs. John McKnight at 2929 A St. A car driven by Bob Horn, former radio and TV disc jockey, collided with theirs. Slated on a drunken driving charge, he was allegedly driving the wrong way on a one-way street.

Injuries from the impact sent the entire McKnight family to the hospital. Six-year-old Jackie had a fractured skull, was there for more than a month. Two-year-old Donna, and her parents, escaped with cuts and bruises. Gail stayed until yesterday.

THE LITTLE GIRL with short blonde hair and deep blue eyes was an armload of excitement as her dad lifted her up the steps of the brick row house.

But she could hardly show her excitement. Gail's right leg hangs awkwardly, almost useless. She can't move her right hand. Once a constant chatterer, she can barely talk.

Aided by an adult, Gail is able to stand. Her pink party dress is now well above her knees. "She's grown so," said her mother almost in disbelief.

The family hadn't seen Gail during the past month. "Both of the other children had chicken pox," explained McKnight, a sales promotion employe of Abbotts Dairy.

TWO-YEAR-OLD Donna, who now out-talks her older sister, was like a roll of adhesive tape clinging to the convalescent. The curly-haired brunette hugged her and kissed her and wanted to show her every bit of the house in the first two minutes.

Donna is the only one of the three children who remembers the accident. At first she had nightmares, crying spells.

Jackie, who still bears the scars on his short-cropped head, wanted to be every bit a big brother. "Let me help her," he'd say in his husky voice. "I think she wants to see the toys in the shed," he'd interpret.

He brought in Gail's roller skates. She smiled. And he strapped them on her small red shoes.

SHE SEEMED content to just sit with them hanging heavily on her feet. She must know that its going to take a long while to get better, including visits three times a week to the hospital for physical therapy treatments.

"She's a fighter," commented one of the few visitors at the intimate homecoming.

209

Bob Horn's Auto Injures Five

Former TV personality Bob Horn was arrested early today after his car collided with another while he allegedly was driving the wrong way on a one-way street.

Two children were seriously hurt. Their parents and another child also were injured. Horn was unhurt.

Police slated Horn on a drunken driving charge at the 30th District, Front and Westmoreland Sts. It was the second time he had been so charged in the last seven months.

Subsequently, however, Dr.

THE COLLISION happened at 1:05 a.m. at the intersection of A and Clearfield Sts. Police said Horn's car, traveling the wrong way on eastbound Clearfield St., collided with an auto operated by John McKnight, 29, of 2929 A St. McKnight was driving south on A St.

McKnight's car spun around, and his three children—Jack, 6, Gail, 5 and Donna, 2, were thrown out. Jack and Gail were

Gennaro Squillace, a police physician, examined Horn and pal Hospital in serious condition.
pronounced him fit to drive. A The boy received a possible hearing was set for later in the skull fracture. His sister has inday. ternal and head injuries.

McKnight, his wife, Jane, and daughter Donna, escaped with cuts and bruises.

HORN, 41, of 66 Sweetgum Rd., Levittown, was slated on the drunken driving charge at 1:50 a.m. He was released at 4:30 on a copy of the charge obtained by his lawyer, Louis Lipschitz, and signed by Magistrate E. David Keiser. Police said the charge was entered on the books on the basis of information given by the arresting officers.

admitted unconscious to Episcopal Hospital in serious condition.

The boy received a possible teen-age girls as a result of last year's vice ring probe. He was arraigned on those charges last Oct. 25.

He was originally scheduled for trial on Dec. 10, but that trial was moved back to Jan. 2 of this year. Subsequently, he was rescheduled for trial next Monday.

Until his arrest on drunken driving charges last June, Horn had been master of ceremonies on the WFIL-TV program, "Bandstand." He was suspended by the station following his arrest.

At present, Horn is awaiting trial on morals charges involving teen-age girls as a result of last year's vice ring probe.

Bob Horn Guilty Again

He Is Convicted Of Drunk Driving

Bob Horn was convicted of drunken driving for the second time this afternoon even though the police surgeon who examined the disc jockey gave him a clean bill of health.

Judge Vincent A. Carroll found Horn guilty over the testimony of Dr. Gennaro Squillace.

Dr. Squillace examined Horn one hour and 35 minutes after an accident at A and Clearfield sts. last January 22 in which five persons in the other car were hurt.

Doctor Called

The defense called the doctor as a witness after the Commonwealth failed to do so. Dr. Squillace said Horn was well oriented, walked in a normal gait and had a normal pulse and temperature.

He said there was alcohol on Horn's breath but, in his opinion, Horn was not sufficiently under its influence to make it unsafe for him to drive.

Judge Carroll indicated by questions and comments that he believed Horn was under the influence of alcohol. The judge termed a "cock and bull story" Horn's account of getting lost in the fog the night of the accident.

Other Driver Testifies

The other motorist, John McKnight, 29, 2929 A st, testified earlier that Horn was traveling the wrong way on Clearfield st, which is one-way eastbound.

Judge Carroll postponed sentencing pending new trial motions. A jury convicted Horn last Tuesday of drunken driving in June, 1956. Formerly of Levittown, Horn, 41, now works and lives in Houston, Tex.

JAN 22 1957

10-8-513

Horn Held as Tipsy in Crash;

PHILADELPHIA DAILY NEWS, TUESDAY, JANUARY 22, 1957

CONTINUED FROM PAGE ONE

jured internally. The hospital reported them "in very poor condition."

McKnight, his wife, Jane, 26, and daughter Donna escaped with cuts and bruises.

WHEN STRUCK by Horn's Cadillac, McKnight's car went out of control. It smashed into the parked auto of Samuel Smith, of 3057 A St., which was pushed into the parked car of James Scullin, of 3058 A St.

Horn's car was damaged in front. The side of McKnight's car was smashed in.

HORN, 41, of 66 Sweetgum Rd., Levittown, was slated on the drunken driving charge at 1.50 a.m. He was released at 4.30 on a copy of the charge obtained by his lawyer, Louis Lipschitz, and signed by Magistrate E. David Keiser.

Horn was arraigned before Magistrate Ellick at the E. Girard and Montgomery Aves. police station. Approximately 70 persons crowded into the courtroom.

Policeman Philip Garvin, one of the arresting officers, said that in his opinion Horn was intoxicated. At the scene of the crash, Garvin said Horn told him he had had "a few beers." But later, at the police station, Horn denied he had taken a single drink.

"There was a strong odor of alcohol on Horn's breath," Garvin testified. The policeman said Horn was not examined by Dr. Squillace for more than an hour and a half after the collision.

HORN'S LAWYER mentioned the fact that the heavy fog might have been a cause for the crash. "Driving was poor, but not that poor," Garvin said.

The report of Policeman Robert Hinchclif said that while Horn was being questioned half an hour before the police surgeon's examination, "Horn appeared to be under the influence of alcohol."

Other policemen who testified backed up the testimony of Garvin and Hinchclif.

McKNIGHT testified he was driving no more than 15 miles an hour and, at A and Clearfield Sts., he stopped and looked both ways on Clearfield. McKnight said he was half-way across the intersection when he was struck.

Assist. Dist. Atty. John R. Sutton asked the magistrate to hold Horn for drunken driving "irrespective of the police surgeon's findings."

Attorney Lipschitz objected, insisting that his client had not been pronounced intoxicated. Despite this, the magistrate held Horn for court.

AFTER THE HEARING, Horn went across the room to Mc-

211

Court Upholds Conviction Of Bob Horn

The State Superior Court today unanimously upheld a drunken driving conviction of former TV disc jockey Bob Horn.

Horn was sentenced to six months in jail, fined $500 last Oct. 25 after being found guilty of drunken driving in a crash that injured five persons. His sentence was stayed pending the appeal refused today.

JUDGE Robert E. Woodside, who wrote the opinion, said there was "sufficient evidence to support the finding of guilt." Horn was found guilty by Judge Vincent A. Carroll at a non-jury trial.

Attorneys for Horn, who now works for a Houston, Texas, radio station, had argued that Judge Carroll was biased, particularly in his questioning of Dr. Gennaro Squillace.

THE CRASH in which Horn was involved took place at A and Clearfield Sts. on Jan. 22, 1957. Five members of the family of John McKnight were injured. One, 5-year-old Gail, still is partially paralyzed.

Horn, 41, a former Levittown resident, also was convicted last October of another drunken driving charge. Last June he was acquitted of morals charges in one of a sensational series of trials.

Horn Story 'Unworthy Of Belief,' Judge Says

Former TV disc jockey Bob Horn was convicted of drunken driving "because his testimony was unworthy of belief."

That's what Judge Vincent A. Carroll has told the State Superior Court. He did so in his denial of a new trial after he'd ordered Horn jailed six months and fined him $500

The jurist said he felt "impelled" to impose that sentence because of a previous drunken driving conviction against Horn. His car was involved in an accident in which five were hurt. Horn 41, formerly lived in Levittown. *1-24-58*

Bob Horn Held Victim of 'Bias' In Trial Conduct

Disc jockey Bob Horn was held out before the State Superior Court as the victim of a "biased, prejudiced judge who refused to give him a fair trial."

Attorney Louis Lipschitz was referring to Judge Vincent A. Carroll's conduct in the trial in which Horn was found guilty of drunken driving.

Carroll last, Oct. 25 jailed Horn for six months, fined him $500. Lipschitz' appeal, which stayed the sentence, was heard yesterday by the higher court.

"ALL THROUGH the trial," Lipschitz said in his plea, "Judge Carroll's conduct and comments indicated bias." Referring to police surgeon Dr. Gennario Squillace on the stand, Lipschitz said:

"In 30 years of practice I've never seen a defendant kicked around like Horn."

Dr. Squillace had testified he found Horn fit to drive following a crash at A and Clearfield Sts. in which a family of five were injured. One girl still is partially paralyzed. MAR 2 8 1958

HORN, a former TV disc jockey here, now works for a Texas station.

He was convicted on another drunken driving charge last Oct. 2, and was acquitted of morals charges in another trial in June, 1957.

The court took the case under advisement.

212

The management of WFIL had won their desire of being rid of Bob Horn in less than eight months from their decision to act at such negligible cost as to be hardly noticed in the station's budget. Did they feel badly about their conquest? Probably not. Did they do anything at all to give Bob Horn credit or recognition for what he had done for WFIL? Why should they, in their opinions? They allowed him to have all sorts of glory and celebrity status between 1949 and 1956. Nearly seven years, with two and a half years on WFIL-AM radio and approaching four years on WFIL-TV. In their minds WFIL didn't owe Bob Horn anything and that's what he received from them — nothing.

Authors Still Don't Have The Story Exactly Straight.....

Back, once again, to Dick Clark's autobiography to reflect the sort of half truths and rumors that sometime become accepted as truths with passing time and no one digging into the past. Mr. Clark said: "Horn never returned to the show. The drunken-driving charge was followed by a statutory rape charge which involved a fourteen year old girl; apparently several local radio and TV personalities were making dirty movies out in the country at a place called Hound Dog Hill. Horn was arrested a second time on charges of drunken driving. He was eventually acquitted on the rape charge when the IRS showed up and accused him of not paying taxes on $392,500 worth of income.

"Horn was exiled from radio and television. He moved to Mc Lendon, Texas (There is no such city in Texas) where he did a local TV dance show for a short time. The station eventually found out about his past and yanked him off the air. He continued working for them as a radio time salesman. He died there of a heart attack several years later, a pauper, and one of his old regular dancers paid for his funeral."

In reality, Mr. Clark's spun tale is about 40% fact and 60% pure fiction.

We know already that Mr. Horn, literally tarred, feathered and run out of Philadelphia by the media responding to how the media people read and played the trumped up charges against Bob Horn, moved to Houston, Texas where he did a radio show for several months after changing his name for the second time in his life, to Bob Adams, only to learn that his style of radio wasn't right for the station's listeners. And, yes, he did sell advertising for that station for some months until he opened his own advertising agency known as **Bob Adams Associates, Houston, Texas.** His premature death, at age 50, in 1966, was caused by a heart attack brought on by a heat stroke. And as for beating to death the old story of Hound Dog Hill, there wasn't an isn't any such place.

What the first alleged drunk driving charge and going through a red light didn't do to get Bob Horn off of *Bandstand* and run out of Philadelphia – the publicity in connection with the statutory rape charge took care of nicely. Someone or more than one someone at WFIL-TV in 1956 did their unconscionable deeds, more devastating than a Watergate, far worse than any Whitewater to a self-educated, self-made man to destroy him and to cause two generations of embarrassment and hurt to the man's wife, his children and to his children's children. And this without even words of credit for what he gave to WFIL-TV, to the Annenberg empire and to all Americans who so much loved (by the departed) and so much love by today's followers of rock 'n' roll.

It is true that Jerry Blavat paid for Bob Horn's funeral (pictured as he appears today in the photo section of this book on page 105, and as he looked when a teenager in the "1955 *Bandstand* Yearbook" section) did pay for Bob's funeral as an expediency move at the time. And whether that money was ever paid back to Jerry or if he decided to make the amount a gift to the family of a man he truly loved, Jerry has never told me. But for Dick Clark or anyone else to say Bob Horn, who in addition to having his ad agency also had a seven acre ranchette (anything smaller than a thousand acres in Texas) where he boarded race horses and show horses was a pauper — that is an insulting mistake.

Outside Of Having To Return To Philadelphia For Court Sessions And To Serve Approximately Three Months Of A Six Months Prison Sentence Meted Upon Losing His Appeal On One Of His Two DWIs – Just What Did Bob Horn Do In Texas And The Southwest?

When all of the scandalous and negative publicity, on top of not being able to gain a steady job in or near Philadelphia, forced Bob to seek a livelihood elsewhere, he moved to Houston, Texas where he was offered a news-talk-music show on a radio station KLIF when it was newly acquired by Gordon B. McClendon, the Scotchman who created the Liberty Broadcasting System, the second largest network in the nation in 1952 with 458 station, and who was a friend of Bob Horn. To avoid rumor problems and people shying away from him or turning him away in his quest to seek a new livelihood, Bob Horn changed his name for the second time in his life to be, Bob Adams.

After settling court matters in Pennsylvania, including making payment and fines to the IRS for previously unpaid taxes on some of the monies Bob received over a period of several years as stipends, tips, commissions or his shares of split commissions (referred to as payola) and serving 3 months of a 6 month prison sentence adjudicated for one of his alleged DWI citations, Bob Adams returned to Houston and KLIF. Bob, however, was too much of a Pennsylvanian for his personality and style to be a quick hit among Texas radio listeners so, according to Mr. Bill Weaver, who was manager of KLIF when Bob worked there, Bob was taken off the air and became an advertising representative for Mr. McClendon's station.

Bob Adams did a good job of selling and one of his major accounts was the chain of Globe

Discount City stores that were later purchased to become a part of the Walgreen Drug Stores chain. Still creative, Bob participated in the openings of all new Globe Discount City stores such as a new one in Phoenix, Arizona, located at 36th Street and Thomas Road, next to Tower Plaza. It was for Globe stores that Bob came up with the successful "**Midnight Madness Sales**," since picked up by chains of stores and independent stores all across America to stimulate sales to people unable to shop easily during regular store hours. At some of the store opening events Bob Adams was the emcee for opening programs and events that drew thousands of people to, usually, parking lot presentations. And Bob Adams still featured the r & b music well, by then, on its way to becoming rock 'n' roll.

Bob, knocked down about as far as a man can be without physical harm, was exactly that, down but coming back up fairly fast.

With him in Houston, after selling off what holdings they had left in Pennsylvania, were Ann and their three daughters. Bob (Horn) Adams, with Globe stores start-up augmentation, opened his own advertising agency, **BOB ADAMS ASSOCIATES**, located at 3030 Woodridge, P.O.B. 26366, Houston, Texas 77032. Telephone: (713) 644-0501.

Bob and Ann had acquired a 7 acre ranchette and home, where after daytime work hours Bob and a helper boarded and cared for several fine horses at a time. Bob Adams was doing okay. Ann told this book's author, that after getting off the air at KLIF (Houston), Bob had no desire to ever return to radio or television. He never said much of anything about his "Bandstand" becoming "American Bandstand." He did, occasionally, have lunch or and afternoon conversation with entertainers visiting Houston who knew Bob and professed, as all of his real friends did, that Bob Horn was railroaded out of WFIL-TV and out of *Bandstand*.

In 1966, ten years away from *Bandstand*, Bob Horn (Adams) had a heart attack brought on by a heat stroke and he passed away at the early age of 50. Just in the month that these words are written your author asked Barbara Horn, Bob and Ann's youngest daughter if she believes the treatment her father received at the hands of the managers of WFIL (Philadelphia) had anything to do with her father's premature demise. Her answer was, "Yes, and it also has impacted every member of the Horn family, since WFIL and Philadelphia in some negative way." Asked if she thought her father deserved to be enshrined in the Rock and Roll Hall of Fame, her answer was "Absolutely, right along with Alan Freed."

This author insists, that Bob Horn was tarred, feathered, and run out of Philadelphia by two grasping, stepping on people, radio-TV station managers working for an ivory tower employer, Walter H. Annenberg, who, of all people should have jumped to Bob Horn's side and support after just having gone through living down a somewhat similar tarring and feathering of his own father, Moses Annenberg, in the years immediately preceding the unjustified and increasingly evidenced criminal ousting of Bob Horn from the *Bandstand* Horn created and from Mr. Annenberg's stations WFIL.

An unknown Philadelphia writer and a girl who was one of the "regulars" on *Bandstand* as best they could of Bob Horn without lots of research:

THE MAN who was originally responsible for Bandstand, its success and the happy memories of the "regulars" died in 1966 in Texas, where he had moved following the scandal-ridden termination of his Philadelphia career.

Bob Horn was Bandstand's first host, prior to Dick Clark's later and longer term with the television show. A TV disc jockey and master of ceremonies here in the 1940s and early 1950s, the then 40 year old Horn was fired from Bandstand in 1956 after a drunken driving arrest. A few months later he was arrested on morals charges, accused of having hade sexual relations with a 13-year-old girl over a period of several years.

Horn's first highly publicized trial ended in a hung jury, but several months afterward he was finally acquitted by a judge sitting without a jury. Later motor-vehicle arrests and a tax-evasion case kept him in and out of courts for the next few years, but in Texas Horn worked for advertising agencies and three years before he died managed to open one of his own.

"Bob Horn was very nice to all of us — not like Dick Clark who never cared for teen-agers," recalled Andrea Kamens, the Bandstand "regular" who organized last weekend's 21st reunion.

He was very straight with us, never any mention of sex. None of us knew that girl he was involved with. She wasn't in with the Bandstand group, We knew nothing about it until it got into the papers."

BOB ADAMS

A S S O C I A T E S

3030 WOODRIDGE P.O.B. 26366
☐ HOUSTON, TEXAS 77032
☐ 713-644-0501

Advertising and Public Relations

CHAPTER TEN

FOUR YEARS OF WFIL-TV HISTORY ERASED
HOW DID THEY DO THAT?
AND
WHAT IS YOUR CRIME VERDICT?

With Bob Horn gone to Texas, and Tony Mammarella assisting with a smooth transition of *Bandstand* to its new host, Dick Clark, life at WFIL-radio and TV facilities was going along smoothly with only murmurs here and there about how much better the show used to be with Bob Horn and a few die-hards wanting to know where he is, what he's doing, and how he's doing. In conversations with former WFIL people while doing research interviews this book's author got the feeling that managers Clipp and Koehler were just happy Horn was gone so they could carry on with *Bandstand* as they would see fit – and they didn't much give a damn about what was or was not happening for Bob Horn.

Their job, in their minds, was to keep a lot of publicity going for *Bandstand* and, now, Dick Clark — and to make that publicity and advertising hot and heavy from the start with Clark on the show to cause viewers, kid dancers and the station's public to forget Bob Horn as rapidly as possible. The effect is that similar to a magician causing an audience to watch his or her left hand so they won't realize what the right hand is doing.

By all means, keep on playing the r & b music on *Bandstand* because the guy who was there before proved that's what today's dance audience wants. For people who seriously want to know about Bob Horn, he's down in McLendon, Texas selling advertising for some little rinky-dink radio station. We understand he's about broke and other than the fact he'll have some court dates coming up here in Philly, we don't know any more about him.

These two managers, and perhaps only Roger Clipp working it by himself, have or has pulled off what might be considered a perfect crime. Clipp, alone, or in concert with Koehler terminated a contract employee with practically no real cost to WFIL at all, and force the terminated individual to leave town — and not be a business threat by being an experienced and qualified professional broadcaster who might go to work for a competing station.

In a full 14 years of meeting with people who were there or nearby when Bob Horn was at WFIL radio then TV, and seeking and reading letters, memoirs, notes, news clippings, magazine articles and going through stacks of photos. While most of this seeking occurred in Philadelphia, much occurred, too, in New York, Houston, retirement communities around the nation, in Hollywood, Jacksonville, Florida, and in bedroom communities within range of Philadelphia. And from person after person and in reading one data item after another the same indications and the same bottom line kept coming up:

**Bob Horn was "railroaded" out of WFIL by one
or more unscrupulous management individuals....**

And while Walter Annenberg, then owner of the stations, might have been a part a devious scheme to depose a television celebrity he employed, it is thought not. Mr. Annenberg had nothing in particular to gain by such unscrupulous actions other than perhaps pleasing a wife whose lady friends made complaints to her about Mr. Horn being too old to be hosting a show with all those teenagers. On another hand, Walter Annenberg, known to have a quick temper, might well have said, "Fire the son-of-a-bitch" if his managers said to him, Bob Horn is doing things to discredit WFIL. Beyond these things there have been indications that Walter Annenberg actually liked Bob Horn because Bob Horn had creativity and intestinal fortitude.

With Bob gone from WFIL all the way to Houston and with no chance of his returning to Philly as a broadcaster, both managers who so plainly wanted hin gone have that wish they shared fulfilled. Roger Clipp continued to move upward within the Triangle Publications (Walter Annenberg) organization, as did George Koehler, also, who would move into Mr. Clipp's former position of General Manager of both WFIL radio and TV stations — then continue on upward in stations management until one day he would be a key individual in the corporation that would acquire from Mr. Annenberg his WFIL properties and several other broadcast holdings of Triangle Publications. Of the quartet spoken of here, of the author's knowledge at this particular time, only Messrs. Annenberg and Koehler remain alive and both are in semi-retirement.

Early in researching efforts for this book there was an occasion to meet with Mr. George Koehler who it was hoped would be able and willing to shed some light upon why Bob Horn left WFIL with no recognition whatsoever for his contributions to WFIL radio and TV, for his creation of *Bandstand*, and his streetwise, quasi-scholarly, one-man-in-Philadelphia effort to bring young people of that post war era the music that would lead to a kind of music of their own. Alan Freed would name it, as Bob Horn would help dispense it. The music these men brought to hungry-for-it listeners and dancers would become rock 'n' roll.

Even fans of the three "B's" in music, Bach, Beethoven and Brahms could, if they were true music devotees and not mere musical snobs, find and recognize in the rhythm and blues music that lead to rock 'n' roll true musical values worthy of recognition, acceptance and refinement. In that latter regard, Mitch Miller, the bearded one, and Bob Horn had something special in common, they could sense a new recording as a hit after hearing only a few bars performed.

But back to George Koehler, today an elderly and respected gentleman, for two hours in conversation this author attempted to lead him into some discussion of Bob Horn and the Bob Horn days at WFIL. But not one word about Horn, the man, or the _Bandstand_ days in Philadelphia. Each time effort was made to make such a conversation it was thwarted by Mr. Koehler preferring to speak of the weather or something far afield. Perhaps it was his age, or perhaps it was something painful to remember but nary a word from Mr. Koehler about Bob Horn. That avoiding talk of Bob Horn was disappointing because Koehler had been Horn's immediate boss for four years and was bound to be able to shed some light on the subject of this book, 'the untold story.'

Both WFIL managers, Clipp and Koehler, were intellectual individuals, well educated, well placed and respected in the community. Both were graduates of the same University of Pennsylvania and both were (are) held in high esteem their peers. By strong evidence today, some tangible and much of it convincing circumstantial evidence one or both of these fine, outstanding, WFIL general managers of the 1950s and 1960s might well be criminals in atleast one aspect of their lives, with truth coming more to light through witnesses and documentary materials with each passing quarter year. The crime or crimes as it may be still further established were in their treatment of Robert "Bob" Horn when they wanted him out as host of _Bandstand_ — and away from Philadelphia. They both wanted him gone, with little expense to WFIL, in order to ease their way for doing "big things" with the show Bob Horn created, named and nurtured to phenomenal success. The show was first **Bob Horn's Bandstand** — then, a first clue of management's intent to "dump Bob Horn" was when the managers changed the name of the show to simply, **Bandstand.** From there on managements treatment of their "golden goose," Bob Horn became similar to hazing a freshman at UP — only much more serious when dealing with a breadwinner, a professional performer and his family.

Many people have tried to convince this author — or otherwise get me to subscribe to the idea or possibility that Bob Horn self-destructed. There have been a few things story research has revealed that momentarily make such a thought appear feasible. But when that has happened, six or seven more things turn up in the studies of the people involved, some living and some deceased, that shoot down any belief or opinion that Bob Horn may have done to himself the things to bring on the end result of a still promising broadcasting career. So, gentlemen and gentle ladies, this author is locked in to his studied and restudied opinion that what happened to Bob Horn was done to him. He did not do it to himself. Sure, as his widow, Ann, told me. "Bob was no angel, but he wasn't the bad things WFIL management people wanted everyone to believe about him either." I believe you, Ann Horn.

As a pragmatic individual in most aspects of life, this author places more faith in the opinions of people who worked every day with Bob Horn — people like Jack Steck, who hired Bob Horn and who spent time with him every day. And people like Anthony "Tony" Mammarella, who worked long hours with Bob every weekday. And, yes, also in what Gerald "Jerry" Blavat tells about Bob Horn who he knew well as a young dancer on **Bob Horn's Bandstand** and who followed in Bob Horn's footsteps to become a popular disc jockey in the greater Philadelphia area. These people knew Bob Horn whereas a Johnny-come-lately like Dick Clark didn't know Bob Horn at all. All Dick Clark knew about Bob Horn was that he would like to have Bob Horn's job hosting *Bandstand*.

And As For Burying The History Of Bandstand, 1950 To October Of 1952 On WFIL-AM Radio And October Of 1952 Into July Of 1956 — That Wasn't Difficult At All....

Stop, as of June 22, 1956 (the day after Bob Horn's traffic violation and his being tabbed 'drunken driver'), any mention of any kind using the name of Bob Horn in any media outlet in a positive manner. Start immediately heavy, fresh advertising and promotion of *Bandstand,* more so than for a long while ever, with moderate mention of the interim host, Tony Mammarella. (As much as WFIL management likes Tony he cannot remain as host very long even though he is the right age, good looking, and knows the show format backward and forward — and the kids like him. No, WFIL can't keep Tony on as host because his name and his appearance are "too Italian" on a show with already a near majority of the dancing kids being Italian. That would never do for WFIL in 1956, being Philadelphia's WASP [White Anglo Saxon Protestant] stations.) Then, when a permanent *Bandstand* host is chosen, let him be the show item to tout all-out for several months. The public is fickle and if his name is no longer mentioned as the *Bandstand* guy for a few month viewers, except for the diehards won't even remember there was ever a Bob Horn on the show. That part of the show history is quickly erased by spending some promotional dollars.

As for burying the records that takes a while because records must be maintained for advertiser's billing purposes and for recordings played royalty requirements. Those records, though, do not need to be available to the public at all during 1956 nor into the future. This author has tried on several occasions to obtain WFIL-AM radio logs and WFIL-TV logs. but to no avail.

Now We Must Evaluate Our Skills As A Jury Person....

A good many clues some as facts, some as conjecture, and some as pure reading between the lines have been presented in the foregoing pages of this book.

As the author found in his researching for the book, certain same answers to questions asked or found in documents read kept coming forth repeatedly from many different sources. Some of these clues are, of course, circumstantial but to get the same answers over and over and over again gives vent to believing such clues are truths or that there is a significant amount of truth within these clues.

Some materials found in published works reviewed, read and studied in preparing to author this book were found to be either somewhat erroneous or 100% wrong. i.e.: Bob Horn was not fired from WFIL; there is no such place as McLendon, Texas; and there never was and is not today any such place as Hound Dog Hill; and Bob Horn did not die a pauper.

Bob Horn, we know from scores of different 'close to him' sources was never an alcoholic and only a light social drinker who, on most occasions chose to drink beer and usually with food. Jack Steck, WFIL Program Director for years, and the man who hired Bob Horn and who saw Bob nearly every week day, said to this author, "Never did I smell alcohol on Bob's breath, and never did I see him drunk." If anyone wanted to nail him for driving after having a couple of beers at early lunch time or of an evening after watching new entertainers perform or hearing new music, it would be easy to do because he did enjoy a couple of beers while (for him) he was conducting business. And, according to Mr. Steck, that's exactly what he believed happened. "Someone at WFIL wanted to shove him out onto the street, and they had him framed by getting cop to stop when he was known to have had a couple of beers. That's how it happened. The poor guy was framed."

I asked Mr. Steck if he knew who framed Bob Horn. His answer was,

"No, but I have my own suspicions."

"Who," I asked?

"I won't tell you that. It wouldn't do any damned good anyway because the people are all dead or dying off fast."

And About The Girl, Lois Gardner....

There's been much learned about her and her mother since 1956 when she took the stand in court to drive stakes into Bob Horn, by saying she had sex with him on many occasions since she was 12 years old. Lois Gardner was what we today call a "celebrity groupy," an individual who hangs around where celebrities work, live, dine or relax in hopes of having them pay attention to her. Groupies do not discuss their age and ordinarily take great pains to look and act like a mature adult. And among girls who are groupies anyway, many of them become promiscuous at an early age. For such girls the very thrill of being alleged to have had sexual relations with a celebrity (whether they have or not) is almost enough to get one of them to lie about having had sex with a target celebrity — even if there is no money connected with the accusation they are asked to make.

There remains, today, only hearsay about Bob Horn and his escapades to Philadelphia area bawdy houses (including the non-existent Hound Dog Hill). Whether he did partake of such entertainment or not nobody seems to know. Ann Horn, Bob's wife, has said on a taped interview, "Bob was no angel but he sure wasn't any of things he was accused of being, and he certainly didn't do any of the things they are trying to make out that he did."

From where your author sits, there is no question in his mind but that one or more executive level people at WFIL radio and TV stations framed Bob Horn as the culprit in at least two of the crimes he was accused of committing. In that, reference is made to the first of his two DWI citations and to his being accused of statutory rape or contributing to the delinquency of a minor.

We know and acknowledge that Bob was at fault and had consumed a couple or a few beers on the evening that he ran into a car on a foggy night. There is evidence, too, that even in this case the police surgeon stated that although Bob was mildly intoxicated he was no so to a level that would preclude his being able to safely drive his auto.

Further, we have knowledge that Bob did fail to pay income tax on some of the money he received from recording hawkers to play their recordings on _Bandstand_ — money that became known as payola — funds that were not in any way illegal to accept prior to 1959 following Congressional hearings on the form of payment. Payola still seems not too bad to this author who is aware the real estate salespeople, auto salespeople and a host of markerting people in other fields do not hesitate at all to split commissions or otherwise pay individuals who help these salespeople consummate sales. What, then, is so different about recordings. Oh well, that's all part of American justice.

Bob Horn paid dearly for the auto accident that was his fault. He ended up in prison for three 3 months as his punishment for his first (frame up) DWI citation. And his expenses for defending himself against (frame up) statutory rape charges and morals charges were tremendous. Then, when piling on top of those things his being taken off of _Bandstand_, the show he created, formatted and polished to perfection, his being fired from the broadcast firm (radio and TV) were he had worked diligently and conscientiously for more than six years, and being forced out of a broadcast career to which he had devote 25 years of his life. The individual or the individuals who plotted and activated the schemes that would move Mr. Horn from celebrity to criminal status was the equivalent of committing a homicide on the part of the frame-up perpetrators. But did they get caught? Absolutely not? Did they go on with their lives, reaping benefits from Mr. Horn's being gone? We can be sure they did.

And to think, that after all of that cruel and vicious treatment, all the Horn family longs for today is that their deceased husband, father and grandfather, Bob Horn, should have his name in the Rock and Roll Hall of Fame. So little to ask for having paid so much. But who is there living today who could nominate Bob Horn's name for acceptance into the Rock and Roll Hall of

Fame? This book's author is trying in the only way he knows at the time of this writing, to rally public and broadcast people's support for getting Bob's name there beside Alan Freed's name in that Hall of Fame. If you would care to assist in this effort, please write to me care of my publisher. The address is in the front pages of this book.

But Now It's Time To Solve This Historical Mystery....

1. Was this a conspiracy by one or possibly two bosses who plotted and carried out this horrible deed to satisfy their own business wants and needs, real or imagined?

2. Has this been the story of a talented man who came too far, too fast and to then self-destructed?

3. Were the plots activated by station management to economically eliminate a question mark (a too old host) from *Bandstand*, a TV show destined to go national and soar to worldwide popularity?

4. Could this possibly have been result of a suggestion by a active-in-social-circles wife of the big boss, responding to a friend's suggestion that Bob Horn is too old to host *Bandstand*?

5. Do you have a theory of your own as to how Bob Horn got dumped?

Based upon 14 years of digging into what happened, this book's author is convinced that the circumstances precluded sheer fortuitous happenings attacking Bob Horn without help from WFIL management. One, at least, if not two of the criminal involvements by Bob Horn in 1956 were either plotted entirely by a WFIL management person or substantially helped along by a WFIL manager or managers. All of my indicators point to Roger Clipp as the one or one of several management people involved in a conspiracy to do away with Bob Horn at WFIL. It is, however, to early to actually accuse Mr. Clipp because additional evidence is still coming in. Data has been coming out of the woodwork since word is out of my effort to restore Bob Horn's good name and to regain credit for his creative talents. *I would like to learn your thoughts about how it all happened. Please let me know through my publisher whose address is in the front pages of this book. Thank you for meeting Bob Horn and some of the people who knew and worked with him though these pages.*

Stanley J. Blitz — July, 1997

AND IN A FRESH, 1997 TRIBUTE TO BOB HORN
AND THE ORIGINAL *BANDSTAND*

Harvey Sheldon and **"Dimples"** who were both dancers
on the original **Bob Horn's Bandstand**
(Both pictured at the far right in the above photo taken on the original *Bandstand* set)
are currently making an effort to bring back, today,
"The Bunny Hop"
as they were there to help introduce that fun dance in 1954
with **Ray Anthony** and his music on **Bob Horn's Bandstand**

To help make the dance and its music return, Harvey and "Dimples" will be
making guest appearances on popular television shows. A recent appearance
was on the popular Crook and Chase (FOX) morning show on June 11, 1997.

225

A LASTING AND MEMORABLE TRIBUTE TO BOB HORN

from the man who was the original Producer for *Bandstand* with the show's creator and original host – and who stayed with *Bandstand* as producer after Dick Clark became the show host. The following letter, written shortly after Bob Horn's untimely death in 1966, was essentially a letter to Mrs. Ann, Bob's widow, from **Anthony "Tony" Mammarella** but it was presented to the people of the 1950s and 1960s broadcasting industry by being published in the August 10, 1966 edition of *BEHIND THE SCENES*, "A Radio and Recording Industry News Letter, still actively published today from Buffalo New York, when Mike and Mickey were the publishers. The following are Tony Mammarella's tribute words to Ann Horn and to "the industry:" (Reprinted here by permission from *Behind The Scenes* and the Bob and Ann Horn Estates.)

++++++++++

Dear Mike and Mickey:

I am not prone to writing letters to the editor or anyone else for that matter, but I feel this is one I must write.

It is my hope that at least you will not treat the death of BOB HORN with a 'chic' or 'pithy' one liner. Although his untimely death perhaps means more to me and some others who were closely associated with him, the Industry should surely take note of his passing and remember.

If Bob Horn was nothing else, he was the originator and creator of Bandstand Shows. It was his idea, his title, his brainchild and it had international significance. Bandstand shows now exist in all parts of the world. Dick Clark replaced Bob Horn as M.C. on Bandstand, which by the way originated in the WFIL-TV's Studios in Philadelphia. Under the guidance of Bob Horn the Bandstand show was the highest rated local daytime show in the U.S.A. Dick took it from there to the top network daytime show as American Bandstand on ABC-TV.

Dig up any story you want about the guy but remember also to print this: He was a pro in every sense of the word. He could smell a hit in the first eight

226

bars and he didn't have to wait for Cashbox, Billboard or the Gavin sheet to tell him. He was a leader and innovator because he was tuned to the people in his audience and not to people in the trade. And Mike, if all you can say about him is that he was a leader, in today's era of the automated follower, that's saying a lot!

I could say more but let me end with this, and all of you guys who are on top listen. Winners loved him. Losers hated him. Nobody ignored him. He found out, the hard way, that very few guys that you meet in this business are really friends. They are like the subjects of the kings of old. The go from king to king. They don't particularly care who is king, they only know they need a king to follow.

Bob Horn was everything you have heard about him but he was my friend. I only regret that I was not close to him these last few years to tell him so. I hope he knew. Perhaps I will be able to tell his wife Ann and their children. It would be nice for all of us who knew the guy to let her know he will be remembered. She needs to know.

Mike, he was also a proud guy so there will be no sad songs. Bob Horn is dead and I will miss him, knowing he is no longer around.

Sincerely,
ANTHONY S. MAMMARELLA
(Original producer of Bandstand)

++++++++++

Note: Ann Horn passed away on February 1, 1997. While she will not read this page her children, with Bob, and their grandchildren will be able to read Tony Mammarella's tribute to Bob Horn and perhaps know more about the man who was their father or grandfather. Ann had one fervent wish after Bob was gone, that he would become nominated and accepted into The Rock and Roll Hall of Fame along with Alan Freed and the others who first brought the music that would be the forerunner of rock and roll to America and the world. This author and this books publisher shares your wish, Mrs. Horn.

Bibliography:

BOOKS

Clark, Dick with Fred Bronson, *Dick Clark's American Bandstand,* New York: Collins Publishers, A Division of Harper Collins Publishers, 1997

Clark, Dick and Robinson, Richard, *Rock, Roll & Remember,* New York: Thomas Y. Crowell Company, 1976

Cooney, John, *The Annenbergs, The Salvaging of a Tainted Dynasty,* New York: Simon & Schuster, 1982

Dawson, Jim and Propes, Steve, *What Was The First Rock 'N' Roll Record?,* Boston: Faber and Faber, 1992

Miller, Jim, Edited by, *Illustrated History of Rock & Roll,* New York: Random House/Rolling Stone Press, 1976

Shore, Michael with Clark, Dick, *The History of American Bandstand,* New York: Ballentine Books, 1985

Swenson, John, *Bill Haley, The Daddy of Rock and Roll*, New York: Stein and Day, 1982

PERIODICALS

Chicago Tribune
New York Times
Phoenix Republic & Gazette
Philadelphia Bulletin
Philadelphia Daily News
Philadelphia Inquirer
TV Guide

PHOTOGRAPHS

Gerald "Jerry" Blavat, Page 105.
Edgar S. Brinker, Philadelphia and the Estates of Robert and Ann Horn,
    Pages 96, 98, 100, 101, 102, 104, 106, 107, 108, 109, 110, and 111.
Bruno of Hollywood, Page 17.
Kathleen "Bunny" Gibson, Page 137.
The Horn family personal photos, Pages 112, 113, 114 and 115.
Schaeffer of Philadelphia and the Estates of Robert and Ann Horn, Page 103.
Urban Archives, Temple University, Philadelphia, PA., Pages 97 and 99.

MATERIALS LOANED FOR REPRODUCTION IN THIS WORK

The Estates of Robert and Ann Horn, though the courtesy of their grandson,
    Robert Graham, Robert "Bob" Horn's personal copy of the Official 1955
    Bandstand Year Book, in its entirety, Pages 139 though 171, and now
    © 1997 as an integral portion of this book.
1955 TV GUIDE counter card with Bob Horn's photo, courtesy of the Robert
    and Ann Horn Estates, Page 75.
Tasty Baking Company, permission to include a somewhat reduced size
    reproduction of two panels of their packaging of TastyKakes, Page 117.

Any omissions of names that should be credited in connection with this work are
unintentional and, if brought to the publishers attention, will be included in subsequent
editions of this book.